D0536638

# practical photography

# PRACTICAL PHOTOGRAPHY

ROBERT A. McCOY
*Assistant Professor*
*Industrial Arts*
*University of California at*
*Santa Barbara*
*Goleta*
*California*



McKNIGHT & McKNIGHT
*Publishing Company*
*Bloomington, Illinois*

**SECOND EDITION**

**Second Printing**



Lithographed in U. S. A.



All illustrations, unless otherwise credited,
are by the author.

TO

MY MOTHER

AND

MY WIFE

# preface

This book is written as a nontechnical text for high schools, a beginning course for colleges, and as a guide for the amateur. It is designed so that the chapters need not be studied consecutively although it is suggested that this is the most logical procedure.

Many good books and pamphlets have been written on the subject of photography and new publications, patents, and ideas are presented each day. No single book could be made large enough to contain all of this information. Most of the publications are technical in nature and tell what is to be done in photography. This book is an attempt to bring together in one volume the essential information to take and make good pictures. It is written in a nontechnical manner to tell you *how* to do the things which are so self-evident for the experienced professional photographer and so difficult for the beginner. Only as many technical terms and formulas as are necessary for clarity are used. More technical books are recommended for those who wish to make a more thorough investigation of the subject. This list is found in Appendix A.

It is the hope of the author that this course will be a source of much pleasure and profit to those who take and make pictures.

Many of the cameras, equipment and supplies are called by their trade name. This is necessary in the interest of clarity. It is the earnest hope of the author that no manufacturer of

*(continued)*

photographic supplies, or any reader of this book, will read into these pages any enmity, unfavorable comparison, or praise of one make at the expense of the other. If such offense is committed, it is not intentional.

The author gratefully acknowledges his indebtedness to Mr. H. H. Mills, Associate Professor of Education, University of Colorado, for his constructive criticism in the writing of this manuscript; Mr. Charles F. Snow, A.S.P., Master of Photography, F.R.P.S., for his very generous and helpful suggestions and criticisms during the preparation of this manuscript and for photographs contributed by him; Mr. Julian M. Blair, Associate Professor of Physics, University of Colorado, for his contribution in checking the scientific material presented; Mr. Frederick A. Reiss, LL. D., University of Michigan for his helpful suggestions and criticism while studying under his direction (many of the suggestions and instructions found in his course have been passed on to the reader in this book) ; Jane Merrick, for her contribution of Sunset in the Bahamas; Mr. Jay M. Clark for his contribution of the animal portrait; Mr. R. C. Jacobson for his contribution of the South Sea sunset; Brooks Institute of Photography, Santa Barbara, California; Norcross Studio, Santa Barbara, California; Tomlinson Studio, Santa Barbara, California; Santa Barbara Medical Clinic, Santa Barbara, California; Burleigh Brooks, Inc., New York City; Charles Raleigh, Graflex, Inc., for their contribution of photographs and other instructional aids which have been reproduced in this book; The Eastman Kodak Company for the use of their photographs of equipment, and formulas reproduced in Appendix B; E. I. du Pont de Nemours & Co. Inc., for the use of their formulas reproduced in Appendix B; and to others who have been helpful in the preparation of this manuscript.

ROBERT A. MCCOY

# table of contents

# table of figures



*(Continued)*

*(Continued)*

# table of illustrations

CHAPTER I

# the story of photography

The story of photography begins about the year 1777 when Scheele, a Swedish chemist began to experiment with the action of light on silver chloride. Scheele discovered only chemical facts and never put them into practice for making pictures. It was more than a half century later before the experiments were again continued. In 1802 Thomas Wedgwood read a paper before the Royal Institution in England in which he explained a process of making profiles by the agency of light upon nitrate of silver. It was not until a little over one hundred years ago, that the first method of making permanent pictures was announced. Since that time great progress has been made. Nearly every family of the civilized world today has a camera for taking photographs.

The development of photography in recent years has progressed so rapidly that we can now have pictures in natural color. We can take a picture in any part of the world and in a few minutes millions of people all over the world can view it in their newspapers. We can take pictures in an extremely small fraction of a second. Compare this with the six to eight hours required in 1814! Photography is used in all sciences, by industry, by doctors and by hobbyists throughout the world.

Photography in the future will be much more extensive than in the past. Because of its great importance, we will examine in this and future chapters something of the processes involved in producing good photographs.

The story of present-day photography centers around the element *silver and its compounds.* This will be recognized as belonging to the science of chemistry. Silver will combine with another element *bromine* to form beautiful three- or six-sided crystals. These crystals are known as silver bromide. If we now place these crystals of silver bromide, which have been struck with light, in a certain liquid (developer) it will be reduced to a spongy black mass of metallic silver. When these crystals of silver bromide are distributed evenly on a glass plate or film and exposed to light of varying intensity, some of the crystals are affected and some are not. The number affected varies with the amount of light. When this plate is developed some places will be of greater density than others. Where no light has struck, there will be no blackness.

The film or plate thus developed is not permanent because the crystals that were not exposed to light are still sensitive. These unexposed crystals, if taken into the light, would at once become exposed and turn black. It is necessary to remove the unexposed silver and all of the other chemicals in the process of development, in order that the image remain permanent. This process is another chemical reaction called *fixing.*

In order to produce an image on the plate or film it is necessary that the light be controlled and directed where it is wanted. This is done by means of a *lens.* The lens is mounted in a light-tight box so that the light going through the lens traces an image of outside objects on the sensitive plate inside. It is necessary to control the length of time the lens allows light to strike the sensitive plate. This can be done by any means of closing the opening or covering the lens. The device used in modern photography is called a *shutter.* This whole mechanical device is called a *camera.*

The technique of photography is based upon the principles of physics and chemistry and application of the principles of art. The controlling of light and the tracing of pictures by means of the lens properly belong to the field of *physics.* The procedures of producing sensitive plates, of developing, fixing and other related processes, are the science of *chemistry.*

The principles of art are often neglected in a course in photography. The application of the principles of art increases the beauty or aesthetic quality of photographs. The first aim in photography is to make a record of some object or scene, but there should be much more to it than that. It should be a record of the object or objects *as that particular person saw it.* Interpreting an object or scene as *YOU* see it leaves great latitude for creative arrangements. A good photograph should show the scene, plus. The plus quality is you, your personality, your likes, your dislikes, your creative ability, your artistic sense. A skillfully composed photograph, properly exposed, developed and printed is a work of art.

You need not travel to distant lands to find something beautiful for a picture. Nature is all about you. Observe the trees, the flowers, a brook running through a field or wood, your pet dog or kitten. Beauty is all about you, if you will only look for it. The technique of producing beautiful pictures will receive considerable attention in the remainder of this book. It is hoped that photography will become a little more interesting, understandable and pleasant for you by reading and studying this book.

In the remaining chapters there will be found instructions for the processes involved in making good photographs. The descriptions and instructions have been simplified as much as clarity will permit. The complicated formulas and computations have been omitted. Although the book has been simplified, the simplification has not killed the adventure, the mystery, and the challenge that photography presents. If more scientific and technical discussions of the mechanics and chemistry of photography are desired, they can be found in the list of suggested references.

CHAPTER II

# choosing a camera

If the purchase of a camera is being considered, the question always arises, which one to buy? The clerk in the photographic stores will probably ask a number of questions concerning your prospective purchase.

One of the first questions asked is, "What type of camera do you wish?" This is followed by, "About how much do you want to pay for it?"

Before you can answer these questions, you will have to ask yourself some questions. The first question is, what do I expect my camera to do for me? Do I want occasional snapshots, sports pictures, portraits or do I just want a camera because the Jones' have one? Do I want a simple camera or one with all the adjustments and accessories that are known to photography? Do I want a large camera or one that will go in my pocket?

Before answering these questions, some consideration should be given to the general characteristics of some types of cameras. They all operate on the same general principle but differ widely in lens quality, shutter and accessories.

### The Pin Hole Camera

The simplest of all cameras is the pin hole camera. Perhaps you will want to make one. If you are careful and accurate in your work, you can get a remarkably good picture with this camera, although it is not practical for general use.

The pin hole camera is made by using any light-tight box (a chalk box is very good) and cutting a small hole in one end. The hole is covered by a very thin piece of metal in which you have punched a very small hole. The thickness of the metal plate must be less than the diameter of the hole.

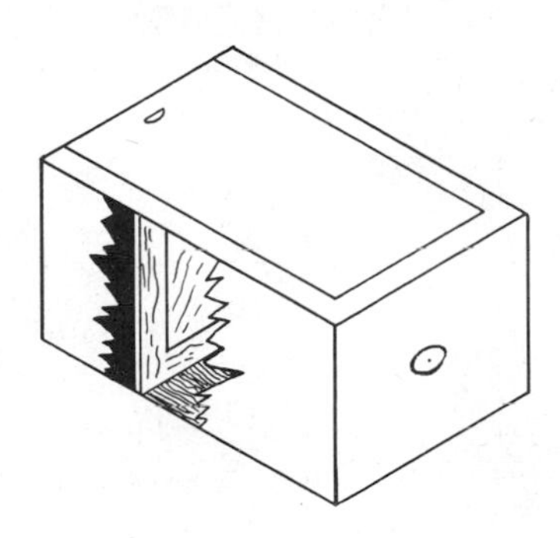

Fig. 2-1. Diagram of a Pin Hole Camera

Use a number nine needle (approximately 1/50 inch in diameter) and place the film at a distance of about five inches. If you use a number ten needle, the distance from the hole to the film should be about four inches. The f-opening for the hole made by the number nine needle is about f/250 and for the number ten needle f/240.

When you get the pin hole mounted in place, you will need something to cover it until you are ready to make the exposure. This can be a rotating disc (shutter), or a piece of tape. When everything is in readiness, take the camera into the darkroom and place the film in its prepared place. It can be taped in place with a small piece of tape on each corner, or held in a small printing frame. Close the camera and place tape over all of the edges where light might enter. You are now ready to take your picture. Do not worry about focusing, depth of focus, aperture, or any of the other adjustments usually found on cameras. How-

A Photograph Taken With a Pin Hole Camera

ever, you must calculate the exposure time. For a bright sunny day with few or no clouds, the approximate time for the number nine hole is about two seconds, using a film with an ASA rating of 200. If a slower film is used, the time is increased according to the film speed rating.

### The Box Camera

The box camera may have limited adjustments for controlling the amount of light transmitted by the lens. Usually the exposure time is fixed at about 1/50 of a second, although different makes may vary slightly from this figure. Some of the better box cameras have limited means of adjusting for distance. If there is no adjustment for distance, pictures should not be attempted closer than about twelve feet.

The view finder is of the simple type. A view finder is a device which shows you the approximate picture you will get on your film. It is a simple lens which forms a real image on a ground glass. A mirror is usually placed so that the image can be seen at the top rather than at the back. In the box camera, the fact that the lens of the view finder is placed at a different place than the lens of the camera makes very little difference. In some cameras this does make a considerable difference.

The box camera is designed for those who know very little about the mechanics of photography, and do not care to spend much time in learning about it. The camera is simple to operate and takes good pictures under favorable conditions. Action shots, extreme close-ups, copying and shots in bad light are out of its range. For the person who wants an occasional picture to keep in the family album, this camera is recommended. It is not expensive.

A modification of the older box camera has become very popular. It is more flexible than the box camera yet keeps the simplicity of operation. The camera is basically a 2¼ x 2¼-inch twin-lens fixed-focus camera. Pictures are taken from 6 feet to infinity. It has a close-up attachment which slips over the lens to permit pictures to be taken from 3 to 4½ feet. The camera has a built-in flash synchronization to permit taking pictures at night. It is so simple to operate that youngsters have very little trouble in using it.

By Jane Merrick

SUNSET IN THE BAHAMAS
Taken With a Box Camera

### The Folding Camera

There are many types of folding cameras made by several companies. The simplest and cheapest folding camera is little more than a box camera. The greatest difference between the box camera and the inexpensive folding camera is the bellows. This is an accordion shaped device which will fold together allowing the camera, when not in use, to take up much less space. The simplest form has a simple lens and a fixed shutter speed. Most have an adjustable diaphragm but some do not. The view finder is similar to the one described for the box camera. There are some advantages of this type camera over the box camera; it occupies less space; it may have a simple adjustment for f-opening; and it might have an arrangement for varying the distance of the lens thus making it possible to take pictures closer than the box camera. It is recommended as equal to or better than the box camera and requires little or no extra fuss in using.

Courtesy, Eastman Kodak Company

Fig. 2-2. An Inexpensive Camera

The folding camera is available in many types — from the simple, inexpensive model just described, to the better high-speed press cameras with highly corrected lenses, fast accurate shutters, and many accessories. Some of the better folding cameras may cost several hundred dollars. The better folding cameras will be described later in this chapter in the discussion of press cameras.

You can choose a folding camera in any price range and quality from a few dollars to several hundred, from the simplicity of the box camera to the complexity of the fully equipped press camera, and from a miniature size picture to eight by ten inches.

### The Reflex Camera

There are two general types of reflex cameras, the type which contains two lenses, and the type which contains only one lens.

Examples of the two lens type are the Rolleiflex, the Argoflex, the Ansco Reflex, etc. They are named by the manufacturer with "flex" as a part of the name. Cameras with "flex" in the name are usually of the reflex type.

Essentially the twin lens reflex camera is a box camera divided into two parts with a lens in each part. The top part has a ground glass on the top and a mirror placed at a 45 degree angle in the box. (See Fig. 2-3.) This mirror is arranged so that

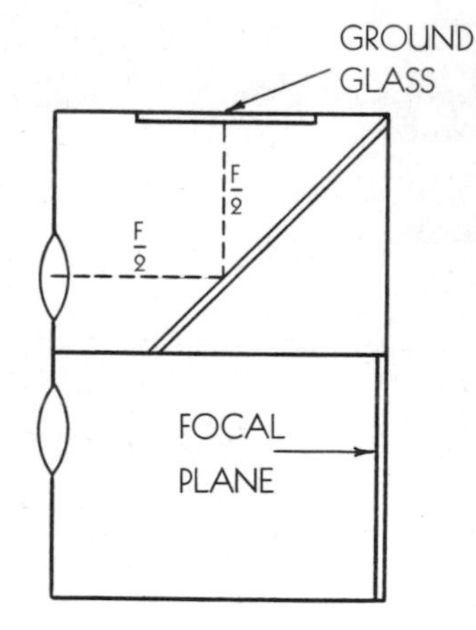


Fig. 2-3a. Design of Reflex Camera

Courtesy, Burleigh Brooks, Inc.

Fig. 2-3b. Twin Lens Reflex Camera

the light has the same distance to travel from the lens to the ground glass as the light from the lower lens travels to the film. The lenses are of the same focal length so that similar images are formed on the ground glass and on the film. This enables you to see your picture in full size. It has another advantage. The two lenses are usually placed in a mount that can be moved, coupled together so that when one is moved the other will move also. This makes it possible to focus the picture on the ground glass and check its composition up to the instant the picture is taken.

Lenses and shutters can be had in various qualities and speeds. Only the lower lens has an iris and a shutter but the lenses are mechanically connected so that when the image is sharp in the ground glass it will also be sharp on the film. If the camera possesses a good lens and shutter, good sport pictures and pictures of fast moving objects may be made. This type of camera is an excellent camera for general purposes.

### The Miniature Camera

A miniature camera is usually thought of as one which uses 35 mm film. This is not strictly true. There are several cameras on the market that have film sizes slightly larger than this. The classification is in the type of construction rather than the exact size of film. The miniature camera has many advantages over some other types. Some photographers insist that it isn't really a camera, but a toy with which you can do everything but take good pictures. Very excellent miniature cameras are now available that will produce excellent enlargements up to 16 x 20 inches.

The camera is usually quite small and compact. Many of them will fit into your pocket. The lens is usually of high quality and has a great depth of field. This camera can be fitted with accessory lenses for wide angle or telephoto shots, thus giving the operator wide latitude.

The miniature camera is sometimes used by the press. It will cover sports events adequately. Using some of the accessory lenses the miniature photographer can do some very commendable serious photography. The miniature camera lends itself admirably to making 2 x 2 inch slides in black and white or color for projection. Many schools are now using it to produce visual aids.

The miniature camera ranges in cost from a few dollars to several hundred. Remember that the smaller a machine, the better it must be built. Everything must be made to precision. Good miniature cameras are usually rather expensive. Remember, too, that the miniature is not a toy or a box camera. It requires careful attention to every detail to get good results.

Courtesy, E. Leitz, Inc.

Fig. 2-4. A Miniature Camera

Courtesy, Eastman Kodak Company

Fig. 2-5. A Miniature Camera (Kodak Flash Bantam)

MT. RAINIER, WASHINGTON
Taken With a Miniature Camera

Most of the companies that manufacture miniature cameras make many accessories for their product. It is wise to learn how to use the camera well before investing in these accessories. When the basic camera has been mastered, then accessories that are required to produce the type of picture that you desire may be purchased.

The accessories, handled by one who knows how to use them, make the miniature camera very versatile.

### The Range Finder

The miniature usually has a device for determining accurately the distance to the object being photographed. This device is called a range finder. It contains mirrors or prisms, and some lenses, placed so that part of them will turn. They are based on the optical effect which technicians call "parallactical differences." This is a little too technical for explanation here.

The operation of these range finders is quite simple. They are of two types, the split image or military type, and the superimposed image type.

To operate the split image type it is necessary to look through the finder and observe that the image seems to be broken in the center and offset. (See Fig. 2 - 6a.) Turn the knob or push the lever (whichever the case might be) until the image comes together to form a complete unbroken picture. When the images are properly lined up the range finder will read the distance in feet.

In the miniature cameras the range finder is usually connected mechanically (coupled range finder) to the lens so that, when the two images are together in the range finder, the lens will be automatically set to the proper distance. The other type range finder is the superimposed image. Instead of the image being split you will see two images, (one may be colored). Adjust the knob until the images are together. (Fig. 2-6b)

## Press Cameras

A press camera is what the name implies, a camera used by press photographers. The press photographer goes on all kinds of assignments to get all sorts of varied pictures. Today they have a top social event, tomorrow it's a horse race, next day a landscape and perhaps some wild life or a tiny flower.

Fig. 2-6a. A Split Image Rangefinder
Left: Not in Focus Right: In Focus

Fig. 2-6b. Superimposed Rangefinder
Left: Not in Focus Right: In Focus

They operate under any and all conditions from the gay party to the rainy day football game. They need a camera that will do all of these jobs.

The most popular press camera for many years was the Graflex. This camera is capable of anything from portraits to prize fights. A description of its operation was given under the heading "Reflex Cameras." It is still preferred by some press photograghers.

In recent years there has been a tendency for press men to shift to the less bulky type of camera such as the Speed Graphic, Crown Graphic, Linhof, or Deardorff. They are usually equipped with a coupled range finder and a flash gun. A synchronized flash gun is a device which contains a flash bulb in a reflector, set off when the shutter release is pushed. They are adjusted so that the shutter opens when the light is brightest (synchronized). Focusing is done by the use of a range finder coupled to the lens, or by a ground glass on the back.

For those who are considering photography as a serious hobby or a business, a press type camera is recommended.

## View and Studio Cameras

The view camera and studio camera differ somewhat from other types of cameras. Thcy havc only one view finder and means of focusing, the ground glass on the back. The bellows usually have a long extension thus permitting several focal length lenses to be used. Both the front and back of the camera have tilts and swings for corrective photography.

Courtesy, Graflex, Inc.

Fig. 2-7. 4″ x 5″ Speed Graphic Press Camera

View and studio cameras are made for deliberate exacting work. They are excellent for beginners learning serious photography. The studio camera is a type of view camera. They must be mounted on a tripod. The larger studio cameras are usually mounted on a stand which can be easily moved about. This stand has various adjustments for height of camera and direction.

### Things in General

Photography is advancing so rapidly that any text book can not hope to keep up to date on the different makes and models of photographic equipment which are offered to the public each year. It is usually best to buy equipment made by companies known to be reliable.

Every reliable company has tested its equipment. When you get a camera or other photographic equipment, read all about how to use it to best advantage. If you have a good camera, it will serve you well. Remember, *you* are the master, the camera is only a machine which will do what *you* make it do. Along with knowing what it will do, know also its limitations.

When you begin to learn photography remember that the keynote to success is *simplicity*. Don't try to do the impossible. A visit to the studio of an internationally known photographer revealed the following interesting facts: The equipment was good, but exceedingly simple; one fluorescent light, two or three reflectors and a handmade spot. His camera was a studio type with two or three focal length lenses. He takes prize winning pictures by keeping things *simple* and *clean.*

## PRACTICAL EXPERIMENT

### Making a Shadow Picture on Printout Paper

*Materials Required —*

1. Any small object.
2. One sheet of printout paper.
3. Sunlight.

*Procedure —*

Place an object in direct sunlight so that a sharp shadow will be produced on a suitable background. Having done this, place a piece of printout paper so that the shadow of the object falls on the paper and so that all other parts of the paper are in the sunlight.

*Questions —*

1. How does this compare with the pictures made by Sir Humphrey Davey and Thomas Wedgewood more than 100 years ago?
2. What causes this paper to change color where it was exposed to light?
3. Can you make the image permanent?

CHAPTER III

# lenses

*The picture you take can be no better than the lens you use.*

A lens is a device, usually made of glass, used to converge light rays and form an image of the object or objects to be photographed on the sensitive film. To treat the subject of lenses thoroughly would require a book in itself. This chapter will concern itself with the fundamental ideas about light and lenses, with some comments on the selection and care of the lens.

Before taking up the lens itself, it is desirable to consider some of the properties of light. Light is transmitted from the originating body in waves. There are many different waves some of which can be seen and some which cannot be seen. In the whole spectrum of radiation, the light that can be seen occupies a very small part. In the longer wave radiations will be found radio waves. Waves which are shorter in wave length are Hertzian waves. Shorter still are the infrared rays. Then come the waves which can be seen, the red, orange, yellow, green, blue, indigo, and violet. These colors, when mixed in proper proportion, form natural white light. Many other rays exist which are shorter than violet and beyond the power of the eye to detect. Some of these rays are the ultraviolet, x-rays, gamma rays and cosmic rays. Only the rays that can be seen plus ultraviolet and infrared will be considered.

### Some Properties of Light Waves

In order to understand the working of the lens, it is necessary to understand some of the basic principles of light. The first principle is that for most practical purposes waves of light

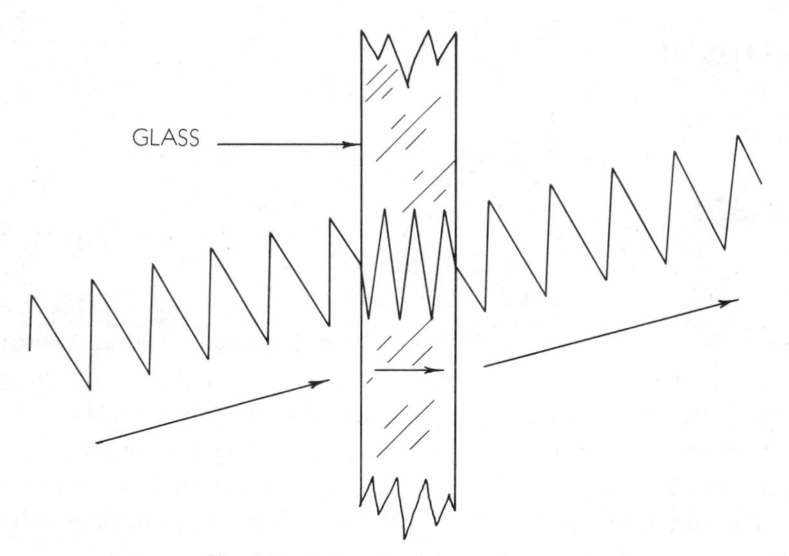


Fig. 3-2. Refraction of a Light Wave

travel in straight lines. The second principle is that rays of light will pass through transparent materials such as glass and water but may be *bent* (refracted) and thus sent on a new path as they pass through, Fig. 3-2. The third principle is that light can be reflected, as by the use of a mirror. All objects, unless totally black, reflect light in varying degrees. It is important to note that the light will leave the mirror at exactly the same angle as it struck the mirror, Fig. 3-3. Some objects reflect very little light but absorb part or all of it. For example, if a piece of cloth reflects all of the rays, it appears white in sunlight. If another piece of cloth absorbs all rays, it appears black. If still another piece of cloth absorbs all rays except red, which it reflects, the cloth appears red. The presence of light is necessary to distinguish any color. No matter what the color, whether it be white, red, green or blue, if there is no light, you cannot see the object.

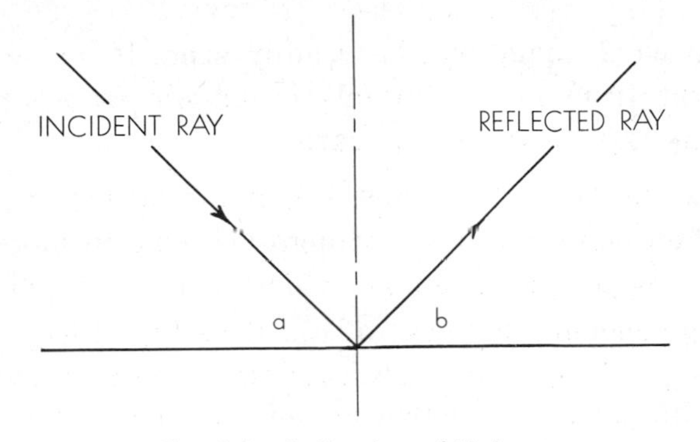


Fig. 3-3. Reflection of Light

The last principle which will be mentioned is that light can be filtered. By the use of certain filters a part of the light can be removed and a part of it, the part selected, can be passed unchanged.

Photography makes use of all of the principles which have been mentioned as will soon be seen in the discussion of the lens.

### The Formation of an Image

Suppose that we take a lighted candle, a piece of metal with a tiny hole in the center, and a piece of white cardboard, and arrange them as in Fig. 3-4 so that the metal with the tiny hole is between the lighted candle and the white cardboard. If the room is now darkened, you will notice an image of the candle on the white cardboard. This image will be inverted. The reason

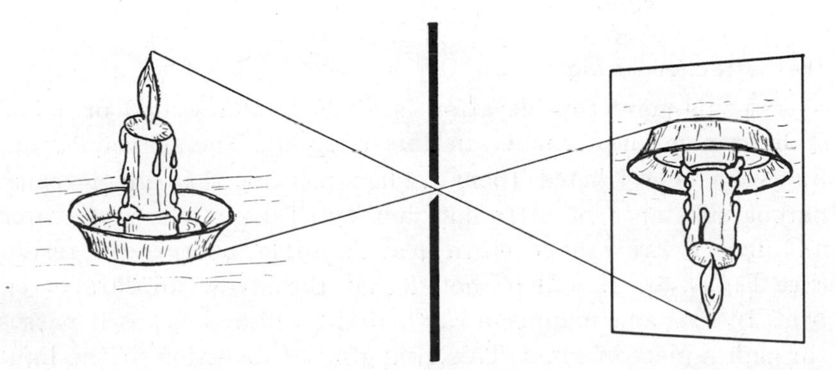

Fig. 3-4. Formation of an Image Through a Pin Hole

for the inverted image will be readily seen, if you will trace a ray of light from any point on the candle *in a straight line* through the hole to the white card.

If now the hole in the metal is made larger, rays of light from a given point can pass through the hole in more than one direction thus giving an image which is not distinct or, if the hole is large enough, no image at all. (See Fig. 3-5.)

If this pin hole is properly arranged, pictures can be taken with it. This device is known as the pin hole camera. The exposures necessary with the pin hole camera are so long that it is not practical in general photography. It is necessary to find another method of letting in more light and still make a sharp image on the sensitive material.

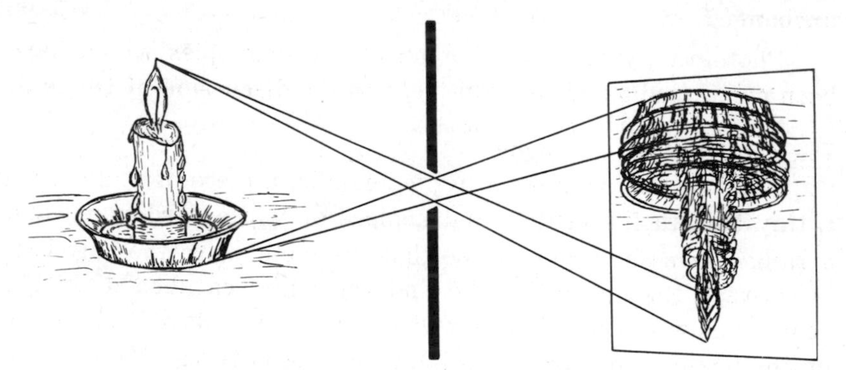

Fig. 3-5. Indistinct Image With a Large Hole

## The Refraction of Light

At this point consideration is given to the second principle of light mentioned earlier in this chapter: The principle that light can be refracted (bent) when passing through a transparent substance of different density. Take a glass of water and place a straw or pencil in it at an angle; observe the result. (See Fig. 3-6.) It will be noted that the straw appears to be bent. In the same manner a ray of light will be bent as it passes through a piece of glass. This changing of direction of the light ray is called *refraction.*

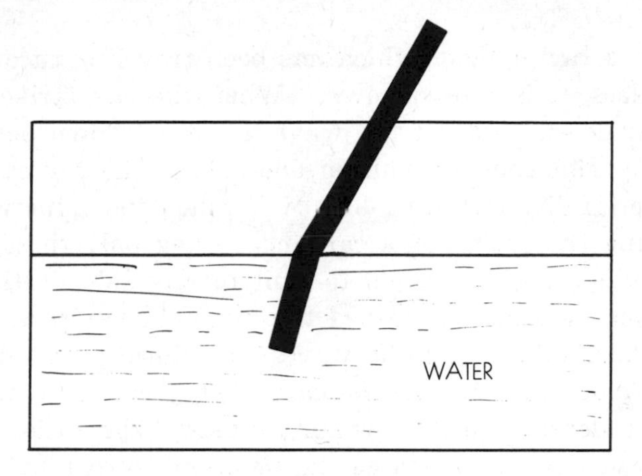


Fig. 3-6. Refraction of Light in Water

Not all materials will change the direction of a ray of light the same amount. Every ray of light coming through a transparent thin material such as air will have its direction changed when it enters a more dense material such as water or glass. When the ray emerges from the dense material again into the thin (less dense) material, it will change direction again, but this time the change will be in the opposite direction. A ray falling upon the glass perpendicular to its surface goes on through without changing direction. If one piece of glass, because of its chemical composition, is more dense than another piece of glass the change in the direction of the ray will be greater in the glass having the greatest density, Fig. 3-7.

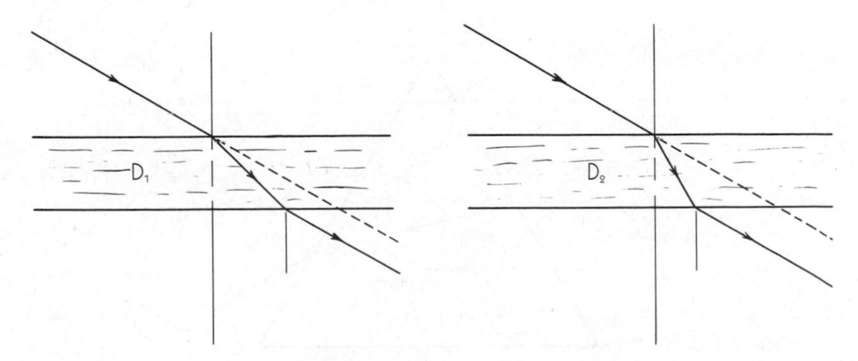


Fig. 3-7. Refraction of $D_2$ Is Greater than $D_1$

When a ray of light, which has been traveling through air, strikes glass, it is slowed down. When the ray strikes at an oblique angle, one side of the wave is slowed down before the other side. This causes a pull on one side of the ray causing it to change its direction, Fig. 3-2. It is much the same situation as applying the brakes of a car and having only those on one side working. The car tends to pull to one side of the road. The harder the brake is pushed the more the car tends to pull to that side. Likewise, light waves are slowed, and direction changed, much the same as the car, when they strike an object of greater density, such as water or glass. The ratio of these velocities of light is known as the *index of refraction.*

Now consider what happens if a prism is used instead of a glass with parallel sides. A light ray strikes the surface of the prism and is refracted toward a line drawn perpendicular to the side of the prism. It passes through the glass in a straight line until it strikes the other surface where it is refracted again but this time, since it is entering a less dense medium, it is refracted away from the perpendicular of the second side. (See Fig. 3-8.)

### The Principle of the Simple Lens

What relation does this prism have to a lens? Consider every lens as being made up of an infinite number of small prisms. If four prisms are placed together, (Fig. 3-9) they resemble a lens. If a thousand prisms are placed together, the result is more nearly like a lens. A true lens can be produced by taking

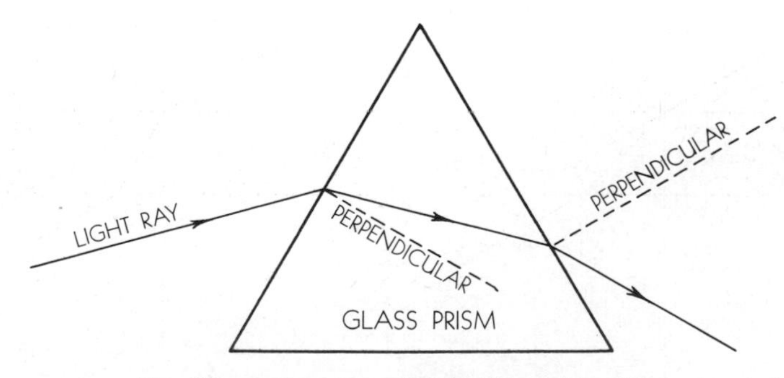


Fig. 3-8. Refraction of Light Through a Prism

an infinite number of prisms and polishing all rough corners. The laws of refraction which have been discussed with regard to plane surfaces and prisms apply equally also to lenses.

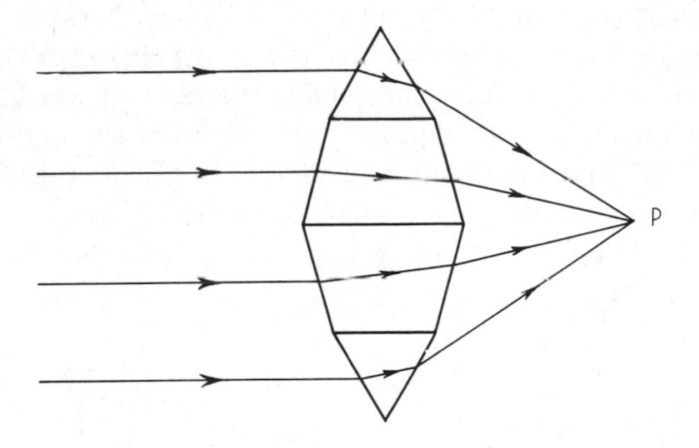


Fig. 3-9. Four Prisms Resemble a Lens

If a simple lens is substituted for the pinhole in the camera, the image is much brighter thus making short exposures possible. Careful examination will show that not all parts of the picture are clear and sharp. Some distortion can also be observed. (See Fig. 3-11.) Since this lens does not meet the requirements of good pictures, it is necessary to add other lenses with different indexes of refraction to correct the defects.

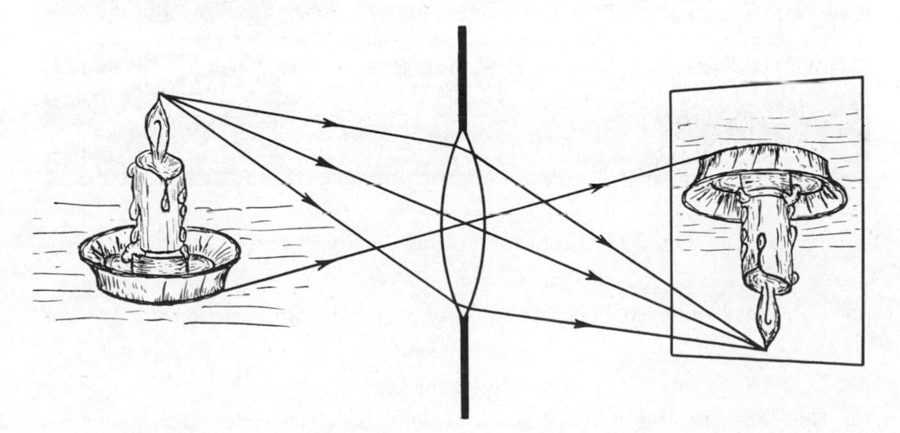

Fig. 3-10. Formation of an Image by a Simple Lens

Lenses are classified as convergent or positive, and divergent or negative (Fig. 3-11). A convergent lens is thicker in the center than at the outer edge. A divergent lens is thicker at the edge than at the center. The convergent lens gathers the parallel rays of light together behind the lens at a point to form a real image, while the divergent lens bends the rays outward, spreads them, so that the light appears to come from a point in front of the lens. The divergent lens does not form a real image behind the lens, but forms what is called a *virtual image*. A virtual image appears to be in front of the lens when one looks

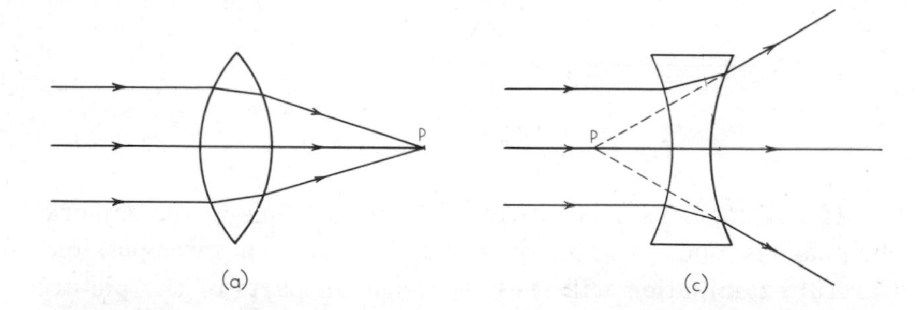


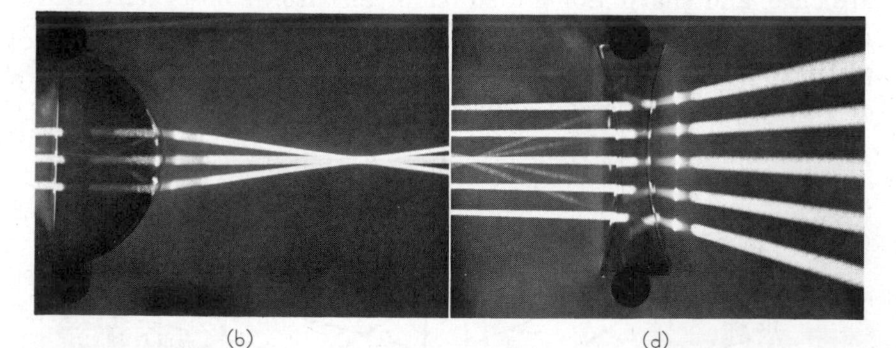


Fig. 3-11. Convergent and Divergent Lenses
(a) Convergent Lens
(b) Light Rays Photographed Passing Through an Uncorrected Convergent Lens Near Its Center
(c) Divergent Lens
(d) Light Rays Photographed Passing Through an Uncorrected Divergent Lens Near Its Center (Note Reflected Light on Entering Side)

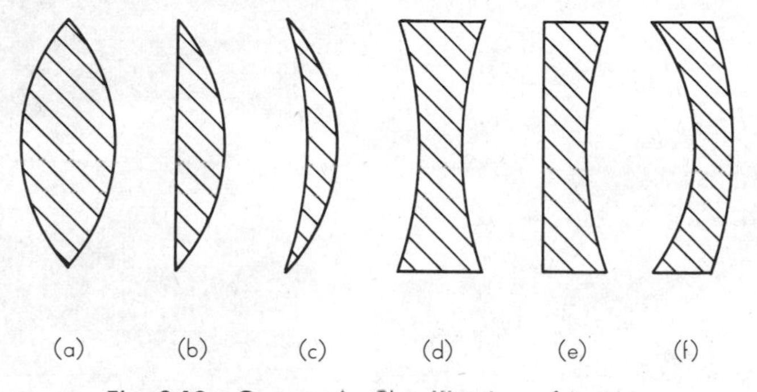


Fig. 3-12. Geometric Classification of Lenses

through it toward the object being viewed. A lens which is made of a single piece of material is called a *simple lens.*

Lenses are classified geometrically by six types as follows: (a) double convex or biconvex, (b) plano-convex, (c) positive meniscus, (d) double concave or biconcave, (e) plano-concave, (f) negative meniscus. See Fig. 3-12.

A line which passes through the center of curvature of a lens is called the *axis* of the lens. A *compound* lens is two or more simple lenses with a common axis.

### Aberrations of a Simple Lens

Simple lenses do not make perfect images. Many irregularities occur. These irregularities, or defects, are called aberrations. Some of the more important aberrations will now be considered in more detail.

### Chromatic Aberration

It was stated earlier in this chapter that light traveled in waves and that white light could be broken up into several colors. Each color has a different wave length. Red has a longer wave length than violet. As these rays strike and travel through a prism or lens, they are refracted differently and, therefore, do not come to a focus at the same point, Fig. 3-14. The image for each color becomes sharp at a different point. This produces a series of closely spaced colored images.

To correct this condition, the better quality lenses combine elements of different kinds of glass which have different indices

Fig. 3-13. (a) Photo Taken With an Uncorrected Reading Glass Lens
(b) Photo Taken With a Highly Corrected Lens

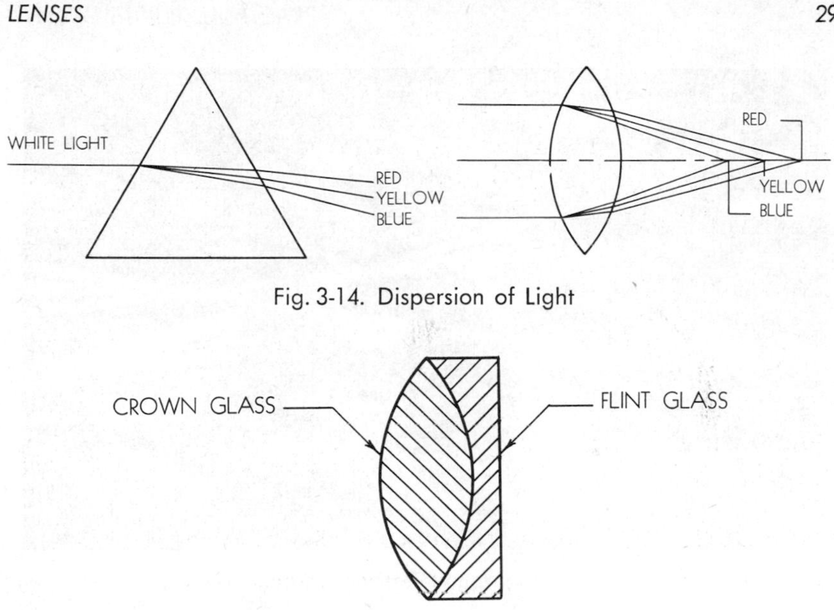


Fig. 3-14. Dispersion of Light

Fig. 3-15. Achromatic Lens

of refraction. The combination corrects the refraction so that the various colored images merge together as a single image. Figure 3-15 shows such a combination. A lens corrected for chromatic aberration is called an achromatic lens.

### Spherical Aberration

Spherical aberration is caused by the fact that light rays entering the lens at the edges come to a focus before those entering near the center, (Fig. 3-16). This can be corrected to a large degree by eliminating the border rays with a smaller diaphragm

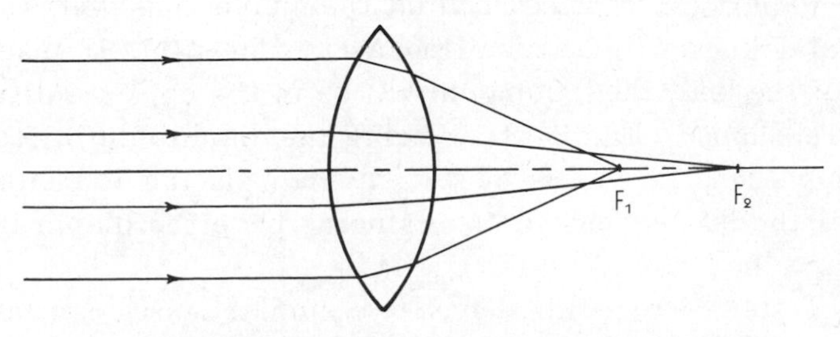


Fig. 3-16a. Effect of Spherical Aberration on Focus

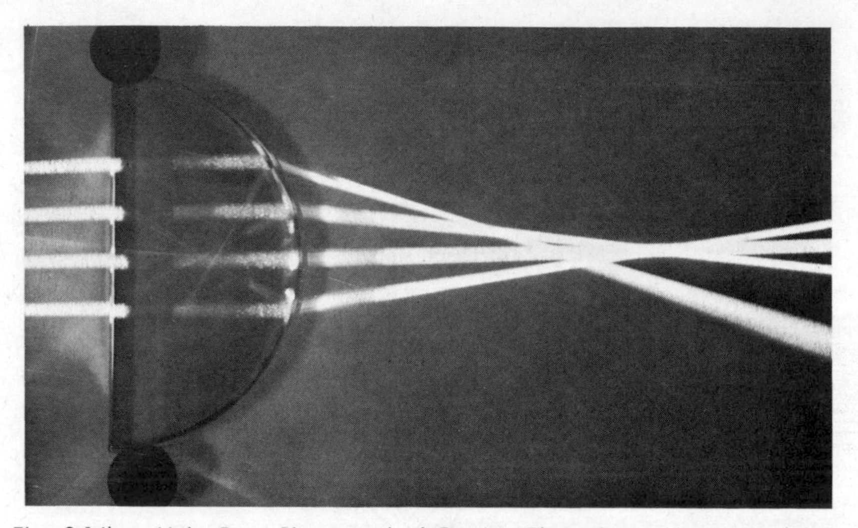

Fig. 3-16b. Light Rays Photographed Passing Through an Uncorrected Lens (Ray Nearest the Edge Does Not Focus at the Same Point as Those Near the Center)

opening. Fortunately, the correction for chromatic aberration also corrects spherical aberration to a large degree. By closing the diaphragm part way, it will make reasonably sharp pictures. Such a lens is often used in box cameras.

### Distortion

In order to regulate the amount of light entering a camera it is necessary to insert a diaphragm in front of, between, or behind the lens. Reducing the amount of light entering the lens by regulating the diaphragm opening is known as *stopping down.* If the diaphragm is placed behind the simple lens, vertical and horizontal lines will be distorted as in Fig. 3-17. If placed in front of the lens, the distortion will be in the opposite direction or barrel-shaped (Fig. 3-18). Placing the diaphragm in front of the simple lens gives less distortion than placing it behind; so most of the less expensive box cameras have the diaphragm in front and the lens behind it.

To better correct this defect two similar lenses can be used with the diaphragm between them. This arrangement is known as

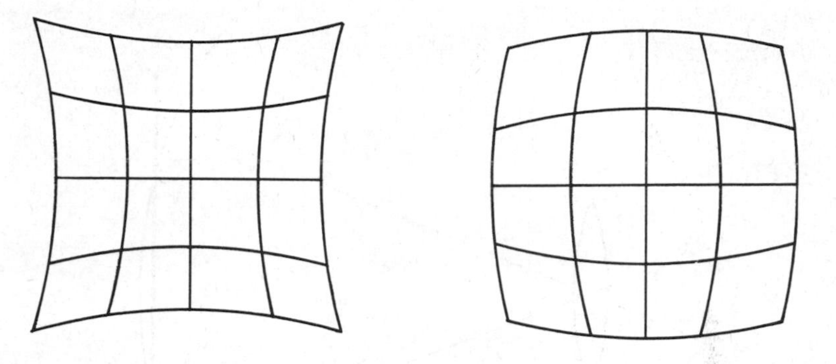

Fig. 3-17. Diaphragm Behind Lens    Fig. 3-18. Diaphragm in Front of Lens

the *doublet* or *rapid rectilinear* lens. The better box cameras and some professional cameras now have the rapid rectilinear lens.

### Curvature of the Field

The image formed by the lens of our eye falls on a curved surface, all points of which are equally distant from the center of the lens. This makes all points equally in focus. Cameras have no such arrangement, but use a flat plate or film. Since the image is formed in a curved line and it is desired on a flat surface, it is necessary that the film be placed at the best average position. This, of course, limits the useful angle of the lens. See Fig. 3-19.

Curvature of the field of anastigmats, described next, is always very much less than the simple lens. The better lenses have been optically corrected to produce a nearly flat field. Stopping the lens down by smaller diaphragm openings further reduces this defect.

### Astigmatism

It is difficult to explain astigmatism in simple terms. Essentially it is the fact that light rays which strike the lens at an oblique angle distort and make a line instead of a point. This distortion may be either vertical or horizontal. The only possible way to correct astigmatism is to employ at least three separated lenses, or, if the lenses are to be cemented together, at least four lenses made of different material each properly placed. A lens so-corrected is said to be *stigmatic* or *anastigmatic*. Most of the better cameras have anastigmat lenses.

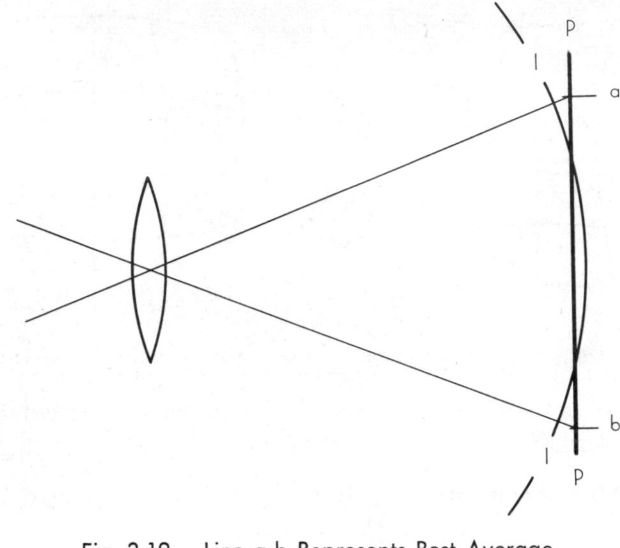


Fig. 3-19. Line a-b Represents Best Average
I Is Curved Image
P Is Photographic Plate

Lenses corrected for astigmatism have also been corrected to produce what lensmakers call a *flat field.*

Remembering what has been said about lenses and their correction, one should hardly be satisfied with less than an anastigmatic lens except for some special types of work. This has most of the corrections necessary for fine work.

## CHOOSING AND USING LENSES

### Focal Length

The focal length of a lens is the distance from the lens to where the image of a distant object is formed. This place where the image is formed in the camera, where the film is placed, is known as the *focal plane.*

### Normal Focal Length

A normal lens is one which will produce a picture approximately as it would look to the human eye. *The focal length of the normal lens is roughly equal to the diagonal of the film to be*

Fig. 3-20a. Photo Taken With Wide Angle Lens (90 mm) Using 4″ x 5″ Film

Fig. 3-20b. Photo Taken With Normal Lens (150 mm) With Camera in Same Position as Fig. 3-20a

*used.* This is the lens that is used for a large majority of the pictures that are taken. Some cameras are sold without lenses and the buyer chooses a lens for the camera. If the buyer can afford only one lens, he should get the normal focal length lens first. All other lenses are for special purposes.

### The Wide-angle Lens (Shorter than normal focal length)

As the name of this lens implies, it covers a wider angle of view than does the standard lens. This lens has some special characteristics that should be known by all who attempt to use it.

Probably the most obvious use of this lens is to include areas that would be impossible with normal lens. Such uses include pictures where it would be impossible to back up far enough with the normal lens to include the area to be photographed or where other objects, not wanted in the photograph, would be included with the normal lens.

Another useful purpose of the short focal length lens is for photographing very small objects to make large pictures of them, such as insects, small flowers, the texture and structure of minerals and plants. This photographing of small objects in life size or bigger is sometimes called *Macro* photography. The short focal length lens is especially suited to this work because it has great depth of field (depth of field is explained later in this chapter). Because of the great depth of field obtainable with this lens, some sports photographers use it for action shots and then enlarge the part that they want.

There are some precautions to be observed when using a wide angle lens. The wide angle lens distorts perspective. This means that this lens should not be used for extreme close-ups of people. The parts of the face nearest the lens will be relatively too large and those parts more distant, such as the ear, would be relatively smaller. The person would appear to have a large nose and little ears. Because of distorted perspective a room of medium size will seem almost twice as long. Distances between objects will be exaggerated. (look longer than they really are). If it is necessary to hold the camera at an angle to the subject being taken, the vertical lines of windows, doors, and corners often take on an objectionable perspective.

Fig. 3-20c. Photo Taken With Long Focal Length Lens (305 mm) With Camera in Same Position as Fig. 3-20a and 3-20b

### The Long Focal Length Lens

The long focal length lens acts on the same principle as a telescope or binoculars. It brings distant objects closer by magnifying them. This gives the photographer many advantages over the wide-angle and normal lens. With the normal lens the photographer must be within a few feet of his subject to make a close-up photo. The longer focal length lenses permit close-ups of people, birds, and animals taken from a distance. Birds and animals will usually not permit a photographer to approach close enough for a good picture with a normal lens. People are uncomfortable when the camera is too close and "freeze." Pictures that would otherwise be inaccessable can be taken. A good example of the latter would be an eagle's nest built where man cannot reach it, or an object across a river or canyon.

The long focal length lens also has special characteristics that the photographer should understand. While it fills the negative with an image of a distant object, it also gives the scene a quality of flatness. This lens tends to bring the separate planes of the composition closer together. This means that objects at various distances in the scene, even though they are quite a distance apart, seem to be very close together. This apparent flatness can be partly overcome by side lighting and the use of filters.

The long focus lens has an apparent lack of depth. Objects at a considerable distance in front of, and behind the object being focused upon will not be sharp. This can also work to your advantage by deliberately fuzzing out unwanted background.

Lenses of the same focal length do not always cover the same area of a negative. This is a very important consideration when the lens is to be used for corrective photography with a view camera. The telephoto lenses, in general, are not suited for corrective photography because the area covered by this type of lens is considerably less than a regular long focus lens of the same rated focal length.

Some cameras are made so that the lens can be easily changed. This allows for the use of either a short, medium, or long focus lens.

#### f-Rating

Up to this point the main consideration has been the focal length. The second major way a lens is rated is its *f-number*. This term has been widely misunderstood, and needlessly so.

The f-rating is a scientific way of stating the relationship that exists between the *focal length* of the lens and the effective diameter of the lens opening. The size of the lens opening may be regulated by a diaphragm placed between the lens elements, with a scale and means of adjusting it attached to the lens housing. *The f-rating is simply a fraction of the focal length.* A lens set at f/4 has an effective diameter which measures $\frac{1}{4}$ of its focal length. A lens rated at f/2 has an effective diameter of $\frac{1}{2}$ of its focal length or twice as much as the one rated at f/4, provided, of course, that the focal length of each is the same. If one lens has a diameter twice as great as the other lens, the area of the opening would be *four* times as great. Since $\frac{1}{2}$ is larger than $\frac{1}{4}$, the lens rated at f/2 is faster than the lens rated at f/4. It is four times faster.

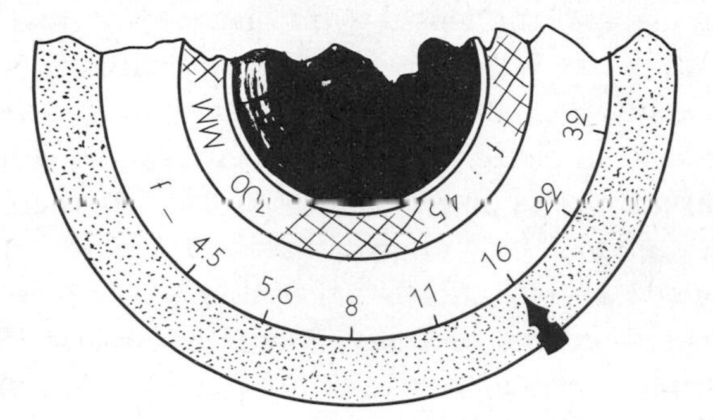


Fig. 3-21. Scale Indicating f-Opening

Remember the *smaller* the f-number the *faster* the lens. It is also important to remember that *closing the diaphragm from one f-number to the next reduces the amount of light striking the film by one half.*

Every lens has a scale which indicates its f-opening, (usually called "stops"), and an indicator for setting it to any opening which you choose, Fig. 3-21.

When the size of the diaphragm opening is reduced it is called "stopping down" the lens.

### Adjusting the Lens Opening

You may ask: Why should I stop down my f/2 lens so that the opening is no larger than the lens of a box camera? The answer is, that in the first place, you probably do not need that much light; and, in the second place, you will get sharper pictures and greater depth of field, if it is stopped down.

When a lens is made to focus the image of distant objects on the focal plane, only distant objects will be in sharp focus. Objects at other distances will be more or less out of focus. The closer the object the more out of focus it will be. Box cameras have fixed focus lenses, (lenses that cannot be moved to bring other objects in focus). When using a box camera no attempt should be made to photograph objects closer than about twelve feet, unless there is provision on the camera for closer distances. A lens will converge light rays from any given point so that they will focus to a point on the film, if the ratio of the object-to-lens distance and the lens-to-film distance is exactly correct. If the film is placed either in front of or behind this point, the rays from a given point will not register as a point but will register as a small circle. These small circles are referred to in photography as circles of confusion. As long as these circles do not exceed a diameter of approximately 1/100 of an inch they are not noticed at reading distance. When they are larger the picture appears blurred or fuzzy. Stopping down a lens reduces the size of the circles of confusion and the picture shows more depth.

### Depth of Field

Most cameras have a means of moving the lens to bring closer objects into focus. When this is done, objects which were formerly in focus may be out of focus. The distance between the nearest object and the farthest object which appear in satisfactory sharpness is called the *depth of field.*

Examine Fig. 3-22a. Notice that when the lens is fully open, a small circle placed in the converging cone is very close to the film, but in 3-22b, the same circle placed in the converging cone of a lens that has been stopped down is at a considerable distance

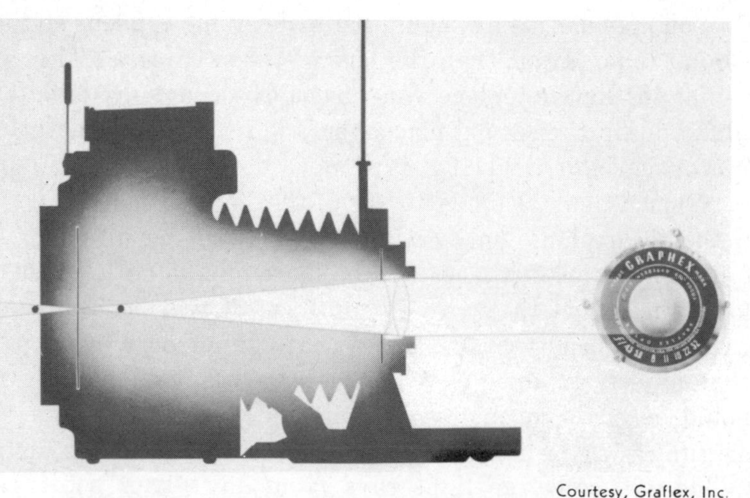


Courtesy, Graflex, Inc.

Fig. 3-22a. Depth of Focus When Lens Is Wide Open

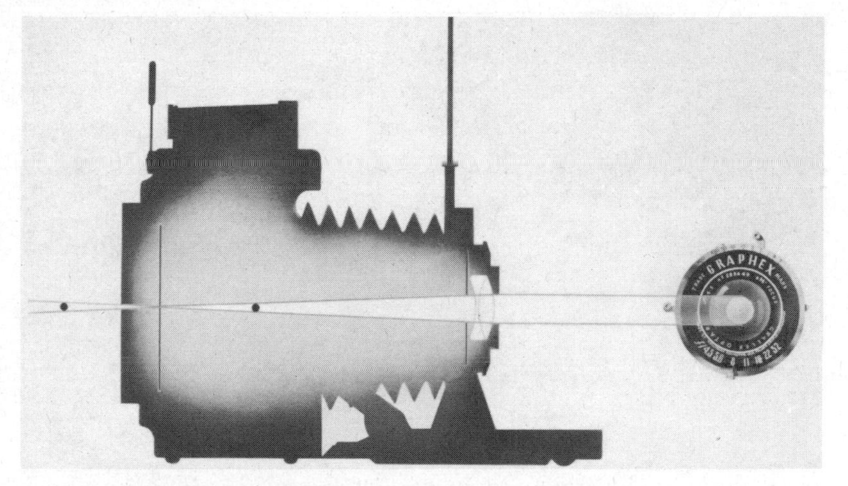


Fig. 3-22b. Depth of Focus When Lens Is Stopped Down

Fig. 3-22c. Graphic Illustration of Depth of Field

from the film. It is within these limits of acceptable sharpness that depth of field indicators are made.

Some cameras have a scale or indicator which gives the approximate depth of field with each lens opening and distance to the principal object. A glance at the illustration (Fig. 3-23) will be sufficient to determine how they are used. As an example, suppose the principal object focused upon was ten feet distant. At a stop opening of f/32, everything in front of the principal object as close as five feet from the camera will be reasonably sharp, while everything to infinity behind the object will be sharp. If, however, stop f/8 is used, objects will be sharp only two feet in front of the principal object or eight feet from the camera, and objects will be in sharp focus approximately four feet behind the principal object or 14 feet from the camera.

Fig. 3-22d. Photograph of Numbers Spaced One Foot Apart Taken at f-4.5

Fig. 3-22e. Photograph of Numbers Spaced One Foot Apart Taken at f-32

If stop f/4.5 is used, objects will be sharp approximately one foot in front and two feet behind the object focused upon. Notice the marked *decrease* in the depth of field as larger openings are used.

Figure 3-22d and e shows two photographs. One was taken with the lens set at its maximum opening. The other photograph was taken with the lens stopped to f/32.

### Supplementary Lenses

It is often difficult to obtain photographs under all conditions with the normal focal length lens. It is difficult to approach a wild animal close enough to obtain a good photograph with such a lens. It is also difficult to obtain a large image of a very small flower with such a lens. Supplementary lenses are used on cameras that have no provision for changing lenses. The general effect is similar to that obtained with the wide-angle

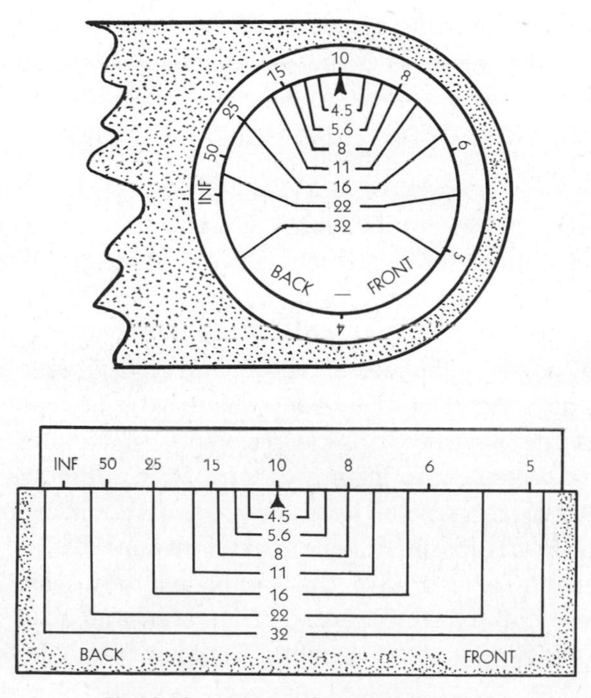


Fig. 3-23. Depth of Field Indicators

and long focal length lenses. These lenses, however, lack some of the qualities of a regular wide-angle and long focal length lens. A number of supplementary lenses are available so that the photographer may choose the effect he desires.

### Portrait Attachment

The portrait attachment is a positive meniscus lens which, when used with the regular lens, permits photographing subjects at a much closer distance than is otherwise possible. They are available in 3/4+, 1+, 3+ diopters.* These lenses are all wide angle lenses. The 3+ lens has the greatest magnification, it also has the widest angle.

When this type lens is used, the focusing scale on the camera cannot be used because the combination changes the focal length. Since the focusing scale cannot be used and because the depth of field is extremely short, *it is necessary to focus on a ground glass or measure the distance carefully.*

The word portrait attachment is somewhat misleading. Portraits can be taken with these supplementary lenses, but the camera must be very close to the subject. This causes some undesirable effects which were explained under the heading wide-angle lenses.

### Supplementary Lenses for Telephoto Effect

Supplementary lenses which convert standard lens to give a telephoto effect are negative meniscus lenses. These lenses are used to photograph distant objects, animals, birds, etc. They have a low power telephoto effect and are obtainable in 1–, 2–, 3–, and 4– diopters. The 4– lens has the greatest telephoto effect; it also has the narrowest angle. In using these supplementary lenses, it is necessary to have a camera with a double extension bellows, or other means of extending the distance from the lens to the film. Focusing must be done on a ground glass.

The image formed with this supplementary lens, especially the –4, may not cover the entire film area and may therefore fall off in sharpness at the corners. Supplementary lenses do not

* A "diopter" is an expression of the power of a lens. It is defined as: 1 ÷ focal length in meters. A lens with a one meter focal length (39.4 inches) would have 1 dioptic power. The + sign indicates a positive lens and the — sign indicates a negative lens.

do the same job as long focal length lenses. They are not recommended where corrective photography is employed.

In using any of the supplementary lenses the effective f - number is changed. In the portrait lenses the effective lens aperture is increased. If negative lenses are used the effective lens aperture is decreased. In both cases the effect is great enough that this change must be considered if correct exposures are expected. A lens guide should be obtained from a reliable dealer or the effect calculated by the use of the following formula:

$$\text{Effective f-number} = \frac{v \times f}{F}$$

Let v = the distance from lens to film
and f = the indicated f-number of aperture
and F = the focal length

The exposure is then calculated by using the effective f-number instead of the number to which you have the lens set. As an example:

When the camera is properly focused the distance from the lens to the film measures $7\frac{3}{8}$ inches. The lens is stopped to f/22 to get increased depth of field. The focal length of the lens is 5 inches.

$$Ef = 32.4$$

Drop the .4 from the calculation. Leave the lens set at f/22 but calculate the exposure as though the lens were set at f/32.

### Care of Lenses

A lens is a precision instrument. Much skill and care have been exercised in making it. It should be kept in the best of condition if it is to perform properly. A few suggestions and warnings should be carefully followed in its care.

A lens is mounted so that it is the correct distance from the film and in proper alignment. A change of alignment of an extremely small fraction of an inch will render pictures which are imperfect. If the parts do not work smoothly, *do not force them.* To do so may throw the lens out of alignment. Care should be exercised not to drop a camera or to let it bang against solid objects. A lens cap and a carrying case are recommended.

It is necessary to clean the front and back surface of the lens occasionally. Great care should be taken so that the lens surface is not scratched. To remove dust or grit gently brush the surface with a soft camel's-hair brush. If a camel's-hair brush is not available, use a piece of lens tissue (which should always be available) wadded to form a brush and used as a brush. If this does not clean the lens, wipe it gently with a wad of lens tissue using a circular motion. Always wipe lightly. Occasionally, finger prints or scum formation on the lens cannot be removed by these procedures. In this case, never wash the lens with water, alcohol, acid or other harsh solvent. Use one or two drops of a reliable lens cleaner on a wad of lens tissue. Do not let finger marks remain on the lens. To do so will eventually ruin the lens.

Protect the lens from spray when near the sea and from sand at all times. Sand driven hard by the wind can ruin the lens in a few seconds.

Keep the camera away from the radiator, car pocket, and other sources of intense heat to avoid ruining the lens. Quick changes in temperature may damage the lens and should be avoided. A camera and lens should be protected from wet weather. One last warning about the care of the lens: *Never take it apart.* It was made, assembled, and tested by skilled workmen with precision instruments and is easily damaged. If the lens is cared for properly, it will last indefinitely.*

## PRACTICAL EXPERIMENTS

### Studying the Formation of an image Through a Pin Hole.

*Materials Required* —

1. Electric light or candle.
2. Pin hole camera.
3. Ground glass or tissue paper.

*Procedure* —

1. Secure or make a pin hole camera.
2. With the back removed, place a ground glass in position

*Note — See Appendix (A) for further references on the subject of lenses.

where the film would normally be placed. If a ground glass is not available, stretch a piece of tissue paper over the back and secure with a rubber band.

3. Place the lighted electric light or candle 10 feet from the camera. Look on the ground glass and observe;
   a. The image of the filament.
   b. The size of the image.
4. Place the light at 5 feet from the camera and make the same observations as before. This may be repeated at 3 feet if desired.

*Questions* —

1. How do you account for the difference in the size of the image?
2. Does the image change in sharpness with a change in distance of the light from the pin hole? Give reason for your answer.

### Discovering Some Characteristics of a Lens.

*Materials Required* —

1. Lens — Any converging lens such as a reading glass is satisfactory.
2. Measuring tape or stick.
3. Candle or lamp.
4. White paper and pencil.

*Procedure* —

Light the candle or lamp then darken the room. With the candle on the opposite side of the room, hold the lens so that it makes a sharp image of the candle on the white paper. Trace this image with a pencil. Measure the distance from the lens to the paper. Place the information obtained in your notebook.

Now bring the candle closer to the lens, (about 3 feet). Again measure the distance from the lens to the paper. Trace this image on a sheet of white paper. Examine the image closely to determine whether it is sharp and clear.

Cut a round hole in a piece of paper so that the diameter of the hole is about half the diameter of the lens. Place this over the lens and note the result.

*Questions* —

1. Why is the image inverted?
2. Does the distance of the object from the lens change the size of the image? Why?
3. Is the distance from the lens to the paper the same in both cases? Give the reason for your answer.
4. Does the small hole over the lens make any difference in the sharpness of the image?
5. What effect does reducing the lens aperture have upon the brightness of the image?

It is suggested that the student consult a physics text or other book related to lenses and image formation to help find the answer to these questions.

### Determining the Effect of the Size of the Lens Opening on the Depth of Field.

*Materials Required* —

1. A camera with a means of focusing and a lens with the apertures marked.
2. Film for above camera.

*Procedure* —

1. Arrange some objects near the camera and include a distant object. Your classmates or friends can be placed about 15 feet from the camera with your school building in the distance.
2. Make one exposure with camera set at infinity and lens set at f/32. Make the second exposure, without moving either camera or objects, with camera set at infinity and lens at its maximum opening. Calculate each exposure so that the exposure is correct.
3. Set up a group of objects so that they are one foot apart and the closest one is 2 feet from the camera lens. The

farthest object should be 10 feet from the camera lens.

4. Make one exposure with camera focused at 5 feet and lens set at f/32. Make another exposure with the camera focused at 5 feet as before and lens set at its maximum opening.
5. Develop and make prints for your notebook.

*Questions —*

1. Is there any difference in the depth of field when the camera is focused on a near object and when set at infinity? Explain your answer.
2. How do you account for the fact that objects vary in sharpness with a change in the size of the lens opening?

CHAPTER IV

# methods of obtaining correct exposure

Exposure means the total action of light on any particular point of the film. This is the beginning of the processes which are necessary to produce a photograph. If the exposure is not correct good prints cannot be expected. No matter how well the other manipulations are performed, no matter how good the position, etc., the pictures will not be perfect unless the exposure is correct. Exposure can mean success or failure.

After the film is exposed and developed, a silver deposit is left on the film. This deposit is black. The amount of blackening of the film depends upon three things; the intensity of the light, the length of time the light strikes the film, and the sensitivity of the film. The intensity of the light is regulated by adjusting the size of the lens aperture. The length of time that the light is permitted to strike the film is regulated by the shutter. The sensitivity of the film is determined by the manufacturer. The film speed rating is published for each film.

### Methods of Regulating Amount of Light

Light intensity is controlled in the camera by the diaphragm or stop. There are two general types of diaphragms in use today — the rotating, and the iris.

The rotating diaphragm is a circular piece of metal with holes of the appropriate size cut into it near the margin and mounted so that the disc can be rotated with the finger. This is the simplest and cheapest type of diaphragm. Usually there is a choice of four openings. This, of course, limits the person using it, but is quite effective with the less expensive cameras. It is sometimes used in the box camera.

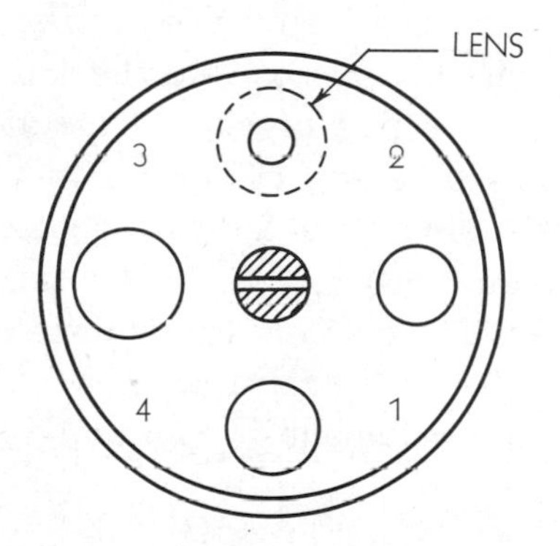


Fig. 4-1a. Rotating Diaphragm

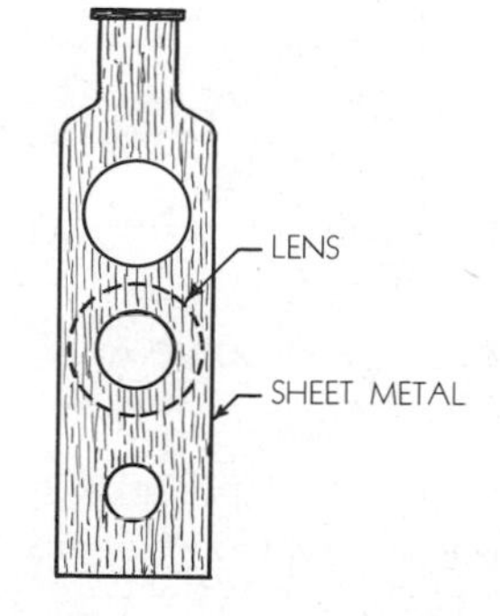


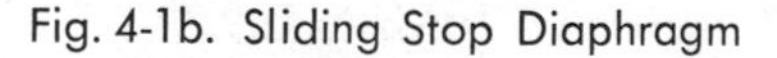

Fig. 4-1b. Sliding Stop Diaphragm

Of historical interest is the Waterhouse diaphragm, named after John Waterhouse its inventor. It consists of a thin piece of sheet metal with a hole cut into one end, and made to fit into a slot in the lens mount. A separate metal strip is required for each lens opening. There are as many of these metal strips as there are lens openings. All that is necessary is to select the proper strip and insert it in the lens mount. This type diaphragm is seldom seen in modern photography. A similar device is sometimes used in box cameras. It consists of a piece of sheet metal with three or four holes in it. To use this device, it is only necessary to pull it out to the desired stop by lifting up on the Small handle. Each stop is marked by a number. Fig. 4-1 (b).

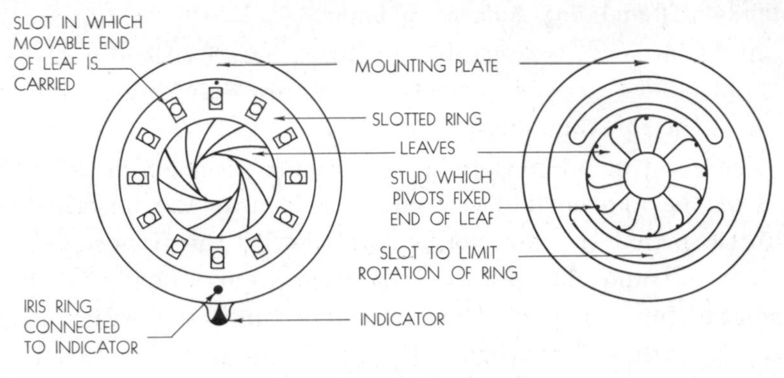


Fig. 4-2. Iris Diaphragm

The iris diaphragm is the one most commonly used today. It is named the "iris" because it opens and closes like the iris of the eye. (Fig. 4-2.) It consists of a series of curved metal plates which are fitted inside the lens tube and connected to a ring on the outside. By rotating this ring or a lever attached to it, all of the leaves are moved simultaneously, thus forming a larger or smaller opening as desired. The opening thus formed is not quite round, but this has no effect on the optical system. The iris type diaphragm is the most convenient to use and is found in most of the better cameras.

## Systems of Marking

There are at least a half dozen systems that have been used to mark the opening of the diaphragm. The diaphragm opening, which is called a stop, is usually marked in numbers on the ring of the diaphragm or on a plate which covers it. If it is marked on the plate, an indicator will rotate about the numbers to show which stop is in use. Included in the systems of marking were the "f", "US", "Zeiss", "Voigthlander" and several others. Since the "f" system is used on most cameras, the other systems will not be discussed.

The "*f*" system, as stated in Chapter III, is a relationship between the diameter of the lens opening, or aperature, and the focal length of the lens. The "f" indicates the speed of the lens or, in other words, the amount of light the lens lets through in proportion to its focal length.

Some years ago the photographer more or less guessed at the size of the lens opening and then guessed at the exposure that would be required. In 1881 some members of the Royal Photographic Society of Great Britain worked out a system of apertures based on a sequence of ratios so that aperature and exposure time could be controlled scientifically. They began with a unit of *one* as an aperture of f/4. The ratio worked out gave each succeeding stop an area of just one-half ($\frac{1}{2}$) of the previous one. Each numerical stop, as the stops become smaller, lets in just half as much light as the preceding one.

The "f" system is used in most of the world today. The following table shows the common f/stops in use today, the fraction of the focal length which each represents, and the ratio of exposures.

| f- | 1.4 | 2.8 | 4 | 5.6 | 8 | 11 | 16 | 22 | 32 | 45 | 64 |
|---|---|---|---|---|---|---|---|---|---|---|---|
| Fraction of Focal Length | $\frac{1}{1.4}$ | $\frac{1}{2.8}$ | $\frac{1}{4}$ | $\frac{1}{5.6}$ | $\frac{1}{8}$ | $\frac{1}{11}$ | $\frac{1}{16}$ | $\frac{1}{22}$ | $\frac{1}{32}$ | $\frac{1}{45}$ | $\frac{1}{64}$ |
| Exposure Ratio | $\frac{1}{4}$ | $\frac{1}{2}$ | 1 | 2 | 4 | 8 | 16 | 32 | 64 | 128 | 256 |

## Methods of Regulating Time

Attention will now be directed to the mechanical devices which control the time the light is allowed to pass.

The oldest method of controlling the amount of time was to have a light-tight cap on the lens which was removed by hand, and replaced when sufficient time had elapsed. This is a very inexpensive method but will hardly suffice with modern high speed films. This might be tried with the pin hole camera.

Inexpensive box cameras are usually equipped with a single metal plate which is attached to a spring. When a lever is pushed the spring rotates the plate allowing the light to enter for about 1/50 of a second. These mechanical devices, which are used to control the amount of time the light is allowed to pass, are called *shutters*. Some of the modern box cameras have a two blade shutter which works on the same principle.

Many of the better cameras have a very complicated device which allows exposure times of from one second to 1/500 second. This is indeed a wide range. In addition they have provision for time and bulb exposures. Some of the more expensive models have still another feature which delays the opening of the shutter for several seconds, and enables a person to take his own picture. The shutter is set to the proper f - opening and time, and the shutter spring lever then pressed. There is time for the operator to take his place with the rest of the group before the click of the shutter. The whole thing is automatic. A detailed

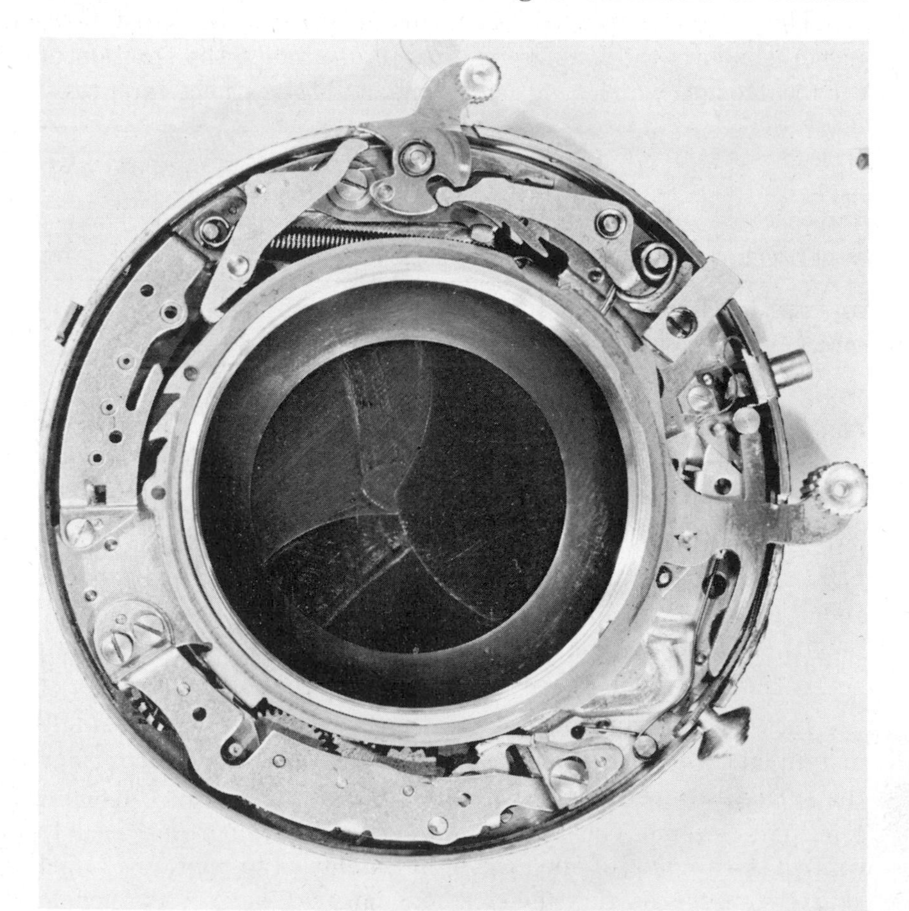

Fig. 4-3. Compur Shutter Mechanism

description of the internal working of this shutter will not be given because the mechanism is rather intricate. A complete description can be found in most handbooks in photography.

The type shutter just described is often combined with the iris diaphragm and mounted between the elements of the compound lens. There is another shutter in general use today which is placed immediately in front of the film (focal plane) and is called the *focal plane shutter.* This shutter is merely a black curtain, very similar to a window shade, which has slits of different widths cut across it. The openings (slits) vary in size from the full size of the film to one-eighth inch in width. The curtain is wound on two spools and is operated by releasing the spring, thus drawing the selected slit across the film. The spring tension is variable and is controlled by a lever or winding key. This type of shutter has some distinct advantages. While the curtain does not move as fast as the between-the-lens shutter, it does not expose the entire film at one time. Because of this fact, extremely short exposures are possible. Shutters of the type just described are used in the Graflex and Speed Graphic cameras, and in some miniature cameras. Several miniature cameras have a shutter designed to change the width of the slit instead of a number of slits.

### Care of the Shutter

Like a fine watch the shutter may occasionally need cleaning and adjusting. However, *the inexperienced person should never try to do this work.* It is a job for experts. Never oil the shutter, for to do so will probably change its speed. Cameras should never be left with the shutter in a cocked or strained position. The spring may become weakened and thus make the shutter inaccurate.

The importance of a good shutter cannot be over-emphasized. Get a good shutter, in keeping with the type of pictures desired. To obtain good pictures it is important to take proper care of the shutter.

**Directions for Using the Shutter**

There are few, if any, adjustments on the box camera. There may be a selection of three or four stops. No focusing is necessary on most cameras. A few box cameras do have a little lever to move which focuses within a speed range. See Fig. 4-4. If the box camera has no adjustments, pictures of objects closer than about 12 feet should not be attempted. A portrait attachment will permit pictures at a closer distance. The shutter speed of the box camera is fixed and is from 1/25 second to 1/50 second.

A folding camera may have arrangement similar to Fig. 4-5. It is necessary to know how to regulate the speed and the stop in order to get the picture. Before buying a used camera test the shutter by ear. It can be detected easily whether each change of

Fig. 4-4. Box Camera With Adjustments for Lens Opening and Distance

speed setting makes a difference in the speed. A highly corrected lens is of little value unless a good shutter is used.

Good shutters have speeds ranging from one to 1/250 or even 1/500 of a second. Near the top of the shutter, Fig. 4-5, is a group of numbers, plus the letters "T" and "B". The "T" is for time exposure. If a picture having an exposure of several seconds or minutes is desired, the pointer is set at "T". This may be done either by moving a little lever or by rotating the outer band, depending upon the make of shutter. Push the release lever or cable to open the shutter. The shutter will remain open until

Fig. 4-5a. Compur Lens-Shutter Assembly

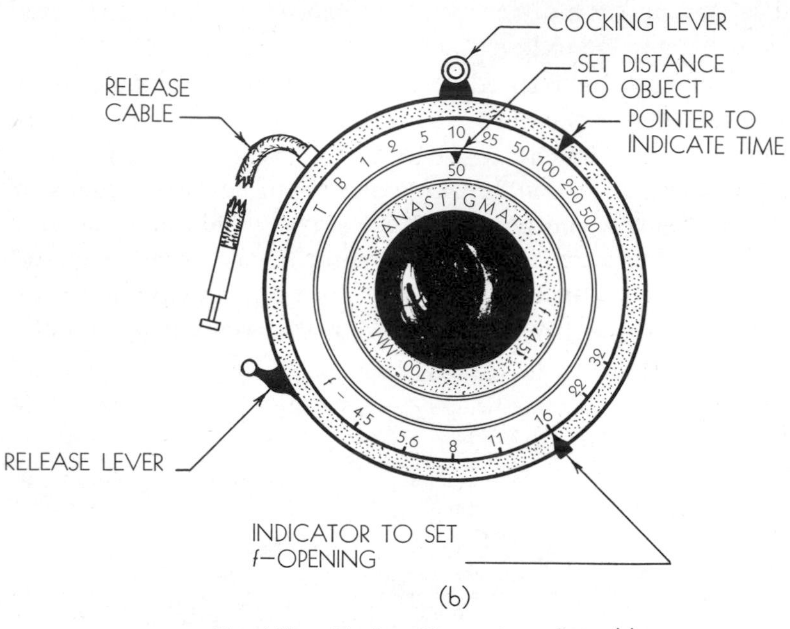


Fig. 4-5b. Modern Shutter-Lens Assembly

the release is again pushed. In order to focus on the ground glass back, it is usually necessary to open the shutter in this manner.

To take a picture which requires an exposure of three seconds, the pointer should be set to "B". To make the exposure press the release lever or release cable down. This opens the shutter. The shutter will stay open only as long as the release is held down. It is better to use the cable release rather than the lever, because there is less danger of moving the camera and spoiling the picture. An exposure of this kind can be timed with a watch, or the seconds may be counted. A little practice in counting seconds may be required but accuracy can soon be acquired by counting out loud — one thousand one, one thousand two, one thousand three, etc. Use a watch for timing in practice.

The numbers on the time scale are fractions of a second. The numerator of the fraction is 1 thus, 1/1, 1/2, 1/5, 1/10, 1/ 25, 1/50, 1/100, etc. These speed steps are graduated so that any step is one-half as long as the preceding one. The whole fraction is not marked on the shutter, just the lower number. The steps of the diaphragm openings (stops) are calibrated in the same proportion, each succeeding stop lets in half as much light as the preceding one. This arrangement is very convenient for tho photographcr.

If the film and light require the camera to be set at 1/50 second at f/16 and suddenly it is desired to photograph a fast moving object, the camera must be reset quickly. To do this just remember: *Next larger stop — next faster speed,* or vice versa. To reset your camera from 1/50 second at f/16 to 1/500 second move the time indicator three intervals. Then open the diaphragm three intervals (f/5.6) and the camera is set. Do not be disturbed that the settings do not seem to fit the mathematical ratio of 2:1, just remember the simple rule. If the speed is increased one interval (one number on the ring) open the diaphragm one interval. If the speed is decreased one interval, close the diaphragm one interval or stop.

The focal plane shutter has a dial or plate that indicates the speeds available. This type of shutter has provision for time exposures and some of them have a provision for bulb. The focal plane shutter has greater range of speeds than the between-the-lens shutter. The range of speeds varies with the make of shutter. As an example: One company makes a shutter that has a range from 1/2 sec. to 1/1250 sec., another company's shutter has thirteen marked speeds from 1 second to 1/1000 sec., still another offers 27 speeds from 12 full seconds to 1/1000 sec.

Focal plane shutters are subject to some distortion, especially with fast moving objects. Stopping the lens helps some. When following fast moving action with a camera that is equipped with a focal plane shutter that travels horizontally across the film, be sure that the shutter curtain travels in the same direction that the subject is moving. It may be necessary to turn the camera upside down to have the shutter direction match the direction of the subject's motion.

The mechanics of setting the focal plane shutter are somewhat different than the between-the-lens shutter but the principle is the same. Usually there is a scale on the camera, which tells how to set the shutter speed. The diaphragm opening is set in the same way as previously described for the "between the lens" shutter. CAUTION — do not leave the shutter in the "set" position; it may weaken the spring.

### Film Speed Rating

There is one thing more which will influence the choice of speed and light and that is the sensitivity of the film. Obviously the camera should not be set the same for a very slow film as for a very fast (extremely sensitive) film. The subject of film speed is discussed more fully in the next chapter.

### Exposure Guides

There are three general devices useful in determining the proper exposure. They are:

1. Tables or Charts
2. Optical meters
3. Photo-electric meters

(See Chapter 5 for directions for flash exposure.)

### Tables and Charts

The simplest guide for finding correct exposure is a chart prepared by the company that makes the film. The chart indicates a shutter speed, the light conditions of the day (bright sun, hazy sun with shadows, cloudy but bright, and dull), and the characteristic of the subject. This type of chart is quite reliable under the conditions listed.

A second chart is used for indoor work using artificial light. This chart indicates the distance of the lights from the subject, size of bulb, and shutter speed.

### Other Factors Which Influence Exposure

The hour of the day may have a considerable influence on exposure. Films are more sensitive to the blue end of the spectrum than the red end. When the sun is rising in the morning or setting in the evening the rays pass through much more air than at noon. This filters out much of the blue and allows the reds and yellows to come through. This change of color affects exposure, and in color films, it greatly changes the color of the scene.

For black and white film during the one hour after sunrise and one hour before sunset, increase the exposure indicated on the exposure guide by at least one stop. That is, if the guide indicates f/11, open the lens one stop to f/8.

The time of year affects exposure. The winter sun, in the latitude of the United States, is low in the sky and shines for a shorter time each day. For winter scenes without snow, using black and white film, it is recommended that the exposure for monochrome be increased one stop.

It is posible that sometime you may be caught without a meter or guide or perhaps encounter some unusual conditions. If this should happen, make one exposure at your best guess, make a second exposure *eight times longer,* and a third exposure *eight times shorter.* The latitude of present day films is such that one of the exposures is almost certain to be satisfactory.

### Optical Meters

The comparison type optical meter is considered reliable. The principle of this meter is the comparison of an unknown light with a light of known brightness. A light of known brightness is fixed in the instrument and the light of unknown brightness comes through a wedge of increasing density. A wedge is a strip of film or paper with different steps of gray ranging *progressively from clear to black.* Select the step on the wedge which has the same intensity as the light in the meter and read the correct setting for the camera. This meter will work in extremely dim light which makes it more reliable than others. With the improvement and reliability of the modern photoelectric meter, this type meter is seldom found.

The success of the extinction type meter is dependent on several conditions. The many variations which affect the reading of this type meter makes it unreliable. It is not recommended. It makes use of the wedge but the principle is different than other meters. It is used by looking through the wedge until the object can just be seen or just fades from view. It depends upon this border line between dark and dim. If the eye is defective or out of focus because of intense light, this method is not reliable.

The meter which is probably most accurate is the photo-electric exposure meter. The photo-electric meter is made on the principle that two metals placed together will generate a small electric current when exposed to light. (Selenium on top of iron is one of the best.) This electric current is used to move an indicating hand over a dial. Some are calibrated to read foot candles and some have other calibrations. This meter has a dial on it which can be set to the film speed rating and also to the intensity of light as indicated by the meter. When properly set, the dial gives several combinations of shutter speeds and f-openings which will produce a good picture.

### Photo-Electric Meters

The photo-electric exposure meter is of two general types: the *incident light* meter and the *reflected light* meter.

The incident light meter measures the amount of light available from the light source. This assumes that every object within the scene will reflect its proportionate share. The reflected light meter measures the amount of light which is actually reflected from the subject. Both types have some advantages and some disadvantages over the other. Both types work very well and are very dependable if the operator will take the time to learn how to use them properly. Many of the meters now on the market can be converted from one type to the other.

The photo-electric meter is not a cure-all for lazy people. It is a fine piece of equipment and will save film and disappointment if used properly. Unless considerable time is devoted to learning to make full use of the photo-electric meter it would be better to use the tables that come with the film.

Because of the mechanical differences that exist in the many meters offered for sale, no attempt will be made in this book to give directions for using each. Each manufacturer publishes a small booklet giving full directions for use of its meter. Read this booklet carefully to be sure that you understand how to operate the meter properly. Remember, too, that it is a delicate instrument built to the precision of your watch; treat it accordingly.

CHAPTER V

# flash

## FLASH

There are times when natural light is not sufficient to make a proper exposure. This is particularly true of fast action. The photographer of a quarter century ago filled a trough with powdered magnesium. At the trip of a switch a spark would ignite the magnesium and a bright flash occurred, accompanied with a white cloud of smoke which filled the room. This magnesium flash supplied sufficient light to make excellent pictures but it was a clumsy, dangerous affair. It was for professionals only. The invention of the flash bulb and later, the electronic flash, has placed flash photography within the reach of every amateur photographer. Flash photography is not difficult, but there are some things which one should know in order to get the best from every flash exposure.

## THE FLASH LAMP

### Classification of Flash Lamps

Flash is classified by class bulb size, light output, and color. Flash lamps may be divided into four classes: F (fast), M (medium), S (slow), and FP (focal plane).

Class "F" lamps should be used with shutters that have "X" or "F" type synchronization. A synchronized shutter is one that

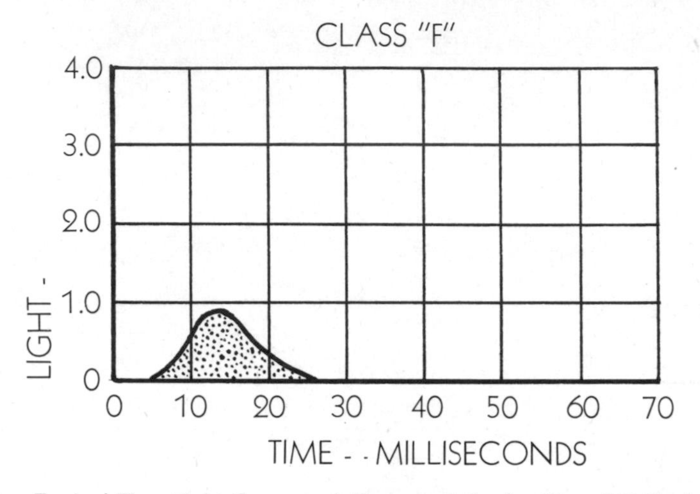


Fig. 5-1. Typical Time-Light Curve and Characteristics for Class "F" Flash Lamp

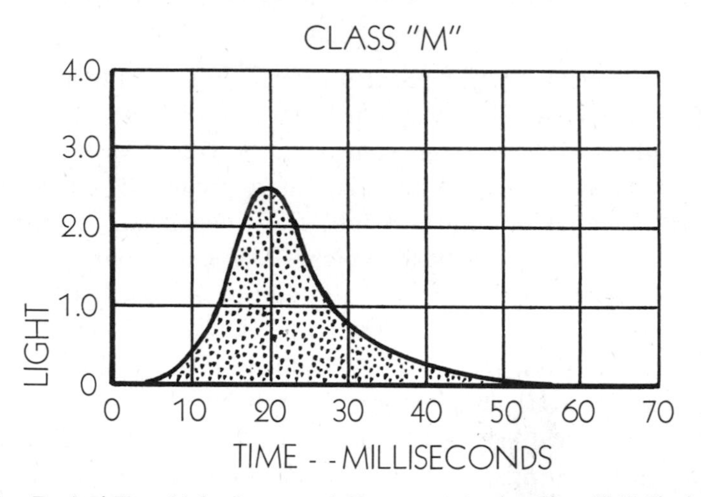


Fig. 5-2. Typical Time-Light Curve and Characteristics for Class "M" Flash Lamp

ignites the flash lamp so that the shutter is open at the proper time to use the maximum output of the lamp. An "F" synchronized shutter closes the contact to light the lamp, about 5 milliseconds before the shutter is fully open. The "X" synchronization closes the contact at the instant the shutter is fully open.

The class "M" lamp should be used with shutters marked for "M" synchronization. This is by far the most used type of lamp. The shutter with "M" synchronization closes the switch to ignite the lamp about 15 milliseconds before the shutter opens. The lamp reaches its peak in about 20 milliseconds.

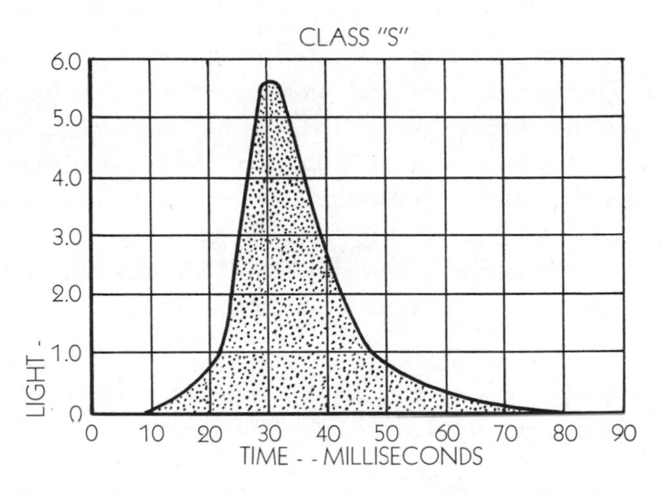


Fig. 5-3. Typical Time-Light Curve and Characteristics for Class "S" Flash Lamp

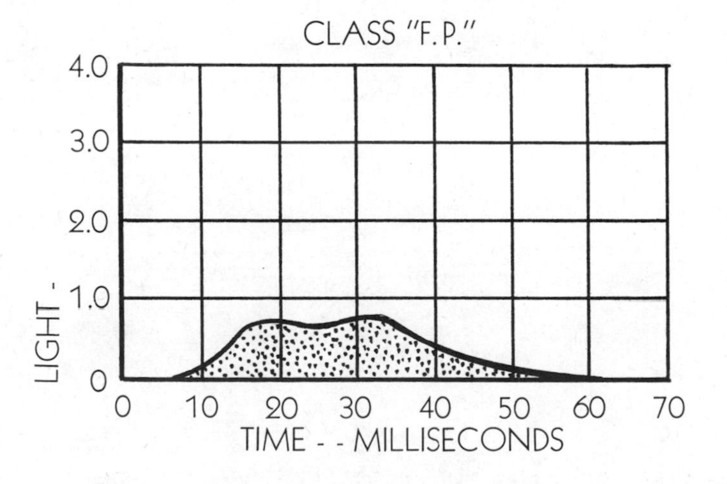


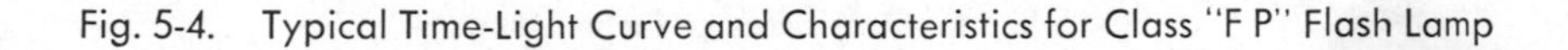

Fig. 5-4. Typical Time-Light Curve and Characteristics for Class "F P" Flash Lamp

The class "S" lamps are best used with slow shutter speeds or open flash. Open flash is often used when the shutter is not synchronized. This class lamp reaches its peak in about 30 milliseconds.

A large number of cameras have the shutter as a curtain near the film. They are called focal plane shutters. The focal plane shutter does not expose the entire film at the same instant but travels across it, exposing the film as it travels. The flash lamp for this type of shutter must maintain a steady light until the shutter has traveled across the film. The class F P (focal plane) lamp is used with focal plane shutters. This class of lamp may retain its intensity for as long as 40 milliseconds.

## Size

Flash lamps vary in size from a very small lamp no larger than the end of a pencil to a lamp 2 5/8″ diameter and 5 3/8 inches

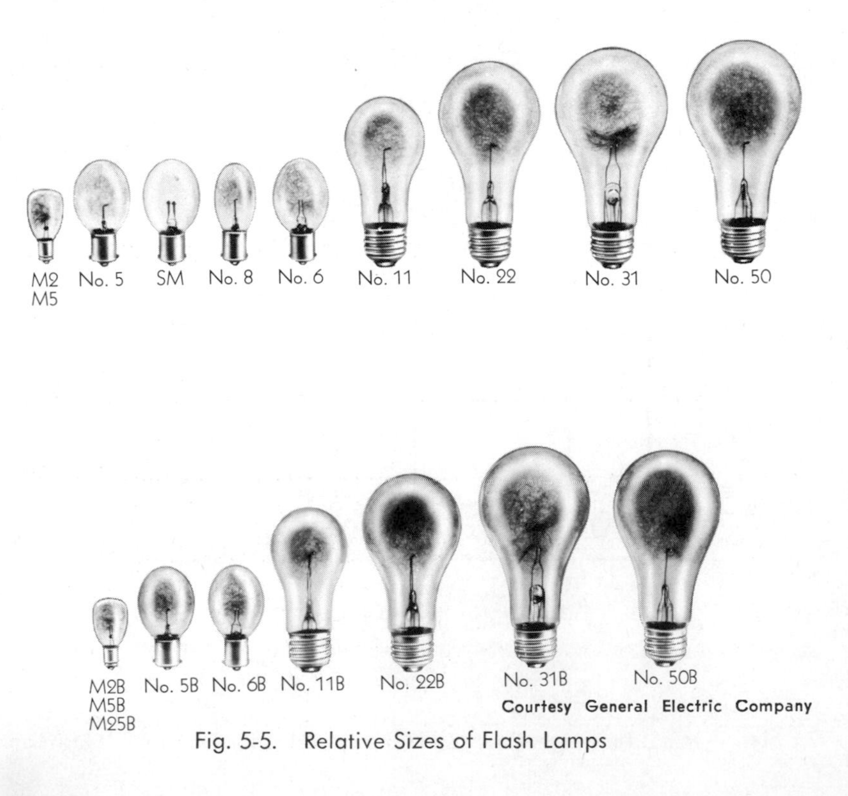


Courtesy General Electric Company

Fig. 5-5. Relative Sizes of Flash Lamps

long. The smaller sizes are usually made in what is known as a bayonet mount while the large sizes screw into a base in a manner similar to the ordinary light bulb. In general, the larger lamps produce more light and are best used in studio reflectors. The smaller bulbs are much easier to carry and are usually adequate for smaller groups. A full dozen may be carried in one pocket.

### Light Output

The output of flash lamps is measured by the number of lumens of light emitted at the time the light reaches its greatest intensity (peak). The very small bulbs emit approximately 550,000 lumens at the peak. The large bulbs may emit as many as 4,000,000 lumens at peak.

### Color

Color temperature is a term used to describe the color of the light. The color temperature is the temperature to which a black object must be raised (heated) so that the light it gives off is the same as the light being considered. The reader is aware that when a piece of black iron is heated it first becomes dull red, then bright red, and when heated very hot gives off nearly a white light. The wire in a light bulb is simply a heated wire. This temperature is measured on a thermometer called the Kelvin thermometer, named after the physicist who originated this method of recording high temperatures. It is based on the absolute scale. Color temperatures of lights are expressed in degrees Kelvin.

Flash lamps usually come in four color temperatures — 3300°K, 3800°K (most clear bulbs fall in this class) 4400°K and 6000°K (Blue/Bulbs).

When using color-film, it is important to have the color temperature of the bulb match that for which the film is balanced. Color films are made to be used at a specific color temperature. Blue colored flash bulbs (6000°K) should be used with film balanced for daylight or when shooting as a fill-in light for film balanced for artificial light that has a conversion filter over the lens. Color films balanced for artificial light are not all balanced for the same color temperatures. Be sure to check with the dealer to determine whether a correction filter is necessary. Light sources also vary.

Photofloods are balanced for 3400°K. Most clear flashbulbs are rated at 3800°K. Standard house lamps are about 2200°K. Noonday sun varies with the latitude. For most of the United States the noonday sun will approximate 5600°K. It becomes quite obvious that light sources for color photography must not be mixed. It should also be remembered that the light from a flashbulb varies throughout the length of the flash. It has its greatest color temperature at its peak and the lowest at the beginning and end of the flash. The camera shutter should be carefully synchronized to get only the peak of the flash.

### The Reflector

The reflector is a very important consideration in flash photography. Some reflectors direct a beam of light almost straight ahead, others spread it widely. In general, the larger the bulb the larger the reflector. As an example, a #5 bulb should have a reflector about five inches in diameter. A very large G.E. #50 bulb should have a ten-inch reflector. Be sure to match the reflector to the bulb to be used; otherwise a "hot spot" may result.

Some reflectors are polished and some are more or less dull. The latter type is usually called a "satin finish." Charts that show numbers to use for obtaining correct exposure may indicate "P" for polished reflector and "S" for satin finish. Other campanies may have a note which tells you how much to vary the exposure if you have a satin finish reflector.

The reflector may be more efficient than the one used to calculate the guide numbers, or it may be less efficient. It is a good plan to make some test exposures to determine whether you should use the guide numbers as they are listed or whether some adjustment should be made for your equipment.

### Guide Numbers

Correct exposure with flash is now quite simple. The manufacturer of flashlamps publishes a chart of numbers as a guide to correct exposure. Figure 5-6 is a typical chart. The numbers

| Tungsten Film Speed Rating | 10 | 12 | 20 | 25 | 32 | 40 to 64 | 80 to 125 | 160 to 250 |
|---|---|---|---|---|---|---|---|---|
| **SHUTTER SPEED** (Seconds) | GUIDE NUMBER | | | | | | | |
| Open Flash and 1/25 Sec. | 85 | 95 | 120 | 140 | 160 | 190 | 280 | 380 |
| 1/50 | 75 | 80 | 110 | 120 | 130 | 170 | 240 | 340 |
| 1/100 | 70 | 75 | 95 | 110 | 120 | 150 | 220 | 300 |
| 1/200 | 55 | 60 | 75 | 85 | 95 | 120 | 170 | 240 |
| 1/400 | 42 | 46 | 60 | 70 | 75 | 95 | 140 | 190 |

Guide numbers are for polished reflectors.
If satin reflector is used, open lens ½ stop.

Fig. 5-6. Typical Guide Number Chart

on the chart are called guide numbers. They are a constant factor for a given bulb and film speed. All that is necessary to obtain correct exposure is to divide the guide number by the distance in feet from the subject. If you have determined the stop that must be used and wish to know how far the bulb should be placed from the object, divide the flash factor by the stop.

As an example, assume that you have decided to use a film speed with an A.S.A. tungsten rating of 25 with a shutter speed of 1/100 sec. After focusing the camera the distance reads 10 feet. Consult chart above (Fig. 5-6). At the top, find the film speed tungsten rating. Follow down this column until you are opposite 1/100 second (shown on left side of chart). The number is 110. Divide 110 by 10 and the answer is 11. Set the lens opening to f/11.

Suppose now that you have a film with a tungsten rating of 80. The nature of the picture is such that you must stop the lens down to f/11 to get the necessary depth of field, and set the shutter speed 1/100 second. How far should the flash be held from the subject? Again consult the chart (Fig. 5-6). Locate the tungsten film speed at the top of the chart and the 1/100 second at the side. Follow these columns and you will find the guide num-

Fig. 5-7. Flash Used as "Fill-in" When Strong Sunlight From The Side Causes Harsh Shadows Left: Without Fill Right: With Fill

ber to be 220. Divide 220 by the f/stop (11) and the answer is 20 feet.

### Check Before You Shoot

There are a number of things that should be checked so that film and bulbs will not be wasted, with resultant disappointment.

Equipment should get a periodic check. Check the synchronization, wires, contacts, and check for corrosion especially of batteries and battery case.

Batteries should be kept fresh. Even though they may fire the bulb, a sluggish battery may cause a slight delay in igniting the bulb thus changing the timing of the flash. With B.C. units the battery is not quite as critical but should be checked periodically.

Distance of flash is important. For very close work it may be necessary to close the lens as far as it will go; yet you still have too much light. Get a smaller bulb if you can. A single white handkerchief thrown over the reflector in front of the flash will reduce the light one stop. Two thicknesses will reduce the exposure two stops. At close distances a plastic covering should be over the reflector to protect the subject from a bulb which in rare cases might shatter.

For distances beyond the distance calculated for correct exposure, acceptable exposures are often possible by aiming the light at the farthest distance to be covered. Raise the light as high as you can reach, or stand on a chair.

Dark walls, a big open hall or gymnasium or outdoors at night call for opening the lens one stop. Light in these situations does not bounce to aid in the exposure.

Flash lamps often cause a rather harsh light. Bounce flash is a softer more natural light. This type of flash is useful when there are reflecting surfaces, such as glass windows, that might reflect the flash back to the camera lens. It also avoids hot spots on glasses. Remember, the angle that you aim the flash at a wall or ceiling, is the angle that most of the light will be reflected. If the wall or ceiling is of medium or light color, hold the flash near the wall or ceiling and calculate the distance from the reflecting surface to the subject. Calculate the f/setting in the usual way then open the lens two stops. This should provide an acceptable exposure.

### Multiple Flash

Multiple flash (more than one bulb at a time) is needed where one bulb will not cover the area, or where it is desired to obtain a given light ratio; for example, for portraits. Calculations are made in the usual way and the lights directed so that the light overlaps and blends together. Lights may be connected to a single battery or may be fired by a special photoelectric cell arrangement.

## ELECTRONIC FLASH

A flashbulb gives only one flash and then must be discarded. Photographers demanded a bulb that would flash more than once. Dr. Harold E. Edgerton partly solved this problem when he conducted experiments with his "Stroboscopic Lamp." Many

Courtesy Tomlinson Studio

Fig. 5-8. Multiple Flash Photograph

improvements have been made in the original design so that today dependable electronic flash units are available. There are many makes and models available and many claims for this product — so many, that the amateur is likely to be confused when trying to decide which is best for him.

## How It Works

The principle of operation is quite simple. A battery or house current builds up an electrical charge in a device which stores electrical energy called a capacitor, sometimes called a condenser. When the shutter is tripped, a contact is made which discharges this current into a flash tube. This device might be likened to a small pump (battery) pumping water into a storage tank (capacitator). It takes time to fill the tank, but when it is full, there is a considerable amount of water available for use. If the bottom drops out of the water tank, all of the water is available in an instant.

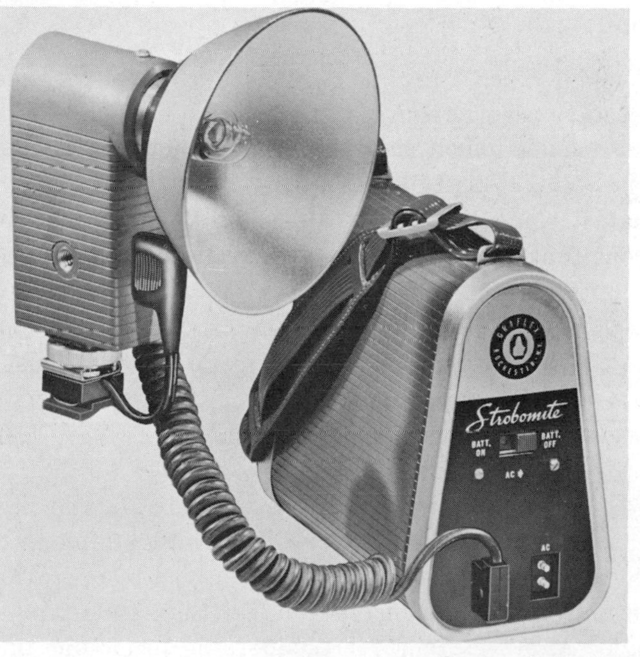


Courtesy, Graflex, Inc.

Fig. 5-9. A Modern Electronic Flash

Some precautions are in order regarding the care and operation of electronic flash units. Unless you are completely familiar with electronic equipment, do not tinker with the internal mechanism. The capacitor stores a large quantity of electricity at high voltages — 100,000 watts is common at flash time. This is enough to do considerable physical damage.

### How It Is Rated

Electronic flash units are rated in three different ways: watt-seconds, lumen-seconds, and guide numbers. Watt-seconds indicates the amount of electrical energy stored in the capacitor. Lumen-seconds is the amount of light emitted by the flashtube. The guide number, as explained for flash bulbs, is a factor that is used to determine the f/opening. It is probably the most useful rating for the amateur. A unit of 100 to 125 watt seconds is capable of very satisfactory results. A guide number of 30 for Kodachrome color film should be considered an absolute minimum.

### Power Supply

There are several sources of power to charge the capacitor. A battery made much like the battery for the automobile is sometimes used. This type of battery has several disadvantages, the greatest being that it contains liquid acid. It also has more equipment that may go wrong. It is, however, more economical for the larger units.

The 110 volt A.C. power pack is fine if the shooting is confined to the inside. Some units are made so that house current may be used when available and the power pack exchanged for a battery operated power pack when shooting where 110 V. A.C. current is not available.

The high voltage battery pack is probably the most satisfactory for average amateur work. It is quite simple in construction which makes for dependability. The cost of operation of this unit becomes rather expensive if fewer than 1000 flashes a year are made. Another item of considerable economic importance is that, if the unit is not used for a considerable period of time,

Photo by Norcross Studio

Sunlight Plus Flash Fill Combine to Make this Delightful Costume Portrait

the capacitor needs re-activating before shooting. This is a heavy drain on the battery. This means that the unit is expensive to operate if only a few flashes are made between long storage periods.

The reflector is important. Be sure that it is correct for the unit.

### Advantages of Electronic Flash

Electronic flash is a soft light resembling daylight. It does not produce the harsh shadows found in flash bulb exposures. With a slight correction filter, it produces excellent color on color films. The duration of the flash is about 1/1000 second. This stops all action and produces extremely sharp negatives. The light itself is the timing device. The unit is ready for another flash in from two to ten seconds. The cost of each flash is relatively small.

### Disadvantages of Electronic Flash

Batteries are expensive. They need attention even though little used. The original cost of the equipment is more than for bulbs. The power pack must be carried around and some of them weigh several pounds. The flash is always of the same intensity and may not carry far enough for a large group.

Negatives made with the electronic flash may be soft (lack contrast). It may be necessary to develop them a little longer than those made with natural sunlight or flashbulbs.

### Synchronization

Electronic flash should be used with shutters indicating "X" synchronization. It is necessary that the shutter be fully open before the flash occurs. Shutters marked "S" or "F" or "M" are not satisfactory for electronic flash. These shutters have a delay to permit the bulb to come to full brightness before the shutter opens. The electronic flash will be gone (1/1000 sec.) before the shutter opens. Result — no exposure.

The only way to use electronic flash with cameras not provided with "X" synchronization is to use the open flash method i. e. open the shutter, flash the light, then close the shutter.

CHAPTER VI

# films

Too frequently, those who purchase films do not know that there is a vast difference in them. It is important to know that films have different characteristics. Then when films are purchased those best suited to particular needs can be obtained.

A reliable company cannot afford to put inferior films on the market. Even though all films are good, it is necessary to know something about the different kinds of film to obtain certain results.

In the early days of photography the photographer made his own sensitive material. Things were not as convenient in those days as now. The photographer took a plate of glass and prepared the coating which he applied to the glass. Some of these plates had to be exposed while they were wet (called the wet plate). No wonder the older photographers laugh at the beginner today. They did not dare make a mistake. They were careful and exacting in their work. The same careful attention to details as practiced by the older photographers will result in greater success with modern equipment and films.

Today some emulsions are still made on glass plates (for plate cameras), but most of them are made on a flexible support.

Cotton is treated with an acid (acetic or nitric) and dissolved in some other chemicals, mostly alcohol and ether. It is then distributed evenly on a large, highly polished cylinder, dried by warm air and stripped off for use as the base of our modern film. The final products of this process are known as cellulose acetate or cellulose nitrate. The cellulose nitrate is flammable, but the acetate will not burn.

The film base is transparent but is not sensitive to light. It must be coated evenly with a sensitive material. This sensitive material, as indicated in the first chapter, begins with *silver*.

Silver is first converted into silver nitrate by dissolving it in nitric acid, then purified.

In order to make the silver compound stick to the film base, it is necessary to have a material that will hold the sensitive material, stick to the film base and be hard and dry when ready to use. This material is *gelatin*. The gelatin is warmed to a syrupy consistency and silver nitrate and potassium bromide added to it. At this stage the very sensitive *silver bromide* crystals are formed. This and all other operations must be carried on in complete darkness. A coating of this emulsion is applied to the film base. It is then cooled and dried and wound into large spools ready to be made into the various sizes of films, packs or sheets.

Film manufacturers have carried on many experiments to produce the best possible films — films that will give the most satisfactory results under a great number of varying conditions. They have treated films with numerous chemicals to give fast films (more sensitive), slow films (less sensitive), films sensitive to all colors, films sensitive to only a few colors, etc. It is necessary to consider some of these characteristics in order to know how to use them properly.

### The H & D Curve

In the chapter on lenses it was shown that the blackening of the film was in proportion to the amount of light striking the film. This is approximately correct but not entirely so. Speed can be increased until a maximum is reached.

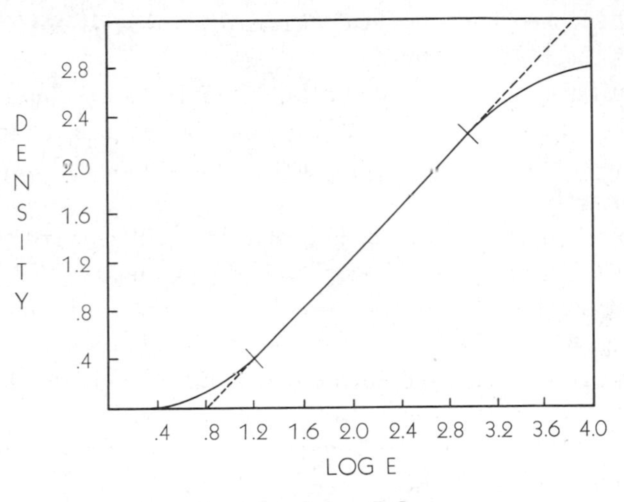

Fig. 6-1. D Log E Curve

Light causes the blackening of the film. The more light the more blackening until a point is reached at which the film is black, and even though additional light may be used it will become no blacker. A little light is required before the film begins to blacken, then gradually the blackening increases, until it is in proportion to the amount of light striking the film.

Hurter and Driffield were the first to measure density or the blackening of the film quantitatively. By a series of experiments they set up a relationship between exposure and the density of the film after it was developed under standard developing conditions. They define density in terms of opacity. Opacity is the ratio of incident light (light striking the film) to emerging light (light that passes through the film). Density is then defined as the logarithm* of the opacity. For example; suppose a silver deposit transmits $\frac{1}{4}$ of the light striking it. The transparency is $\frac{1}{4}$, the opacity is 4, and the density is the common logarithm of 4 or .6. They further discovered that the densities, as defined, were proportional to the *logarithm of the exposure* for the straight line section of the curve. These findings have been plotted on a curve which is known as the H & D curve or some-

* A logarithm is a mathematical term meaning the exponent of that power of a fixed number (called a base) which equals a given number (called the antilogarithm). The abbreviation for logarithm is log.

times called the characteristic curve, Fig. 6-1. It may also be known as the D log E curve.

Manufacturers have tested all of their films and have plotted characteristic curves for each. Much can be learned about a film by carefully examining these characteristic curves supplied by the manufacturer.

If you look at this curve, Fig. 35, you will notice that there are three main parts; the beginning of blackness called the *toe,* a straight section in the middle called the *straight line section,* and the curved section at the top called the *shoulder.*

If the film is exposed to too much light, you use the upper section of the curve. If you underexpose, you use only the toe section. *Correctly exposed negatives use only the middle or straight line section of the curve.*

Very small quantities of light make no impression on the film. When a minimum quantity of light acts upon the film a faint gray will be visible when developed. *The smallest quantity of light energy which is necessary for the slightest blackening of a film is called the threshold value.* The threshold value is different for different films. The less light that is required to produce blackening, the more sensitive the film.

In order for us to know how to expose a film, we must know something about its characteristics, its speed. To help us in this matter each film has been given a speed rating by the manufacturer.

Several methods have been used to rate film speed. Hurter and Driffield defined the speed of a film in terms of inertia. This resulted in the H & D ratings which are still used by some companies.

Scheiner film speeds were based on the first perceptible density which could be seen above fog. This method used a step tablet which was numbered. A negative was exposed with this step tablet and the highest number which could be read was the film speed. This method was not entirely consistent as there was chance of considerable variation. Scheiner speeds were used to a considerable extent in Europe. The American Scheiner rating is not the same as the European.

In 1931 the German Government appointed a committee to work out a uniform system of rating film speed. This committee developed the DIN system. This system is standardized on the exposure required to produce a density of 0.1 above fog. This system is more accurately standardized than most of the other systems.

Weston Electrical Instruments Company developed a system which was used to a considerable extent in the United States. General Electric Company had another. The American Standards Association has developed a standard, based on the minimum exposure necessary for an excellent negative, for all companies in the United States to follow in publishing the speed ratings for their films. The A.S.A. rating is now standard in this country. Most companies that manufacture film, include a data sheet with their film giving some of its characteristics including one or more speed ratings. In the United States the American Standard Association ratings are listed, and occasionally the DIN. The European manufacturers list the DIN and usually the A.S.A. also.

For purposes of comparison suppose that in a normal film the straight line section would be an angle of 45°. Some films are made so that the blackening increases faster than the proportional amount of light. In this type of film the contrasts are greater than in reality and the film is called *hard*. If the contrasts are less than in reality the film is called *soft*. Hard and soft do not refer to the transparency of the film but the difference in contrast. Differences in contrast can be influenced by many factors other than the film characteristics, such as developing, kind of light when taken (example; rainy day), overexposure, printing, etc. However it is necessary to know the characteristics of the film. A hard contrasty film should not be selected for a delicate portrait.

If a film is drowned in light, say a hundred times more than it can take normally, a strange thing happens. Beyond this point of maximum blackening an increase in light cannot produce more blackness, but actually causes the film to become lighter. If this is properly done, a negative can be changed to a positive.

Beautiful Photograph Spoiled by Solarization

This strange occurrence is called *solarization.* Usually a film is not exposed to that much light, but this very strange thing can happen to a part of the picture. Solarization can happen if a picture is taken in a dark room with a window which has a brilliant sky as a background, or it can happen when the negative is being developed and someone opens the door for a few seconds. The solution is not to take that kind of picture; and lock the darkroom door.

### General Film Characteristics

The beginner in photography is likely to be confronted with so many makes of films, so many different claims of the manufacturer, so much advise from his friends that he is likely to be confused when he starts out to buy a film for his use. Modern science has developed some wonderful films, but they haven't developed a single film which will solve all problems.

Films do not always see as the eye sees. In some cases films see more and in other cases less. A picture can be taken in a room completely dark to the eye. A film that does everything and solves all of the problems may be desired but as yet no such film is made. Some of the general characteristics which distinguish one film from another are speed, graininess, color sensitivity and contrast.

### Speed

Speed, as it relates to films, is the sensitivity of the film. A fast film means that good pictures can be taken with less light. The slower the film, the more light is required to take a good picture. In the process of preparing the emulsion, the longer the emulsion is "cooked" before coating, the larger the grains of silver bromide become. The larger the grain, the more sensitive it becomes. There is a practical limit, though, because the grains will become large enough to cause trouble.

If a photograph requires a fast film and none is available, the speed of the film can be doubled by treating it with ammonia fumes. To do this take the film into the darkroom and place it on a reel or spool so that the fumes can attack all parts. Place the film and a blotter which has been soaked with strong ammonia water in a tank, or similar container. After a few minutes of this treatment the film will have acquired its extra speed. It must be used within an hour or it will return to its original speed. This is an emergency measure and is not recommended for general use. With the very fast films manufactured today, the above procedure is seldom necessary.

### Graininess

With increase in speed the grain size may increase. Grain is not usually visible in small prints, but in large scale enlargements it becomes a real problem. It makes a mottled effect over the entire picture. Three things are desirable in photography, large image, speed and depth of field. One of these desirable qualities is gained usually at the cost of another.

Manufacturers have made much progress in reducing graininess and still retaining speed but speed still means graininess. This can be reduced to some extent by choosing a "fine grain" developer.

### Color Sensitivity

In general, films may be classed as blue-sensitive, orthochromatic, or panchromatic. This refers only to films for monochrome (black and white) photography. Color films will be discussed in another chapter.

It is important here to understand that the film responds (sees) only the relative brightness of the scene while the eye responds to both brightness and color. By adding certain chemicals to the silver bromide it can be made sensitive to different colors and record them as shades of grey.

### Blue Sensitive

Silver bromide is ordinarily sensitive only to ultraviolet and blue light. A film made in this way does not respond to other colors. Yellow, red, and green all come out as black on the print. Violet and blue record as white in the print. This type of film has a high contrast. This makes the film especially suited for reproducing drawings, manuscript, and other similar material where color makes no difference. Acceptable portraits could not be made with this film. Since it is not sensitive to red, it may be developed using a red safelight.

### Orthochromatic Film

Orthochromatic film begins to register a little more nearly as the eye records the scene. It is sensitive to all colors except red, but extra sensitive to blue and violet. By using a proper filter the over-sensitivity to blue and violet can be largely corrected. (See Chapter VII "Filters".) Because it is not sensitive to red, it can be developed in a red light. This is an excellent film for the beginner. It is used quite extensively for ordinary snapshots, for night photography and occasionally by portrait photographers, especially for portraits of men.

### Panchromatic Film

Panchromatic (pan) film is sensitive to all colors. It is a little less sensitive to green than the eye, but more sensitive to blue and violet. This over-sensitivity can be corrected by taking away some of the blue and violet by the use of a yellow or orange

# Anno xxxv. Reginæ Elizabethæ. Chap. j.

## An Acte to retaine the Queenes Maiesties Subiects in their *due obedience*.

### The first Chapter.

OR the preuenting and auoiding of such great inconueniences and perils as might happen and grow by the wicked and dangerous practizes of seditious sectaries and disloyall persons, Be it enacted by the Queenes most excellent Maiesty, and by the Lords Spirituall and Temporall, and the Commons in this present parliament assembled, and by the authoritie of the same, That if anie person or persons aboue the age of sixteene yeeres which shall obstinately refuse to repaire to some Church, Chappell, or vsuall place of Common prayer to heare diuine seruice, established by her Maiesties lawes and Statutes in that behalfe made, and shall forbeare to doe the same by the space of a moneth next after, without lawfull cause, shal at any time after fortie daies next after the ende of this Session of Parliament, by Printing, writing or expresse wordes or speeches aduisedly and purposely practise or go about to moue or perswade any of her Maiesties subiects, or any other within her Highnesse Realmes or dominions, to denie, withstand, and impugne her Maiesties power and authoritie in causes Ecclesiasticall, vnited and annexed to the Imperiall crowne of this Realme, or to that ende or purpose shall

Part of a Page Copied With Commercial Blue-Sensitive Film

From Statutes XXXV of Elizabeth
By Christopher Barker,
"Printer to the Queens Most Excellent Majestie, 1593."

filter. When properly filtered, this film reproduces the values of black and white nearly as the eye sees them. It makes pictures that look most natural. This film has many uses, one of its greatest use is for fine portraits. It is available for amateurs in rolls, packs or cut film.

### Antihalation (No Halo)

Sometimes a strong light striking the film will penetrate the emulsion and reflect back to further affect the film, causing a halo. This is often seen in photographs of street lights or other bright objects. To prevent this, the manufacturers coat the back with a light absorbing material "antihalation base." This is usually a dye applied to the backing of the film. The dye bleaches out in the processing solutions with the exception of the blue-gray dye used on some 35 mm films. The presence of this blue-gray dye has no effect on the printing quality of the negative.

### Overcoating

Most manufacturers apply a thin gelatin layer over the sensitive emulsion to protect it from scratches.

### Noncurling Backing

A gelatin layer is applied to the back of the film to compensate for the emulsion on the front and in this way prevent serious curling. The film still has a tendency to curl toward the emulsion side.

## LOADING FILMS

Films are prepared in rolls, film packs, plates and cut films (sheets).

### Roll Films

Roll films are packed in a box, usually with a sheet of instructions. Around the film will be a heavy paper or perhaps metal foil. The film is protected by a paper which is rolled with the film. This paper is usually held tight by a piece of tape.

The steps in handling the film properly are as follows: First, make the camera ready to receive the film. Put the empty spool in its proper place and see that the camera is free of dust and grit. Roll the empty spool with the winding key to see that it turns properly. Second, remove the wrapper from the film but do not break the tape. This should never be done in direct sunlight. If there is no shade, perform this operation in the shade of your body. Third, place the film in its proper place and turn it to make sure that it is properly fitted in its bearings. Fourth, place your thumb on the roll of film and remove the tape. This is done to prevent the paper from unrolling. Fifth, unroll the paper about two or three inches longer than the distance between the spools and thread it into the empty spool. Sixth, turn the winding key until the paper is tightly stretched. Then, and not until then, remove your thumb from the roll. Close the camera securely and turn film to first exposure.

When the last picture has been exposed, continue turning the winding key until a sign appears in the little window indicating the end of the film or until you feel a light resistance. This happens just before the paper comes out of the slot. Stop turning at this point and open the camera (in the shade). To remove the film, again place your thumb on the roll to prevent the paper from becoming loose, roll the remaining paper onto the spool, fold it on the designated line and fasten it with the tape that will be attached. When this operation is complete, remove the film for processing.

### Film Packs

Film packs are wrapped in heavy paper or metal foil. When the adapter or holder is ready to receive the film, remove the paper and place the pack in the adapter or holder and close securely. Always hold the pack by the edges and never exert pressure on the face (paper). Be sure the slide is properly inserted then pull the first tab to the mark that says "tear off along this line." It is well to hold the thumb against the other tabs so that they will not accidentally become displaced.

One of the biggest sources of trouble with film packs is that the snap-on bar becomes loose and will not hold the pack securely, spoiling the film. To make sure that the pack is held securely, hold the pack in position with the thumb when removing the slide or when pulling the tabs.

### Cut Film

Cut film used in holders is packed in a box and sealed in metal foil or wrapped in a heavy black paper, and may be wrapped a second time in another heavy black paper. The film must be loaded in the holders in the darkroom. Remove the slides from the holders and place them all in order. If panchromatic film is being used the loading and handling of films must be done in *total darkness.* It is better to practice with an old piece of film until the handling becomes easy. After everything is in readiness turn out all lights and open the box of films. *The box is opened only in total darkness.*

There are some notches on the film. When these notches are on the right side of the top edge, the emulsion side of the film faces toward you. Now slide it in the holder. Remember to touch only the edges of the film. The notches on the slide handle should be to the outside. Wrap the remaining films in the black paper, and replace them in the box. There are three parts to the box. Be sure to assemble it properly otherwise the films may be spoiled.

Fig. 6-3. Holding Film

Fig. 6-4. Sliding Film in Holder

In using holders, one side of the slide is black and the other white or a light color. On the light side will be found some notches or raised spots. You can tell whether a holder has been exposed by the way the slide is put in the holder. When the film is loaded, the light side (notches or raised spots) are out. When the film is exposed, place the black side out.

A mark should be made on the box cover for each film used, thus, ~~////~~ /, so that a definite record is available as to how many films have been used out of the box.

### 35mm Film

Thirty-five mm. film is usually purchased in casettes. These are sold with 20 or 36 exposures in them. In Europe some companies make a casette with 12 exposures. The company has added enough film so that the user will get the proper number of exposures after the camera has been loaded properly. Not all 35 mm. cameras are loaded in the same way so detailed instruction will not be given here. Follow the manufacturer's instructions carefully.

A few points should be checked in loading any 35 mm. camera. After the film is in place, try the winding knob or lever while the camera is still open to be sure that the sprockets catch in the perforations in the side of the film. When loading the Leica camera, tip the camera and look down in the box to observe the sprocket engagement. After you are sure that the film is transporting properly, close the camera and set the exposure counter. Some cameras set this counter automatically.

When the counter indicates the last picture, or when the film no longer will transport, it is time to rewind the film into its casette. *Do not try* to force the film to get "one more." Chances are that it would break and you could take no more pictures until the film had been removed in a darkroom. *Never open a 35 mm. camera unless it is empty or the film has been rewound.*

## PRACTICAL EXPERIMENT

### Making a Photographic Emulsion

This exercise is intended for those who wish to explore the principles of film manufacture.

*Materials Required* —

1. Gelatin.
2. Potassium Bromide.
3. Potassium Iodide.
4. Silver Nitrate.
5. A piece of thin glass.

*Procedure* —

1. Dissolve 10 grams of gelatin in 360 cc of warm water.
2. Add 32 grams of potassium bromide.
3. Add 0.8 grams of potassium iodide.
4. Increase the temperature of the solution to 55° Centigrade and maintain.

Note — The following steps must be carried out in the darkroom using a ruby light or Wratten #2 safelight.

5. Dissolve 40 grams of silver nitrate in 400 cc of water and add to the bromide solution at the rate of 20 cc per minute. Stir the solution constantly.

6. Hold the temperature at 55° centigrade for 12 minutes and let cool slowly.
7. Add 40 grams of gelatin to the emulsion so that it will set. It may require several hours to set thoroughly.
8. After the emulsion has set (3 to 4 hrs.) place it in cheese cloth and force it through. This will form small shreds.
9. Pour 3 liters (3 qts.) of water over the shreds and let set for three minutes then pour off 2 liters. Add two fresh liters. Repeat this until the emulsion has been washed five times.
10. Heat for 15 minutes at 55° centigrade then cool to 40° C.
11. Pour 5 cc. of the emulsion on a 4″ x 5″ glass plate. Spread it uniformly then chill until set and dry. It is now ready to use.

Note — The exposure time for this emulsion will be about 1/25 at f-8.

*Question —*

1. What type of emulsion have you made?

CHAPTER VII

# filters

Did you ever take a picture of a beautiful scene with a blue sky with a billowy cloud formation and then, when the picture came back from the finisher, discover that those beautiful clouds, which really made the scene, were gone? If you have been to Yellowstone, did you take a picture of Old Faithful in all its grandeur, only to discover when the picture was finished that Old Faithful was not there? The people were there, the rock formations good, but the water shooting up into the blue sky just did not register. Why is it that pictures for sale at the souvenir counter have clouds, and Old Faithful is clear? Why do the pictures you take lose so much detail? Certainly it is disappointing, but there is a reason, and a reason which can be corrected easily.

You will recall that films do not register the same as your eye. Even the panchromatic film is more sensitive to blue than the eye. It is nearly as sensitive to blue as it is to white. That is the reason that the clouds and water did not register as you saw them. You can correct this over-ambition to register blue by preventing some of the blue from reaching the film. This can be done by slipping a filter over the lens.

## FILTERS — HOW THEY WORK

### The Additive Process

In a previous chapter it was explained that light travels in waves and that white light is a combination of several colors. The length of the wave determines the color. Red waves are the longest and blue waves are the shortest. If three projectors are set up so that they will project on the same screen and overlap, the fundamentals of adding color can be observed.

It is important to understand that mixing wave lengths of light is not the same as mixing paint. The results are entirely different. Place a blue slide in one projector and project it on the screen. In the second projector place a green slide and project

Fig. 7-1. Additive Process

it on the screen overlapping part of the blue. It will be discovered that where these colors overlap on the screen, neither blue nor green results, but a new color, a blueish green called cyan is produced. A red slide is used in the third projector so that its color overlaps the other two. The results are even more startling than the first. Where the red overlaps the green a new color — yellow is produced. Where the red overlaps the blue still another color — a purplish red called magenta — is produced. Where all three colors overlap, the result is white.

### The Subtractive Process

If a yellow filter is placed between the source of light and the viewer, the yellow filter will permit its own color to pass through and those which produce yellow by addition — red and green. The yellow will stop its complement — blue. If another filter, magenta, is placed to partly overlap the yellow filter, it will pass its own color plus yellow and blue. Where the magenta and yellow filters overlap, the red rays pass through, since both yellow and magenta will pass red light. The magenta filter will stop the green waves. Now if a third filter, cyan (blue-green), is placed so that it will overlap both the yellow and magenta, the cyan filter will transfit its own color plus blue and green. Where the cyan and magenta filters overlap, blue light comes through. Where the cyan and yellow filters overlap, green light comes through. Where all three filters, yellow, magenta and cyan, overlap, all wave lengths of light are blocked and the result is no color, or black. (See Fig. 20-2.)

Since white light is a combination of the three primary colors, a substance can be placed in front of the lens to absorb some of the rays and soften the light. In the case of white clouds and blue sky, it is desired to hold back part of the blue so that it will register as the eye sees it. A light yellow filter will absorb some of the blue and allow the red and green to pass. A darker yellow absorbs more blue and makes the sky darker than normal. In this case the film has been *over-filtered.* By over-filtering it is sometimes possible to create striking pictorial effects, but it should be done with artistry and good taste.

### Types of Filters

There are two principal types of filters: those that are made of colored glass, and gelatin filters. The gelatin filter is made of a thin layer of dyed gelatin. The thin gelatin filter is very fragile and easily damaged. The thin gelatin is usually cemented between two pieces of optical glass, then mounted inside a metal ring.

Gelatin filters are relatively easy to make and can be made in all shades of a color. The optical colored glass filter is difficult to make, especially in many shades of colors. The glass filters, because of the difficulty of producing accurate shades of colors, are only made in the most used colors. The glass filters do not fade and are not affected by the humidity and fungus of tropical countries.

Each type of filter has its advantages and disadvantages. In general, the gelatin filters are used for color correction and the colored glass filters for general photography. Be sure that the filter that you buy is of a quality equal to the lens of your camera.

### Selecting Filters

Most of the modern panchromatic films are more sensitive to blue than to the other colors. This makes blue appear too light in the print. The other colors come out darker than the eye perceives them.

A filter passes its own color of light and absorbs all other colors. Colors that pass through the filter appear lighter in the finished picture. Those colors that are absorbed by the filter appear darker in the finished print.

For outdoor photography, the yellow filter will correct the films sensitivity to blue. Thus, it will darken the blue sky and allow clouds to show. Some photographers prefer the green filter to a yellow one for outdoor photography. The green filter will darken the blue sky and at the same time lightens the green foliage. The green filter will hold skin texture. It also works out very well in preserving the delicate tone separation of the varied hues of sunrise and sunset.

Sometimes we wish to use filters for special effects. As an example, suppose a sailing vessel with its beautiful white sails is to be photographed. We desire a very dark sky. A color opposite

Fig. 7-2. Colors of Original

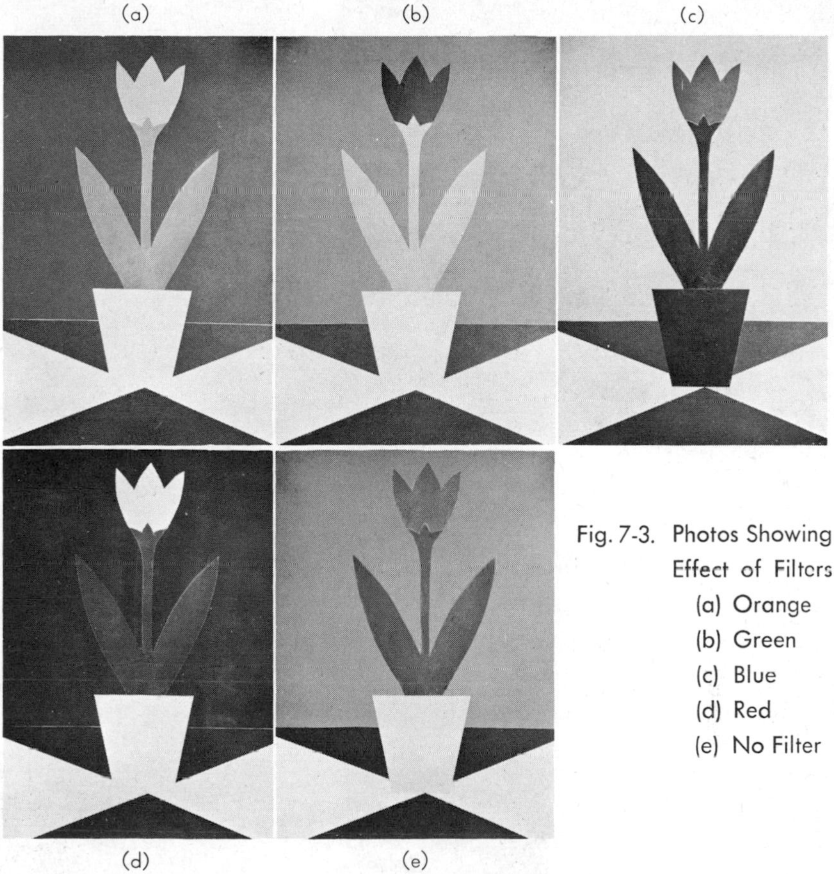

Fig. 7-3. Photos Showing Effect of Filters
(a) Orange
(b) Green
(c) Blue
(d) Red
(e) No Filter

to blue is needed. This calls for an orange or red. The blue sky would then be rendered very dark leaving the clouds and sails to stand out strongly in contrast.

### Filters and Their Effects

| *Filter* | *Lightens* | *Darkens* |
|---|---|---|
| Yellow | Red, Green, Yellow | Blue |
| Orange | Red, Yellow, Orange | Blue, Green |
| Green | Green | Red, Blue |
| Blue | Blue | Yellow, Red, Green |
| Red | Red, Yellow | Blue, Green |

Landscape Scene Taken With Various Filters

Above, top: No Filter
Below: Blue Filter

Facing, top: Orange Filter
Center: Green Filter
Below: Red Filter

### Filters for Infra-Red Photography

Infra-red film is sensitive to blue and infra-red. To get the true infra-red effect, it is necessary to block the blue and pass the red and infra-red. This calls for a red filter. If a partial infra-red effect is desired, a medium red filter will suffice. This filter may also be used for other black and white photography.

If the true infra-red is desired, as in medical photography, crime detection, copying, and analytical work, a dark red filter is needed. The *Wratten No. 87c* is suitable for this work.

The exposure for infra-red is difficult to calculate. The exposure meter will be of little help here. For outdoor scenes in bright sunlight with a medium red filter, try 1/25 second at f/8. It is well to experiment with a number of exposures.

### Special Filters

There are many filters used for special purposes. Two of the most used special filters are the polarizing filter and the diffusion filter.

The polarizing filter is used to subdue or eliminate glare. Ordinary light which is reflected from a surface, such as glass

Fig. 7-4. Photo Taken With and Without Diffusion Filter
Left: Without Diffusion — Center: Medium Diffusion — Right: Full Diffusion

or water or other non-metallic surface is mostly polarized. The angle varies depending on the surface from which the light is reflected. Much of the clear blue light from the sky is polarized. The polarizing filter is rotated visually to get the desired effect. Read carefully the instructions that come with this filter.

Diffusion filters are used to soften definition. They are often used in portraiture to produce a soft diffused image. The same soft diffused image is used many times for landscape and pictorial work. This type of filter may be used either on the camera or the enlarger. If used on the camera, the filter will affect the light colored objects. When used on the enlarger the shadows are affected most.

Both the diffusion filter and the polarizing filter may be used with other filters and both may be used with color film. The effect of the polarizing filter on color film is that it makes the sky a much darker blue without changing other colors.

### Filter Factor

When a filter is used over the lens, the amount of light striking the film is reduced. The exposure must be increased in proportion to the amount of light which has been eliminated by using a filter. The number of times the normal exposure must be increased when a filter is used is called the *filter factor.*

The filter factor depends upon three things:

1. Filter
2. Film
3. Source of light

The color and density of the filter will affect the filter factor. A film which is especially sensitive to red will have a different filter factor than a film equally sensitive to all colors. Sunlight, being a bluish light, will have a different filter factor than a light bulb which gives a reddish light. A table of filter factors will usually accompany the film. This factor must be applied to the calculated exposure to get good results.

In calculating the exposure using a filter with a factor of 2, the calculation would be something like this:

Suppose the basic setting calculated is 1/100 second at f/16. The factor is two, which means that the filter absorbs half of the light, and the lens must be opened to allow more light to enter, or the time of exposure must be doubled. This would mean 1/50 sec. instead of 1/100 sec. or opening the diaphragm one stop (f/11 instead of f/16). Thus, a factor of three requires $1\frac{1}{2}$ stops, a factor of four requires 2 stops, a factor of eight requires 3 stops, etc.

An easy way to adjust for the filter factor when using a meter is to simply divide the film index rating by the filter factor and set the result on the exposure meter.

Example: Film is rated at A. S. A. 200
Yellow filter with factor of 4
$200 \div 4 = 50$
Set 50 on the meter as the index of the film.

## PRACTICAL EXPERIMENT

### Studying the Effect of Filters.

*Materials Required —*

1. A camera of any make or model.
2. One roll of panchromatic film for above camera. If your camera uses cut film, load four sheets of each type.
3. One set of filters (yellow, green and red).

*Procedure —*

1. Place a color wheel or some colored objects in such a position that, when photographed, the scene will include a section of the sky, preferably with white clouds. Include red, yellow, blue and green. With orthochromatic film make exposures as follows;
2. Expose one film correctly without a filter.
3. Expose one film with a yellow filter. Be sure to apply the filter factor.
4. Expose one film using a green filter.
5. Expose the last piece of film using a red filter.

   The films just exposed will be developed in a later experiment.

*Questions* —

1. How do you account for the fact that clouds are more prominent in some of the negatives?
2. Which filter produces the darkest sky? Explain.
3. If you were required to reproduce a page from an old book which contained yellow stains, which filter would you choose so that the stains would be eliminated?

CHAPTER VIII

# the darkroom

Since film and photographic papers are sensitive to light, it is necessary that they be handled in the dark. The darkroom doesn't have to be elaborate. The main requirement is that it is really *dark*. Not even a pin hole of light must enter. It should be remembered that 1/1000 of a second was long enough to produce a picture in a camera. It will require from five to twenty minutes to develop the film.

One can use some baking dishes and the kitchen sink, or the bathroom on occasion, to finish pictures. To make a darkroom in the basement is the ambition of most amateurs.

How can you know when the darkroom is dark? When it appears that all light has been shut out, go inside, close the door and turn out the light. When the eyes have been adjusted to a bright light, it will take about fifteen minutes for them to become perfectly accustomed to darkness. If any light can be seen after about ten or fifteen minutes the room is not dark enough. It is a good precaution to test the darkroom, just to make sure. To do this, take a piece of film and place it on the work table with a piece of black paper over it. Each minute for fifteen minutes move the black paper so that a small additional part of the film is exposed. Develop this strip of film as described in the next chapter and observe the results. If the film is clear, the room is dark. If the film appears gray, it is evident that too much light is getting into the darkroom for satisfactory work. The number of minutes to where the gray begins is the length of time for handling sensitive materials in the darkroom without danger of ruining the pictures.

Another quick test for determining whether the darkroom is dark enough is to take a sheet of white paper into the darkroom. If you cannot see the sheet of white paper after ten minutes the room is dark enough.

The darkroom should be well ventilated. If you are using a room in your home (kitchen or bathroom) and have a ventilating system, the problem is solved. If you are making a room in your basement, you will need to provide for ventilation. There should be two openings, one near the ceiling for air to escape and one near the floor for the air to enter. These openings must admit *no light.*

A good ventilator to the outside is made of hollow tile, or a similar form made of wood, with a baffle plate on the outside and a similar plate on the inside, Fig. 8-1a.

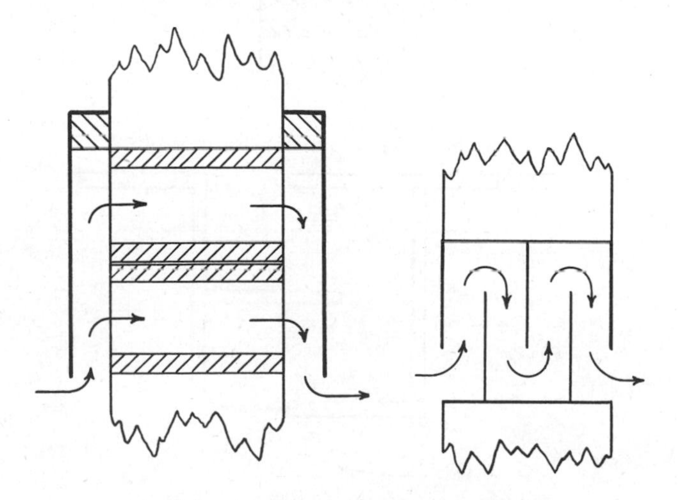

Fig. 8-1. Ventilators for Outside Walls

Another arrangement equally as good is a sheet metal or wooden box to fit the opening, with baffle plates in the box itself, Fig. 8 - 1b.

A ventilator the thickness of the wall can be made in similar manner with fewer baffles, Fig. 8 - 2. In all of these arrangements, the inside walls of the passages should be painted a flat black.

The door to the darkroom should be double, if possible. If this is not possible, a black curtain will help. An arrangement similar to Fig. 8 - 3 may be used.

Since the temperature of the various solutions affects their speed of reaction the darkroom should be of uniform tempera-

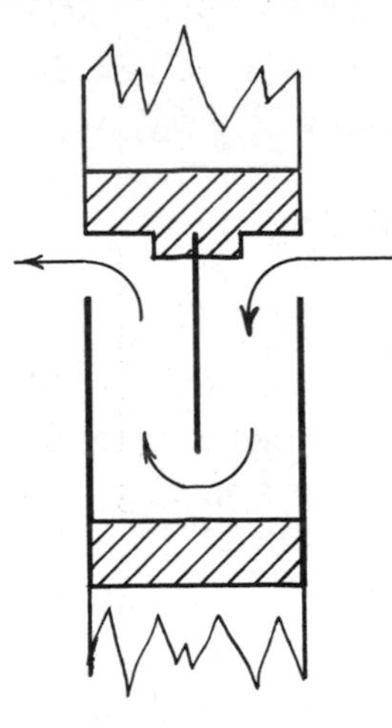

Fig. 8-2. Ventilator for Inside Wall

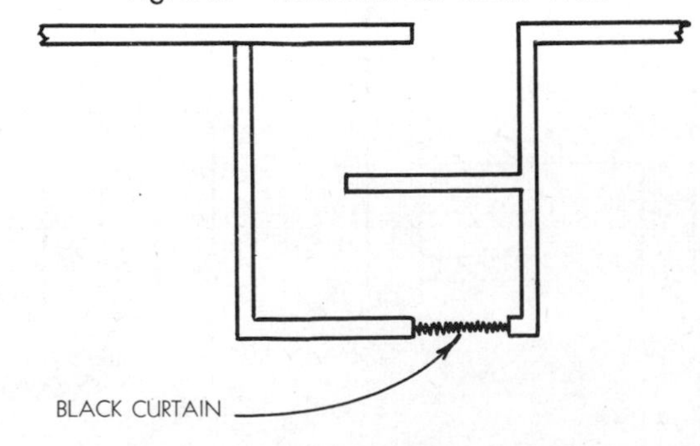


Fig. 8-3. Darkroom Door Entrance

ture. Sixty-five to sixty-eight degrees is recommended. Do not use a coal or wood stove to heat the darkroom. The dust from these stoves will cause many disappointments.

### Equipment for the Darkroom

The equipment for the darkroom can be very modest or very elaborate. The equipment listed here will be a minimum for efficient operation. One can get along with even less. The equipment recommended is as follows:

1. Four trays of good enamelware, china or glass large enough for the largest print desired. If color prints are to be made increase the number of trays to eight.
2. Two graduates (to measure liquid), one small and one large.
3. A good thermometer.
4. One safelight (if only one light is used, it should be made so that the glass can be changed to give a different color light).
5. Bottles for storing solutions.
6. A printing frame or box.
7. One soap dish and towel.
8. One timing clock.
9. One or more ferrotype tins.
10. Necessary chemicals.
11. One glass funnel.
12. Later on it may be desirable to add an enlarger.

The darkroom is not a suitable place to store papers and films. There should be another room for doing all work that does not require darkness.

Make the darkroom so that it is easy to clean. It must *never* be dirty or dusty. Avoid all unnecessary drawers and shelves. Two small drawers and a place to store the darkroom equipment are sufficient.

### Laboratory Dress

Do not wear street clothes or office clothes into the darkroom because they will become stained. A laboratory coat or apron is recommended. Some people find that the chemicals used in photography irritate their skin. In such a case rubber gloves are recommended.

### Arrangement of the Darkroom

First of all the darkroom should have a sink. It is true that explorers have developed beautiful pictures in a tent and without running water. Running water is not essential, but it is a tremendous aid. There should be enough space to set the four trays side by side. Most photographers prefer a sink large enough to hold all four trays, or a space available on each side of the sink. It is well to cover the bottom of the sink with a wooden rack, and the drain pipe with a dome shaped cover to prevent scraps of film and paper from clogging the drain. Immediately under the sink should be a rack for the trays. On one side there should be two drawers, on the other side a space for the equipment. The articles in the darkroom should be sufficiently spaced to make it easy to pick up any one without moving another. *Have a place for everything and keep each thing in its place.* This is important. It should be remembered that articles will have to be found in the dark. Have in the darkroom only that which is necessary.

When developing some films, it is necessary to work in *total* darkness. Other films will permit a red light. A green light may also be needed. The safelight should be at least three feet above the work. Safelights are available with interchangeable filters which makes it possible to change the colors. Other units have separate lights with a control for each. Have the light switches conveniently located but placed so there will be no confusion of the location of each. The table used for loading and unloading film should be far enough away from the sink that it will not be splashed with chemicals.

Clean towels are important. It must be understood that the hands should be entirely free of chemical when the towel is used. *Always* wash the hands first, then wipe them on the towel. Change the towels often.

Once the darkroom is arranged the most interesting part of photography, finishing the pictures, can be done.

## PRACTICAL EXPERIMENT

### Determining the Safety Factor of the Safelight

The object of this exercise is to determine how long you can work under your safelight before objectionable fog results.

*Materials Required* —

1. The safelight that is to be used for contact prints and (or) enlargements.
2. Facilities for making prints.

*Procedure* —

1. Place a piece of contact paper and a piece of enlarging paper side-by-side under the safelight at normal working distance.
2. Place a piece of black paper so that it covers a portion of one end of each piece of paper.
3. Turn on safelight.
4. After one minute move the black paper to cover an additional strip of the sensitive paper. Repeat this each minute until you have five or more periods.
5. Develop the paper in the dark.
6. If the test strips show any grey, the safe time is the time of the exposure just before the placc that shows grey. You may make a similar check for a safelight for handling film.

CHAPTER IX

# developing the negative

When the film was exposed, the light affected some of the crystals of silver salts forming an invisible image called the latent (concealed) image. This image will remain in that state for a year or more, but for best results, the film should be processed as soon as it is convenient to do so.

### What the Developer Does

When light strikes the silver salts they are affected in such a way that when the film is placed in a chemical solution, called the *developer*, the crystals that have been affected by light are reduced to small irregular particles of metallic silver. Silver in this form is black. This makes it easy to see the image on the film. The deposit of silver is heaviest, and therefore darkest, where the most light hit. In areas where the original scene was dark, the areas on the film have much less silver and are therefore lighter. This is just the opposite of the original scene and that is why we call it a *negative.*

### What Fixing Means

When we take a picture, the light from the original scene does not affect all of the sensitive crystals. The film, after it has been developed, still contains many light-sensitive crystals that were not affected during exposure. These light-sensitive particles, if exposed to light, would turn dark and ruin the negative. To prevent this, the film is immersed in another chemical solution which will remove these un-used light-sensitive particles. This solution is called the *fixing* solution. After the fixing process, the negative is no longer sensitive to light.

During the development process the gelatin becomes soft and is easily scratched. The fixing solution usually contains a chemical which will harden the gelatin. This makes the negative less likely to become scratched.

## CHEMICALS

### Developer

The developer contains chemicals to perform four functions:

1. The reducing agent is the chemical which produces the small grains of silver. There are a number of chemicals which will do this job. Two of the most used ones are Elon (sometimes called Metol) and Hydroquinone.

   Elon (Metol) builds up density very slowly. This gives a negative which lacks contrast. Hydroquinone, (also called Hydrochinon and Quinol), after it begins to develop, builds up density rather rapidly and produces high contrast. With the proper balance of these two chemicals, a developer can be made to serve many purposes. Small changes of temperature affect the activity of Hydroquinone greatly. For consistent results, developer should be used at the same temperature each time it is used.
2. The preservative is necessary since the reducing agent by itself spoils rather quickly. The developing agent oxidizes (rusts) very quickly in the presence of oxygen. This chemical prolongs the useful life of the reducing agent by retarding oxidation or "rusting." The chemical most used for this purpose is sodium sulfite.
3. The activator assists the reducing agents, which are not very active by themselves; but in the presence of an alkali they spring into action. The more alkali that is

used, the more energy they develop. There is a practical limit though. Too much alkali produces an all-over veiling which the photographer calls fog. Sodium carbonate is the chemical often used for this purpose. There are several other chemicals that may be used. Sodium hydroxide, the strongest of the alkilis produces an extremely active developer which also produces a very high contrast.

4. The restrainer is usually potassium bromide. With an active developer it is possible that some of the unexposed silver bromide crystals might also be reduced. This condition the photographer does not want. The restrainer is used in the developing solution to prevent the reduction of un-exposed light-sensitive crystals.

### Fixing Bath

The purpose of fixing is to remove the light-sensitive salts from the film or paper. One single chemical, sodium thiosulfate (usually called hypo), will do the job. The usual fixing solution contains some added chemicals to (1) harden the gelatin so that it will not be as easily damaged, and (2) to keep the solution in good condition.

In addition to the hypo the fixing bath usually contains the following:

1. An acid which stops development, almost always acetic acid.
2. A hardening agent which makes the gelatin hard so that it is not easily damaged. Caution — hardening is *not* desired in some toning operations. If a print is to be toned, be sure to determine whether a fixing solution with hardener should be used. One of the most used chemicals for hardening is potassium alum.
3. A preservative, for which sodium sulfite is the most used chemical. It serves two purposes: (a) It prevents any developing solution which is carried over from the fixing bath from turning brown, and (b) prevents the acid from destroying the sodium thiosulfate (hypo).

### Mixing Chemical Solutions

Chemicals may be purchased ready to dissolve in water or prepared in accordance with any of the formulas published by various companies, some of which are included in Appendix B. Follow the directions exactly. This part of photography is chemistry. Although it is not necessary to become a chemist or study chemistry, learn to be as *clean* and *accurate* as a chemist.

If prepared developers are used, mix the chemicals in the order indicated on the package. If this is not done, the solution may be spoiled. If you mix the ingredients yourself, *always mix the chemicals in the order listed* unless otherwise stated in the formula. *Never pour water into an acid.* To do so may cause violent action and spatter acid all over you and the equipment. *Always pour the acid into the water.*

It is best to use chemicals recommended by the company that made the film or paper. Occasionally you may wish to experiment with other products, or compound your own formula. It is not good practice to be constantly changing from one product to another. You are more likely to get good consistent results if you standardize much of your working material.

## TRAY DEVELOPMENT

Prepare the darkroom in the following manner: use a red safelight (for orthochromatic film only), arrange three trays so that they can be found easily and can be reached from one position. If photographic trays are not available, use some dinner dishes. Have a thermometer and a clock.

After the solutions have been prepared, fill the trays. In the first one on the left pour enough developer to cover the film. A half inch deep is enough, although more does no harm. Fill the second (middle) tray with water, and the last tray with fixing solution. Be sure the solutions are the temperature indicated on the package. This is usually about 68°F (20°C). It may be necessary to use a little cracked ice or set the trays in cold water until this temperature is reached.

Wash your hands thoroughly. Cleanliness is very important.

The following description is for orthochromatic film. If panchromatic film is to be developed, *no* light may be permitted and development must be timed.

Turn out all lights except the red safelight. Inspect the darkroom to be sure all doors, etc. are light tight. Here's a tip — lock the doors. Others in the family or friends who might drop in unexpectedly may wish to see how the developing is done. Take the roll of film, rip the tape which holds the roll closed, and begin to unroll the paper. Soon the film will be seen. Continue the unrolling until you come to the place where the film is attached to the paper. When this point is reached, carefully tear the paper from the film and discard the paper. You no doubt have observed long before this that the film has curled and that, if you try to straighten it, it curls some more. A spring clothespin or a photo clip on each end will help keep it straight. Now completely wet the film in the tray containing the water, holding the film by both ends, and moving the hands up and down with a seesaw motion with the curved part of the film always submerged. This will stop the curling. Caution — always handle film by the end or edge. Never put the fingers on the face of the film. Now check the time on the watch, or start the timing clock, and immerse the film in the developer. Start one end through and draw the entire length through the developer. Continue drawing the film through the developer in a seesaw motion until the time for development has expired. This motion need not be rapid but should keep the entire strip of film wet with the developer at all times.

If you prefer to stop development by observation, or if you have no means of timing, you may do so by carefully observing the development of your film. First you will notice the highlights beginning to appear (black in the negative) and soon one side of the film will look black. Now begin to look at the back of the film. The margins of the film were not exposed. When you see the exposed section (from the back) in the form of a rectangle, development is nearly finished. Stop when you see the unexposed margins begin to tarnish. At this same time, you should observe darker spots appearing in the rectangle. These are the

Fig. 9-1. Developing Film by the Tray Method

highlights of the picture coming through. This is another indication of the time to stop. Do not allow the rectangle to become a dark gray or the film will be over-developed. The time required should be very close to the time indicated on the package of developer. **For DK-50 the time should be about six minutes.**

At the instant the development is complete, remove the film from the developer and wash in the clear water. Draw the film completely through the water two or three times. This removes the developer which, if not removed, will "kill" the fixing bath and cause spots on the negative. Never allow developer to drip into the fixing bath, or fixing bath into the developer. The developer is a base and the fixing bath is acid. When the two come together they neutralize each other and form new compounds which cause much trouble. After the film is washed in water, transfer it to the fixing bath (Hypo). Here the coating will disappear and the negative will become clear. When the negative becomes clear, the room lights may be turned on to inspect the results. The seesaw action should be continued until the negative is clear, and the fixing should be continued for twice the length of time that it requires to clear the negative.

After the negative has been completely fixed it should be washed in running water for about thirty minutes, then hung in a *dust-free* room to dry. Do not cut the washing time short because if chemicals are left on the negative, stains, spots, and fading will result. Another caution — do not hang the negative over or near a radiator. Remember that a coating of gelatin holds the image to the film base and it does not take much heat to melt gelatin. The saddest of all things that can happen in developing pictures is to find the negative weeping big black tears which means that it is ruined.

The method just explained can be applied to cut films, plates and film pack. Instead of the seesaw action, agitation is produced by a gentle rocking of the tray.

## TANK DEVELOPMENT

The foregoing method of developing is rather crude and old fashioned but it is effective and still in use. The trouble starts when panchromatic films are developed, or miniature films. Panchromatic films must be developed in total darkness, and imagine how difficult it would be trying to handle five feet of miniature film in the manner just described. A much more convenient method is to use a tank.

### Equipment

There are several types of developing tanks. Three types are most common:

1. The tank that has a drum with spiral grooves in the side. The film is pushed into the spiral from the outside of the drum. (See Fig. 9 - 2a.)
2. The metal tank with a spiral formed from stainless steel wire. The film is started from the center and threaded outward (Fig. 9 -2b).
3. The reel of this tank has a plastic blanket with small round protrusions molded on the edges. The film and blankets are wrapped together on the reel. The protrusions of the blanket keeps the emulsion of the film

Fig. 9-2a. Film Pushed Into the Spiral of the Reel

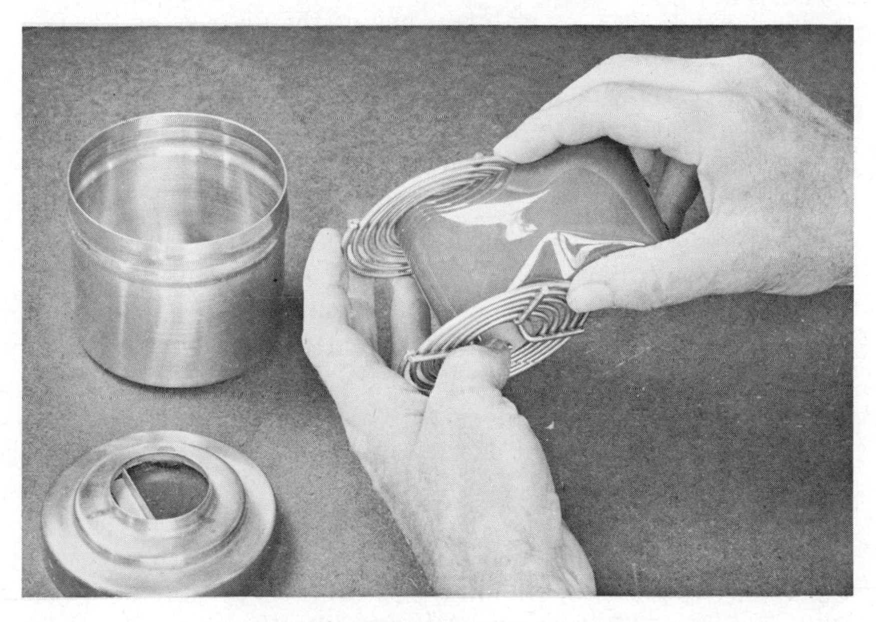

Fig. 9-2b. Film Started at the Center

from touching the blanket and keeps it separated so that the developer can make contact with all parts of the film. (Fig. 9 - 2c.)

### Loading the Tank

All of the tanks mentioned have light-tight lids. The lid has a place to pour chemicals into the tank without removing the lid. This permits all of the steps of processing to be done in daylight after the loaded reel is inside and the lid securely in place.

The reel may be fixed, or may be adjustable for different sizes of films. The flanges (discs) of the drum contain spiral grooves. Insert the film in the groove and gently (never force) feed it into the spiral. This takes some practice. Use an old film and practice this in daylight until you can do it without error with your eyes shut. The new film will curl and cause some trouble, so practice until you can do it perfectly in the dark. *Be sure the reel is dry.* It is good practice to clip the corners of the film. This prevents it from catching on the reel. See Fig. 9 - 2d. A single drop of water in one of the grooves of the reel will cause the film to stick at that point and give trouble. Do not risk an exposed film in total darkness until you are familiar with the operation of the tank.

Chemicals should be prepared as before but this time left in the bottles.

When confident of your ability to handle the film, take an exposed roll of film into the darkroom and arrange the tank so that you can find all the parts in the dark. Turn off all lights. Rip the holding tape on the film. Hold the spool between the thumb and forefinger of the left hand. Now unroll the paper from the spool and roll it up again with the right hand until you feel the film. At this point one feels the need of extra hands but with a little practice the operation is quite simple. Unroll the film for about two inches, not more. Now take the spool of film and the paper roll in one hand and the tank reel in the other. Guide the two inches of film in the spiral groove of the tank reel. With the thumb and finger of the hand which holds the tank

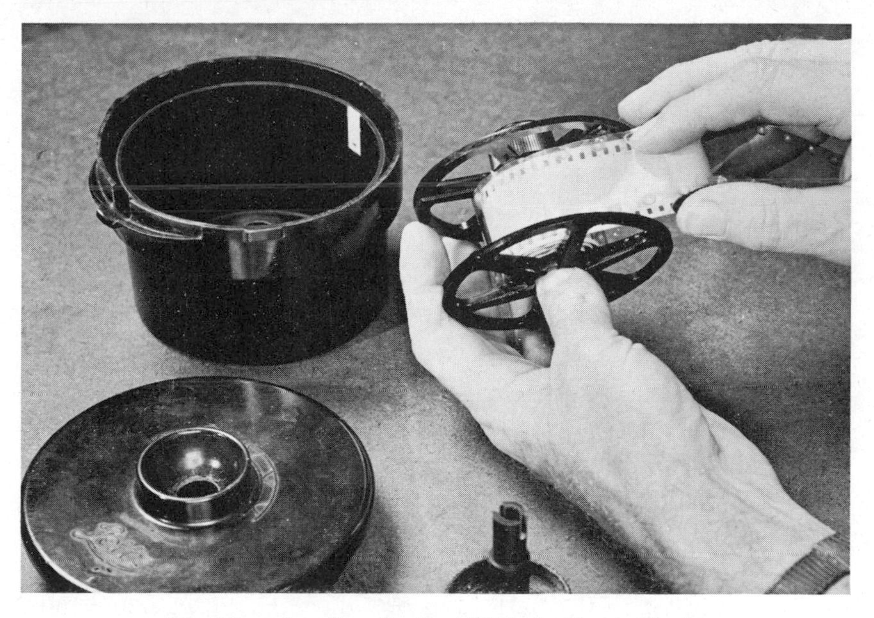

Fig. 9-2c. Loading the Reel With the Plastic Blanket

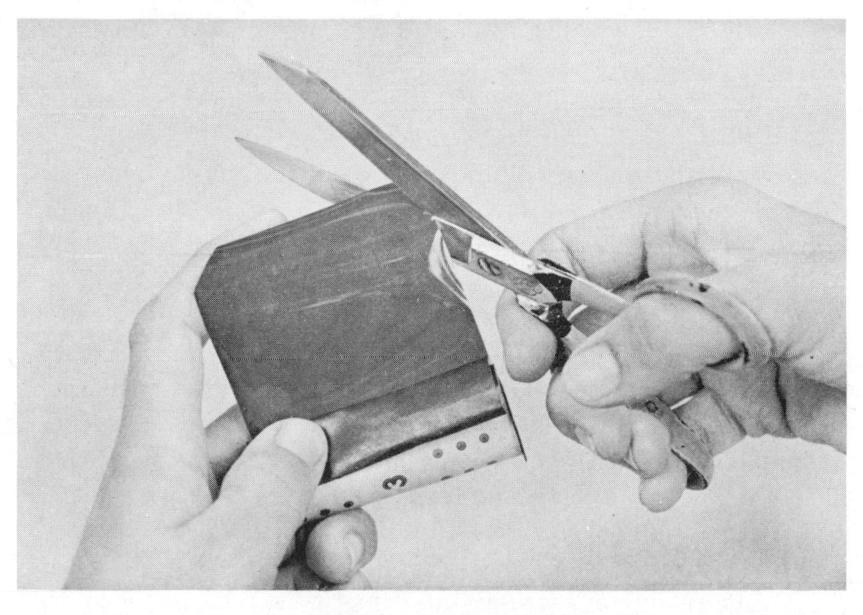

Fig. 9-2d. Clipping the Corners of the Film

reel, hold the film in place while you unwind another inch or two of film from the spool and guide it into the spiral. See Fig. 9 - 2a. You can now drop the paper roll and feed in the remainder in any way you like.

The emulsion should be on the inside. Film tends to curl toward the emulsion side. Try not to touch the coating of the film as it is easily damaged.

Another method sometimes used to load a tank is to remove all paper from the roll of film letting it coil up, then threading it into the spiral of the reel. This method is much simpler but there is more chance to damage the film.

Once the film is threaded into the spiral grooves, insert the reel in the tank and securely fasten the lid in place. Some lids snap on, some screw on, and some are fastened by a nut which is screwed tight. At this point the lights can be turned on if needed. Threading the drum takes only a few minutes. It can be done at night in the bathroom or in a dark closet made light tight. A regular darkroom is not an absolute necessity.

The second type of tank requires a different technique. The roll of film is handled in the same way, but, instead of pushing the film into a groove, the film is bent slightly with the thumb and index finger and clipped to the inside of the reel. (See Fig. 9-2b.) With the thumb and finger resting lightly on the edge of the reel and the film slipping between the thumb and finger (do not pull) turn the reel with the left hand. The film will spread into the spiral grooves as it flattens out. It takes considerable practice to do this properly. Practice with some old film until the technique has been mastered otherwise some of the film will be spoiled.

The tank with the plastic blanket is probably the easiest to load. The film spool is handled as described before. The film is wound together with the plastic blanket. Be sure the protrusions of the plastic blanket are facing the emulsion of the film. Wind the two (blanket and film) together loosely on the reel and place it in the tank, Fig. 9 - 2c.

When ready to process the film, it is recommended that the tank be filled with clear water. This will wet the film which

Fig. 9-2e. Agitating the Film

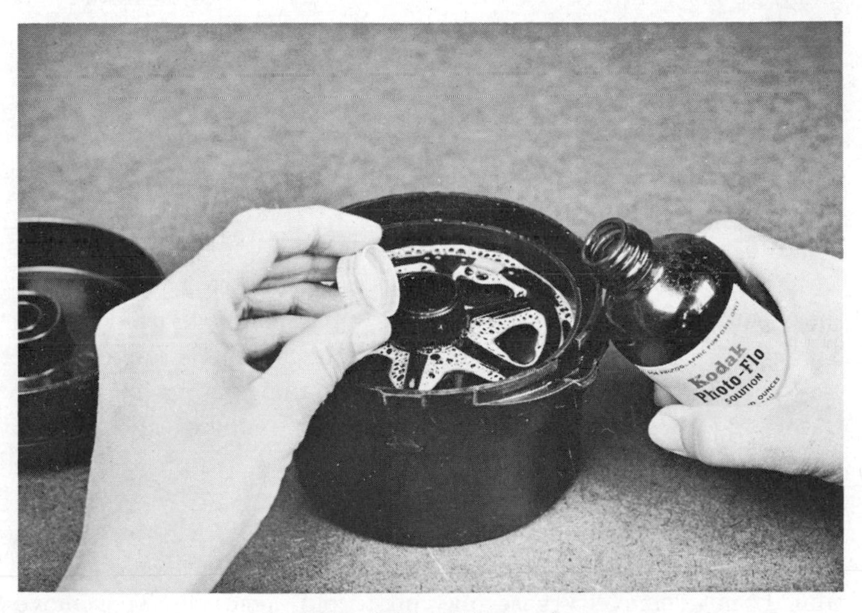


Fig. 9-2f. Adding Wetting Agent

will insure an even distribution of developer over the film and prevent air bubbles. Pour the water from the tank.

Be sure the developer is the correct temperature; then fill the tank. Check the time. The film should be developd the exact length of time stated on the developer for a given temperature. The film should be agitated continuously in the tank during the first minute or two of development and about once each minute for the remainder of the development time. Tanks are usually fitted with a small knob on the top which can be turned with the fingers. This rotates the reel in the tank. (Fig. 9-2c.)

After development is completed, pour the developer from the tank into a bottle marked "used developer." Used chemicals require more time for development than fresh chemicals. Place the tank under the faucet and wash the film for about thirty seconds, then pour all of the water from the tank and fill it with fixing solution (Hypo). An acid hardener is recommended with the fixing solution. Fixing should last ten to fifteen minutes. More time does no harm, but should not exceed thirty minutes. The temperature of the fixing bath is not as important as the temperature of the developer, but it should be approximately the same. The reel should be rotated in the tank several times during fixing. In a tropical climate extreme care is required to keep the correct temperature. The addition of alum to the fixing solution is recommended. If you are to be in the tropics for only a week or two it is best to wait until you return home to process your films.

After the films have been in the fixing bath for the required time, pour the fixing solution into a bottle marked "used hypo." You can use it again, but each time it takes a little longer. You may open the tank at this point. A half hour washing in running water and the process is complete. Your negative should last for many years.

After the washing is complete, hang the negative up to dry in a dust-free room. Remember not to hang it over or near a radiator or in the sun. You will notice drops of water over the film. If not removed, these may spot your negative. To remove this water, use cloth chamois or cellulose sponges, placing one on each side and gently, slowly wiping the film from top to bottom. Another method preferred by many is to soak the film for a half minute in a wetting agent. This causes the water to drain off evenly and does not require sponging. (Fig. 9-2f.)

## DEVELOPING SHEET FILM

Film packs and cut films may be developed by the tray method as described for roll film. The only difference is that instead of seesaw motion you rock the tray gently during the development and fixing. A much better way is to use a tank.

The equipment needed for developing sheet film in a tank includes: three tanks, film hangers of the proper size, an interval timer, and a place to hang the negatives to dry.

The following procedure is recommended:

1. Fill the tank on the left with developer, the middle tank with water, and the tank on the right with fixing solution. Put enough liquid in the tanks to just cover the films when the hangers are in place.
2. Check the temperature and adjust if necessary. The tank can be placed in a bath,either hot or cold water as the case requires.
3. Set the interval timer and turn out the lights.
4. Remove the film from the holder (in total darkness of course) and place it in the film hanger. Hold the film only by the edges. Snap the clip over the top. (Fig. 9-4.)
5. Place the loaded hanger on a rack until all films have been similarly loaded. (Fig. 9-5.)
6. Lift all of the hangers off the rack and place them in the developer. Rap the hangers sharply against the tank to dislodge any air bubbles. (Fig. 9-6.)
7. Start the interval timer. (Fig. 9-7.)
8. Agitate the film continuously for the first minute and once each minute thereafter for the remainder of the development time. A good way to do this is to lift the hangers (together) out of the developer and drain (see Fig. 9-8) for about three seconds, then return them to

Fig. 9-3. Unloading Film from Holder

Fig. 9-4. Placing Film in Hanger

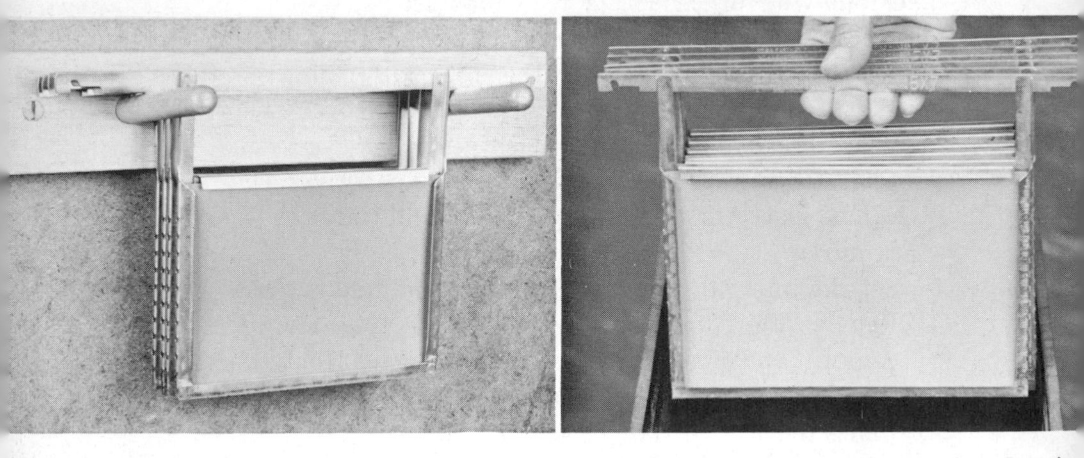

Fig. 9-5. Place Hangers on Rack

Fig. 9-6. Lowering Hangers into Developing Tank

the developer. The next time they are lifted, drain in the opposite direction. Agitation is very important.

9. When developing time is up, lift all of the hangers together, drain for five seconds and place in the rinse. Dip them up and down in the rinse several times.
10. Remove from the rinse and place in the fixing bath. Leave in this bath about 10 minutes. A little more time is required as the bath becomes exhausted. When fixing time

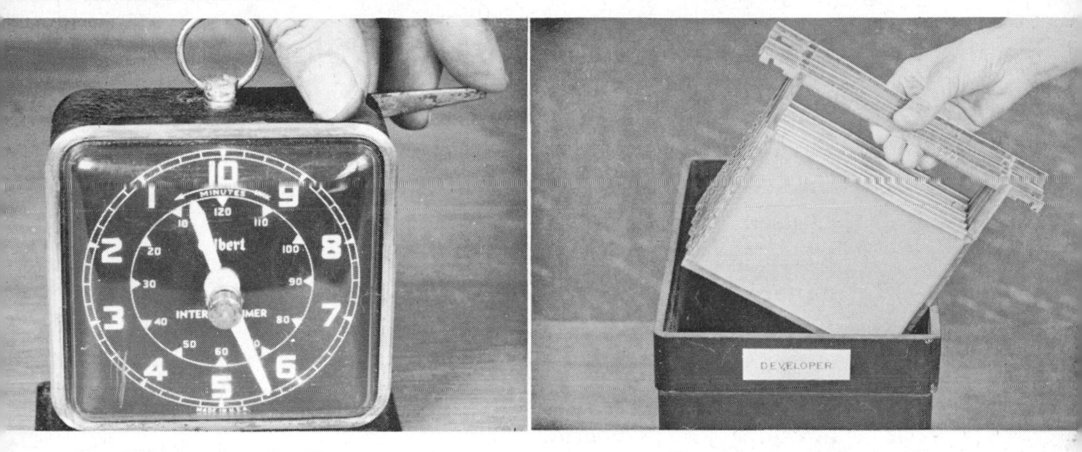


Fig. 9-7. Starting the Timer

Fig. 9-8. Draining the Film

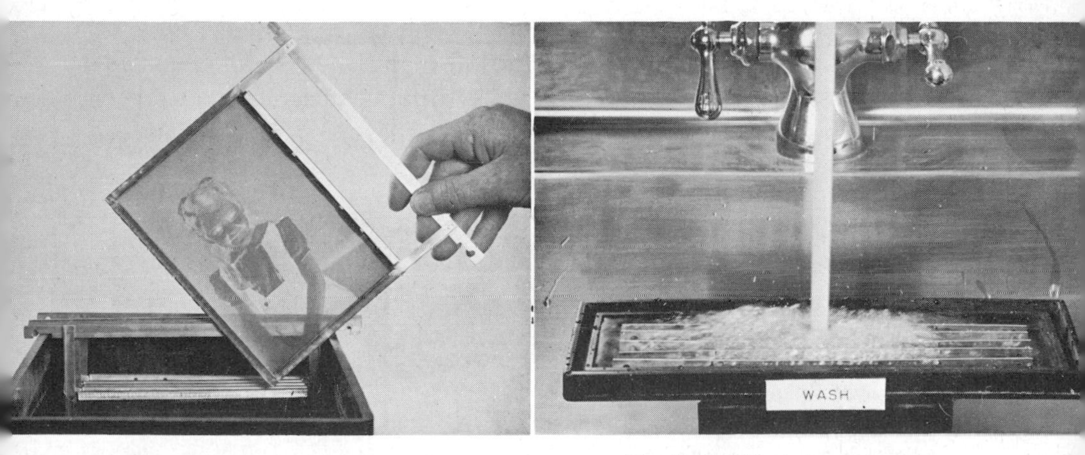


. 9-9. Films May Be Inspected After They
ve Been in the Fix for Three Minutes

Fig. 9-10. Wash for Thirty Minutes

ig. 9-11. Hang Negatives in a Dust-Free
Room to Dry.

Fig. 9-12. Place Dry Negatives in Glassine Envelopes for Protection

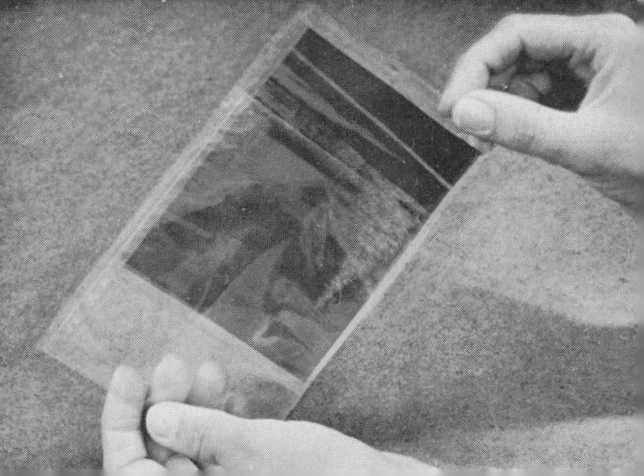

reaches 15 minutes, discard the fixing bath and make a new one. (If quick-fix is used, the fixing time is about 3 minutes) Agitate the films several times during fixing.

11. Turn on the white lights.
12. Transfer the negatives to the washing tank. (Same tank as used for the rinse) Wash for 30 minutes. (Fig. 9-10.)
13. Rinse the films in a bath of wetting agent for one-half minute.
14. Hang up to dry in a dust-free room. Keep one corner pointed down. (Fig. 9-11.)
15. When negatives are dry, place each negative in a glassine envelope for protection. (Fig. 9-12.)

## DEVELOPING FILM PACKS

The process of developing film packs is the same as for cut film with a few exceptions. The film in film packs is much thinner and a little larger than sheet film. It doesn't fit into the same hangers. It becomes necessary to either use a different type

Fig. 9-13. Remove Metal Clip

Fig. 9-14. Remove Film from Pack

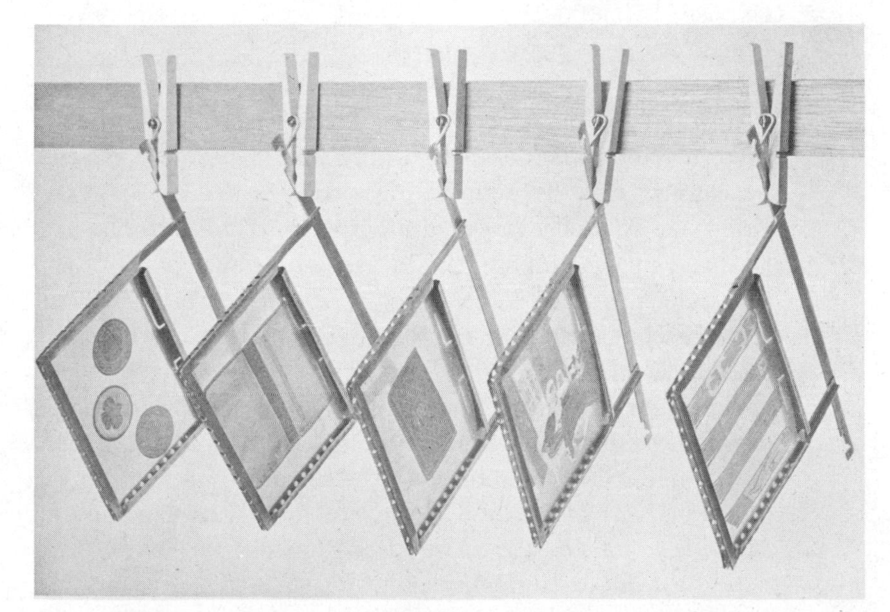

Fig. 9-15. Film from Film Packs Is Left in Hangers to Dry (Hang With One Corner Down)

of hanger or to trim off the tab in a paper cutter. Remember this must be done in total darkness. A guide can be fastened to the paper cutter so that the trimming can be easily done.

To open a film pack and remove the exposed film, remove the metal clip on the top. A gentle pull and it will slip off. Remove it only in the dark. You can now lift the back of the pack and remove the film. Each film has a black paper attached. The black paper should be separated from the film before developing in the tray or before loading in the hangers. Be careful to handle the film only by the edges. (Figs. 9-13 and 9-14.)

The remainder of the developing procedure is the same as for sheet film with the exception that the films are usually left in the hangers to dry so that they will remain straight. (Fig. 9-15.)

## PRACTICAL EXPERIMENT

### Developing Film in a Film Tank

*Materials Required* —

1. A developing tank suitable for film to be processed.
2. Exposed film.
3. Chemicals previously prepared.

*Procedure* —

1. Load the tank in accordance with instructions previously given. (Note) If daylight tank, the remainder of the processing may be done in daylight.
2. Fill tank with developer and agitate at once to insure that the entire film surface is wet with developer.
3. Start clock.
4. Agitate film continuously for the first minute and then once each minute for the entire developing time.
5. Develop for the time recommended for the type film, the developer, and the temperature of the developer. When development is complete pour the developer into a bottle labeled *Used Developer*. This developer may be used again.
6. Wash the film for a half minute. Pour out the water.
7. Fill the tank with fixing solution. The temperature of the fixing bath is not as critical as the temperature of the developer. Rotate (agitate) the film in the fixing

solution. You may open the tank after the films have been in the fixing solution for 3 to 4 minutes. Note when the films are clear. Leave them in the fixing solution for twice the time it takes to clear them but not more than 20 minutes.

8. Pour fixing solution into a bottle marked *Used Hypo*. You can use it over. Wash for 30 minutes.
9. Hang up to dry. Sponge off the droplets that adhere to the film, or rinse in a wetting agent.

*Question* —

1. Inspect the negative. Note and explain any irregularities such as spots, streaks, areas of the negative that are clear, etc.
2. Explain how you might develop a panchromatic film by inspection (using a light).

### Comparing the Results Obtained by Agitating and Not Agitating Films During Development.

*Materials Required* —

1. Camera for making exposures.
2. One sheet of film.
3. Trays for development.
4. A pair of scissors.

*Procedure* —

1. Set up scene and make an exposure.
2. Fill two trays with developer. Be sure that both trays are the same temperature.
3. When ready to develop, cut the exposed film in two pieces (darkroom of course).
4. Slip one half of the film, exposed for the experiment, in each tray. Agitate one tray constantly for the recommended time but do not touch the other tray until you remove the film from the developer.
5. Fix and wash in the usual way.
6. Arrange both halves of the negatives together in the contact printer and make a print on one piece of paper.

*Questions —*

1. Do you notice any difference in the density of the two negatives?
2. Do you notice any difference in the contrast of the two negatives?
3. Explain your observations.

### Optional Exercise. Developing Films Using a Desensitizer and Observing the Results of Special Development

*Materials Required —*

1. Camera to expose films.
2. Usual tray development equipment except two trays will be needed for developer.
3. A fast working developer.
4. A slow developer which produces low contrast.
5. A solution of pinakryptol green.
6. Stop bath.

*Procedure —*

1. Expose a scene that has extreme contrasts. (Usually in bright sunlight and include some deep shade.)
2. Expose a scene that has very little contrast. (Interiors or scene on a rainy day.)
3. Arrange one tray with a high contrast fast working developer. Fill the tank or other tray with a slow developer of low contrast. Include the proper concentration of desensitizer.
4. Develop both films for three minutes in a total darkness in the slow working developer. Turn on a green light and observe the development as it proceeds.
5. One negative will appear flat when the development time is half over. Transfer this negative to the fast working developer and *watch it carefully*. Very soon the contrast will build up. If it appears that the contrast is building up too much it can be returned to the slow working developer. When it is to your liking remove it and place in a stop bath.

Examine the other negative. If it is to your liking, fix it in the usual manner. If you would like just a little added snap or contrast, place it in the fast working developer *for a few seconds*. Then to the stop bath.

6. Make a print from each for your notebook.

*Questions* —

1. Do you like this method of development? Give your reasons.
2. Why does one developer work faster than another developer?

### Preparing Solutions DK-50, F-5.

*Materials Required* —

1. The following chemicals;
   Elon, Sodium sulfite (desiccated), Hydroquinone, Kodalk, Potassium bromide, Sodium thiosulfate (Hypo), Ammonium chloride, Acetic acid, Boric acid crystals, Potassium alum.
2. Two suitable containers.

*Procedure* —

1. Follow the directions for these solutions exactly as given in Appendix B.

### Developing Orthochromatic Films.

*Materials Required* —

1. Solutions prepared in previous exercise.
2. Three suitable trays.
3. Darkroom with suitable safelight.

*Procedure* —

1. Follow the directions given in this chapter for developing film in a tray.

CHAPTER X

# contact printing

Take a negative that has been developed and look through it. Everything that was white in the original scene is black on the negative. Everything is exactly opposite. In order to have a picture which resembles the original scene, it is necessary to carry out another process called printing.

The negative is placed on a piece of paper which has a light sensitive coating and exposed to light. Light passes through the negative and affects the sensitive paper in proportion to the density of the negative. The paper is then developed, fixed and washed, differing only slightly from the method used in processing negatives. A print thus made is called a *contact print.*

The negative may be placed in an optical instrument called an enlarger and a print made by projecting the negative image on the sensitive paper. A print thus made is called a *projection print - an enlargment.* The two processes, although similar, differ considerably in detail. Each process has its advantages and disadvantages. Both processes will be explained in considerable detail. This chapter will deal with contact printing, and Chapter XI will deal with projection printing.

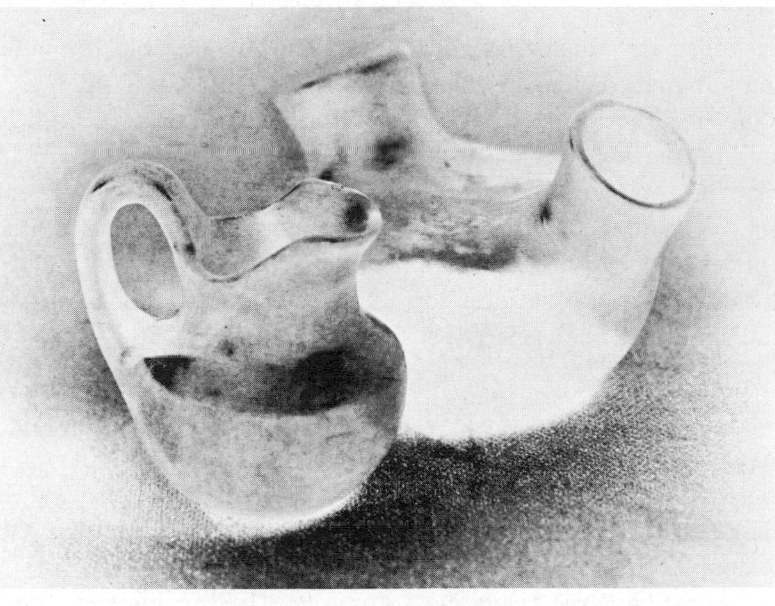

Fig. 10-1a. The Negative

Fig. 10-1b. The Positive

## THE DARKROOM

Most any room that can be darkened is suitable for making contact prints. The kitchen at night is quite satisfactory. The room need not be as dark as for film. In fact, quite a high level of illumination may be used provided it does not contain blue. Draw the window shades at night to keep stray light from entering the room. Safelight bulb or filter should be used. An OA safelight made by the Eastman Company or an S-55-X made by duPont are quite satisfactory. The bulb should be 10-15 watts and should be about four feet from the paper.

### Chemicals

It is best to use the developer that is recommended for the paper you select. You may, however, use a developer manufactured by one company on another company's paper. The Eastman Company's D-72 or 55-D by duPont are satisfactory. Other companies manufacture equally good developers.

Arrange three trays close together. In the tray on the left pour the developer. The developer is usually different for papers than for films. It is usually a fast working developer. If a universal developer is used for the films the same may be used for papers. They are all tested and all good. Just select a developer suitable for the job and prepare it according to the directions given.

In the second tray place a stop bath. A stop bath is a weak acid bath which quickly neutralizes the developer, thus stopping development very quickly. To prepare a stop bath pour 1½ ounces of 28% acetic acid into 32 ounces of water. By the metric system, use 48 cc. of 28% acetic acid to one liter of water. If glacial acetic acid is used, prepare the 28% solution by adding three parts of glacial acetic to eight parts of water.

In the third tray pour the fixing bath. The same fixing bath which was used for films may be used for the prints or a special solution may be prepared.

### Photographic Paper

Paper used in photography is not ordinary paper. A newspaper will soon lose its stiffness and become a wad of pulp when wet but not so with photographic papers. They are made especially to hold the original shape, even after being soaked in water and chemicals for several hours.

Papers made for contact printing are coated with sliver chloride. They are often referred to as *chloride* papers. Papers used for projection printing (enlarging) are coated with the much more sensitive silver bromide and are called *bromide papers*. Other papers may be coated with a combination of silver chloride and silver bromide and are called *chloro-bromide* papers. Your photo supply store has samples of all of these papers. Have them shown to you.

There are several factors to be considered when selecting a photographic paper. If you consider the following points, you will have a much better idea of the paper you should select for your particular job.

1. *Size.* Paper is made and packaged for all standard sizes of film. You may, if you desire, get larger sheets and cut it any size you wish. The edges of most papers are cut straight, but some may be had with deckled edges or edges that looks like it had been torn.
2. *Surface.* Some papers are made to have a high gloss surface when finished. The glossy surface shows the clearest detail which makes it desirable for small prints. A glossy surface is usually required for photographs to be reproduced in newspapers, magazines, and books.

   Other papers may have a sheen or luster surface. Still others may have a medium dull surface called semi-matte. A matte surface is dull with no shine or sheen.

   The surface texture varies considerably. Some papers have a surface that resembles silk, others resemble canvas, still others have a surface that resembles suede leather. These special surfaces are for special effects. Become familiar with these various surfaces so that you may choose intelligently. The method of marking these surfaces is not standard with the different companies. Each company has their own method.

   A further variation of the surface may be had by using

texture screens. These are put in contact with the paper surface during exposure and may be had in a variety of effects.

3. *Tone.* This refers to the color of the paper stock and the color of the image. Most papers are made in pure white and the following colors: almost white with a shade of cream, cream color, ivory, tan, and buff. Some special colored papers may be grey and blue tints. The blue tint papers are effective for snow scenes and those having fog. The warm tone papers, (tan and buff) are useful for scenes on the red end of the spectrum, *i.e.,* sunsets and autumn scenes.

   The image of some papers develops in various shades of brown and may be further colored by a process known as *toning.*

4. *Contrast.* If we always made perfect negatives, we would require only one contrast paper. Sometimes the best photographers make mistakes and produce negatives that are not quite normal. When this happens we have two choices: (1) Make the picture over or, if that can not be done, (2) print the negative you have on a different type of paper.

   Manufacturers realize that we sometimes miss and have made papers in varying degrees of contrast. Contrast grades usually are from 0 to 5. Number 0 has a very low contrast while number 5 has a very high contrast. Number 2 is normal contrast and is the grade you should expect to use if you make good negatives.

   If you should by chance make a negative that has a very low contrast (perhaps made when it was very cloudy or raining), a negative that produces a print that looks grey, has no sparkle, and lacks brilliance, it might make a fairly good print if printed on number 3 or 4 paper. On the other hand, a negative of very high contrast may make a better print on a number 1 or number 0 paper.

   The photographer sometimes calls a low contrast paper

a "soft" paper and a high contrast paper a "hard" paper. Contrast in a paper has nothing to do with its surface texture, tone, or weight.

5. *Weight.* The weight of a paper refers to its thickness. Single weight (sometimes marked "SW" on the box) is the paper usually used. It is less expensive than double-weight. If a stiffer paper is needed (slip-in folder for example) a double-weight paper may be more appropriate.

### The Printing Frame

A good printing frame is necessary. If one is not available it can be made easily. Get two pieces of glass a little larger than the negative and two small spring clamps to hold the two pieces of glass together. This is all the extra equipment needed. Of course a printing box is more convenient, if sufficient funds are available to purchase one.

Take a piece of thin black paper and cut a rectangle out of the sheet slightly smaller than the negative. This is easily and quickly done by folding the paper; then accurately cutting the opening. This piece of paper is called a mask. (Plastic masks to fit all sizes of negatives are available at the photo store.) For special effects it may be cut for numerous designs — heart

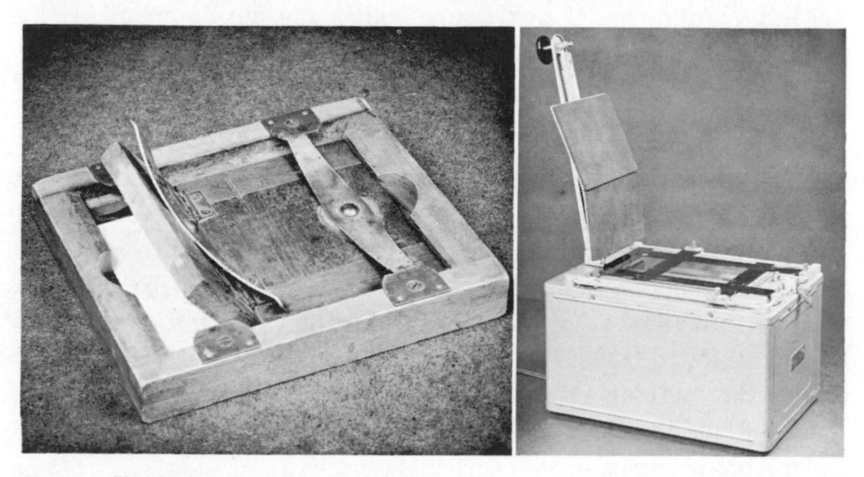

Fig. 10-2. (a) Printing Frame (b) Contact Printer

shaped, clover shaped, etc. Clean the glass; then fasten the mask to one piece. Place the negative over the mask emulsion (dull) side up and arrange it as desired. If the camera was not held in the proper position, the image on the negative will be out of alignment. This can be corrected by adjusting the negative to fit the mask. When the negative is placed in position, turn off all white lights. A red or yellow light may be left on. Sensitive paper is carefully enclosed in a series of two or three envelopes to insure thorough protection from light. Only one sheet should be removed at a time; after which the envelope containing the sensitive paper should be enclosed in the other envelopes so that it will not become damaged. Now place the sensitive paper on the negative,emulsion side down. See Fig. 10-4. *Always place the emulsion of the film toward the emulsion of the paper.* This rule holds true in almost all cases. Fasten the clamps on the printer. Everything is now in readiness for a very exciting experience.

### Making the Exposure

Place the printing frame about two feet from, and facing a 25 watt light. Turn on the light. For the first print make the exposure about four seconds. Count; one thousand one, one thousand two, one thousand three, one thousand four. Turn off the light. Following the exposure comes the development of the print. A metronome used in music study is an excellent counting device for proper timing. Set it to tick every half second.

### The Contact Printer

The operation of the contact printer is essentially the same as the printing frame. The printer is a box containing a red light and white printing lights. The box has a glass top with arrangements for masking to any size. A hinged cover holds the paper in position and when fully closed, turns on the white light inside the box to make the exposure (See Fig. 10-2b.) The steps in using the contact printer are as follows:

1. Place the negative, emulsion (dull) side up on the glass plate.
2. Adjust the masks.

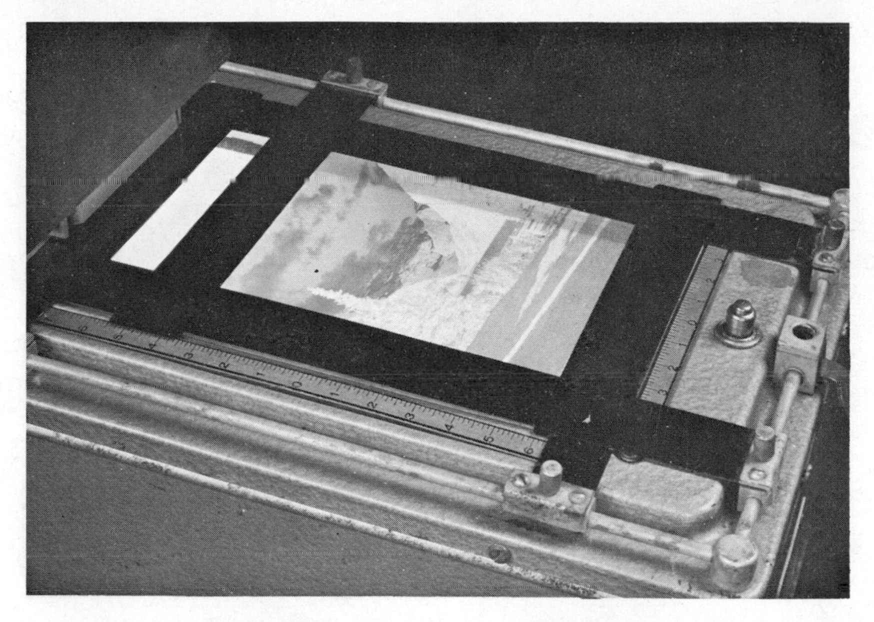

Fig. 10-3. Negative in Place on Printer

Fig. 10-4. Placing Paper Over the Negative

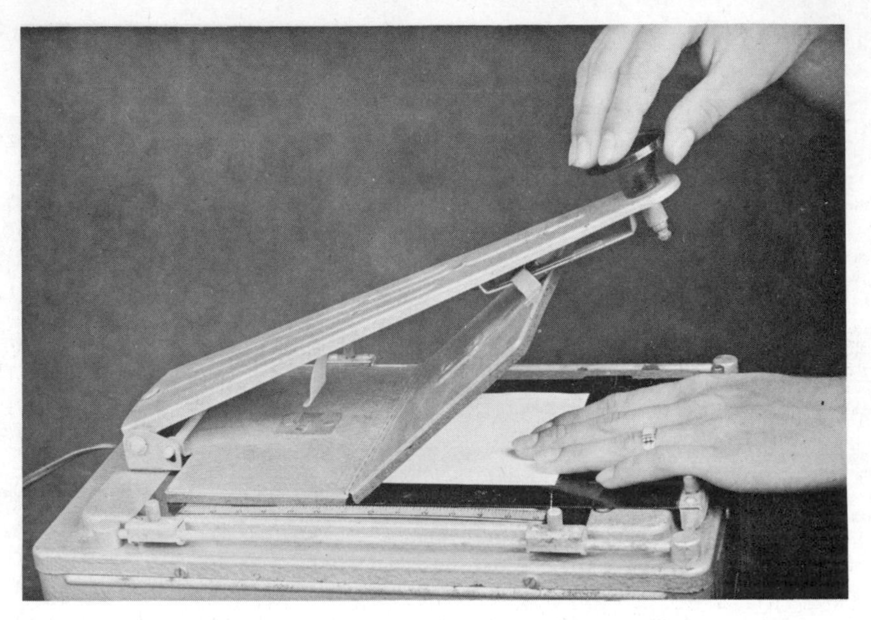

Fig. 10-5. Hold Paper in Place Until Cover Holds Paper

3. Remove a piece of contact paper from the package and place it emulsion side down on the negative. Be sure that the remainder of the paper in the package is protected from any light.
4. Hold paper in position with one hand and bring the cover until it holds the paper in place. (Fig. 10-5.)
5. Bring the cover all the way down to the locked position. This begins the exposure.
6. Time the exposure and release the cover catch. The exposed paper is now ready for developing.

### Developing and Fixing the Print

Check the temperature of the developer in the tray. Developer works differently at different temperatures. Here is the basic rule: *cold concentrated developer yields contrasty pictures, warm diluted developer makes flatter, grayer pictures.* Remove the exposed paper from the frame and slip it into the developer with a sliding motion. Do not drop it flat in the developer or bubbles will form on the surface of the paper. Be

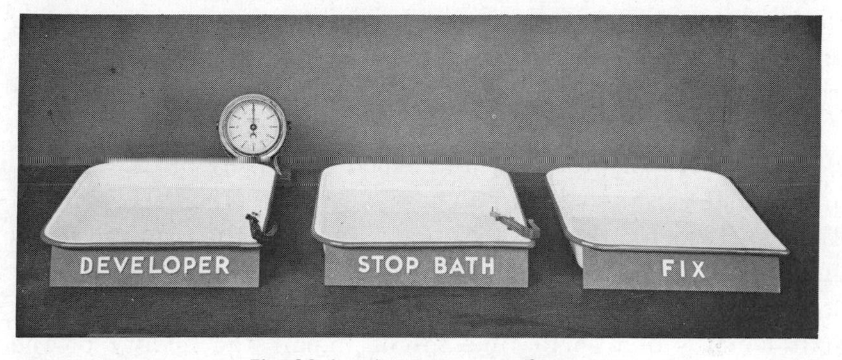


Fig. 10-6. Arrangement of Trays

sure that the entire paper becomes wet at the same time. Rock the tray gently and watch the results closely. Agitation is very important. In about twenty seconds the picture should begin to appear. It should be fully developed in forty-five seconds to one minute. If duPont 55-D is used, the development time is $1\frac{1}{2}$ to 2 minutes. When the image looks just right, transfer it quickly from the developer to the stop bath (next tray). This will stop the development. The dim light makes the print appear darker than it really is, so do not remove the print too soon. Rinse it for a few seconds then transfer it to the hypo fixing bath. After it has been in the fixing bath for five minutes, it is safe to turn on the light for a better inspection of the results. Examine the print. Is it a good one? If it is not entirely to your satisfaction,

Fig. 10-7. Slide Paper into Developer

Fig. 10-8. One Pair of Tongs for Developer, Another for Stop Bath and Fix

perhaps you can make a better one by changing the exposure time, or by using a different grade of paper. The print should remain in the fixing solution for about fifteen minutes after which it is washed in running water for an hour.

The durability of the print depends entirely on the proper fixing and washing. It is not possible to see when the print is fixed sufficiently. Some additional fixing over the required minimum does no harm so it may be left in the fixing solution as long as a half hour. Prints should be removed at the end of a half hour as additional time might impair the quality of the print. The paper is thoroughly soaked with hypo. If the slightest trace of hypo is left in the paper, the print will turn yellow. Be sure to wash it a full hour. Prints can be checked to determine whether all of the hypo has been remove by the use of a product known as "Hypo-check". More time than one hour will do no harm. If running water is not available, the water should be changed about every five or ten minutes during the hour. Many photographers prefer to use a hypo eliminator after washing, but

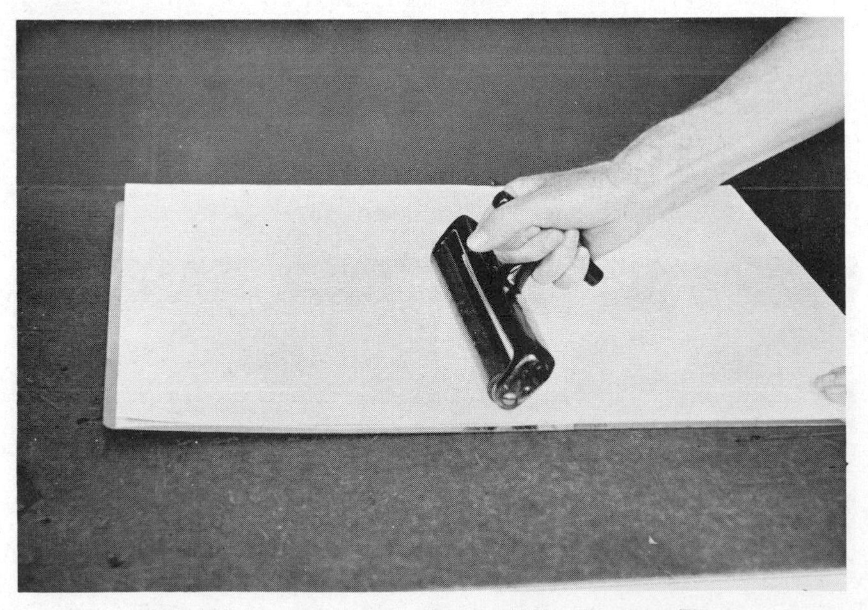

Fig. 10-9. Roll Prints in Contact With Ferrotype Tin

this is not necessary if proper precautions are taken in washing. To insure long life for the print, though, it may be advisable to use hypo eliminator. See Appendix B for formula.

### Use of Tongs

Some few people are allergic to photographic chemicals. If you happen to be one of those unfortunate individuals, you should use tongs to transfer prints instead of the fingers. Two pair are required. Mark some identification on them. One pair for developer and another pair for hypo. When a print is transferred from the developer to the stop bath, drop the print in the stop bath. Do not get any stop bath or hypo on this pair of tongs. To do so may cause brown stains on the print. Use the other pair of tongs for the stop bath and fixing solution. *Keep these tongs out of the developer.*

### Drying the Print

When the print is removed from the wash water, let it drain for a few seconds, then place it on a clean, white, water-absorbing cloth, or on a clean photographic blotter. Do not place it on a newspaper or similar material. It may be placed between two ink blotters if regular photographic blotters are not available.

In order to produce glossy prints, it is necessary to select the proper paper. Not all papers will produce a glossy surface. Papers prepared for glossy prints have an extra coating of clear gelatin on the surface. While the paper is still wet, place it face down on a highly polished "ferrotype tin". Place a photo blotter over the prints. Run a hand roller lightly over the blotter to remove excess water and set the prints. Now roll hard. The better the contact, the better the glossy surface. Set the tin on edge to dry. When dry, the print will peel away from the tin easily. They usually snap off without aid.

An electric dryer is very desirable if one can be afforded. It is essentially a heating unit over which a ferrotype tin is placed. The print is placed face down on this tin and the cover drawn tightly over it. Turn on the current and in a few minutes the print will be dry.

Fig. 10-10. Place Tin on Edge Until Prints Snap Off

Prints made with matte-surface paper are laid face up on a blotter. Wipe the surface with a clean sponge to remove excess water and dirt particles. They may now be dried in a blotter roll or by laying them face down on a clean towel or cheese cloth.

Place prints between two pieces of cardboard and place a weight on top. Leave overnight and prints should remain flat. If the borders are uneven, they may be trimmed with a paper trimmer or scissors.

### Some Suggestions for Improving Your Prints

The developer chosen will have accompanying instructions for the temperature and time of development. If these instructions are followed with a normal negative a normal print should result. A normal print is one which will show all the details, the half tones, and the shadows that it is possible to get from the negative. For about ninety-five per cent of the cases normal development gives the desired result. It may happen in the remaining five per cent of the cases that the aesthetic qualities can be improved by deviating slightly from the normal. There are usually some exceptions to rules. For example: a portrait taken in bright sunlight will have harsh shadows. A picture of this kind can be improved somewhat by reducing the contrasts. On the other hand, a building or statue taken on a very cloudy day results in the negative being a little flat. This type of picture can be improved by increasing the contrast.

Even with the same grade of paper the final result can be changed by changing the concentration of the developer, by changing the temperature of the developer, by changing both concentration and temperature, and by changing the time of development. Here, indeed, is opportunity for experiment, which may result in disappointment, or satisfying improvements in your prints.

A developer which is more concentrated than normal will produce a print of higher contrast. It also works faster. There is a danger of the deep shadows becoming entirely black and losing detail, before the lights are sufficiently developed to show any detail. A developer which is less concentrated than normal works much slower and gives less contrast than normal.

A warm developer works very rapidly, but with low contrast. There is danger of fog in using a warm developer — the print may look gray all over. A cold developer, on the other hand, works slowly and gives more contrast. Delicate details in the lights appear after a relatively long time. As might be expected, a cold developer will *prevent* fog.

When a low concentration is combined with a higher-than-normal temperature, the results are extremely soft. It must be remembered that when the temperature is increased that fog is likely to result. This combination with a very high temperature is seldom necessary.

The last method is to change the time of development. This method requires good judgment, because the results can be very disastrous. When development begins, the picture appears quite rapidly. Near the end of development, however, the process slows down considerably. When detail appears in the lightest parts, additional development will only make the whole thing darker with the danger of an overall fog.

Over development produces additional contrast. Underdevelopment tends to produce less contrast. Some of the best printing papers are made only in normal contrast. If the negative is slightly flat (lacks contrast) or is excessive in contrast, manipulation of exposure time, temperature, developer concentration, and length of development time, may be necessary to produce an excellent print.

The exact instant to remove the print from the developer can be determined only by you. This provides opportunity for individual artistic touch in the finished product.

It might be reasonably asked how cold is a cold developer and how warm is a warm developer? Normal temperatures are from 65° to 70°. The temperature can be reduced (usually with ice cubes) to 50° F. It can be raised to 80° F. Above 80° F. there is danger of damaging the gelatin and also producing fog.

A general rule can be given for developing time. Do not extend development to more than twice the time indicated by the formula or shorten to less than half the normal time.

All of the processes and comments in this chapter, beginning with developing, apply equally well to making projection prints.

These variations are mostly emergency measures. Rarely is it necessary to deviate from normal, but to be a good photographer one should know how to handle some abnormal situations.

Be sure to master the art of contact printing before "graduating" to projection printing. Contact prints should be made before attempting an enlargement.

## PRACTICAL EXPERIMENT

### Making Contact Prints Illustrating the Characteristics of Different Contrast Grades of Paper.

*Materials Required* —

1. Darkroom with suitable safelight.
2. Normal negative.
3. Contact paper, contrast grades, #0, 1, 2, 3, 4, and 5.
4. Necessary chemicals.

Note — It may be necessary for the student to prepare a developer suitable for contact paper.

*Procedure* —

1. Select a negative of normal contrast and place it in the printer *emulsion side up*. Make all necessary adjustments to mask the negative properly.
2. Cut ten (10) pieces of contrast grade #2 paper so that they are slightly larger than the negative. Place the first piece of paper over the negative *emulsion side down*. Expose each piece in succession as follows:
   1st piece for one (1) second — write grade of paper and exposure time on the back.
   2nd piece for two (2) seconds — write grade of paper and exposure time on the back.
   3rd piece for three (3) seconds — write grade of paper and exposure time on the back.
   Continue until all pieces have been exposed.
3. Develop each print for exactly one minute in D-72, or one and one-half minutes in 55D.
4. Transfer to stop bath at the end of one minute and wash for one half minute.
5. Transfer to fixing bath and fix for ten to fifteen minutes.
6. Wash for one hour and dry on blotters or cheesecloth.
7. Select the print you consider the best and read the exposure time which you have written on the back.
8. With the best print as a guide, try to make a good picture from each of the other grades of paper. Grade #0 and #1 take less exposure than #2. Grades #3, 4, and 5 each take progressively more exposure.
   When all prints are dry mount them in your notebook with appropriate remarks.
9. It may be well to repeat this exercise using a negative of low contrast and again using a very dense negative.

*Questions* —

1. How do the speeds of the different papers compare?
2. Explain how glossy prints are made.

**Discovering the Effect of Over- and Underexposure on the Printing Quality of a Negative.**

*Materials Required —*

1. Camera for making exposures.
2. Three sheets of film.
3. Tank for development.

*Procedure —*

Set up camera for a scene of your liking and make three exposures as follows:

1. Calculate accurately the exposure for the scene and film being used. Make one exposure at this setting.
2. Reset your camera to underexpose by two full stops.
3. Again reset your camera so that you will overexpose by two full stops.

   Develop the three films in the same tank for the recommended period. (See Chapter IX, *Developing the Negative.*) Make a print from each for your notebook.

*Questions —*

1. Does a normal paper make a satisfactory print from all three negatives?
2. Explain why it may be necessary to use a different grade of paper to obtain a good print from each negative.

CHAPTER XI

# enlarging

The ambition of all photographers is to view their photographs as only an enlargement can show them. Contact prints are viewed at short range, but an enlargement can be viewed at a distance. It is more impressive, more real. It comes nearer to being the scene which inspired the picture in the first place.

Enlarging is fascinating because it presents an opportunity to exercise considerable control in finishing prints. If there have been some errors, enlarging provides opportunity to partially correct them. It affords further opportunity for individual artistic ability

The process of enlarging is quite simple. The negative is placed in a projector and focused on a sensitive paper. The paper is then developed, fixed, and washed in the same manner as a contact print.

### Enlargers

Enlargers are essentially cameras working in reverse. Some cameras make good enlargers. The essential parts of an enlarger are: a source of light, a device to hold the negative, a means of focusing, and a means of adjusting the distance of the enlarger lens from the sensitive paper.

The light source is usually an incandescent light but fluorescent can be used. Clear, opal or frosted bulbs may be used. The bulb is contained in a light-tight box called the light house. This is attached to the camera part of the enlarger so that the light is directed through the negative. In the lower part of the light house will be found a means of distributing the light evenly over the negative. In the simpler forms, this is merely a piece of opal glass, occasionally two pieces, one above the other and separated from each other. The distance of separation may vary with different makes of enlargers. An enlarger so made is usually referred to as a *diffusion enlarger*. Another method is to use a condensing lens. This type of enlarger, known as the *condenser enlarger,* has no diffusion. It is optically more efficient but has some decided faults. The other type is the *diffusion-condenser* enlarger. This uses an opal bulb which diffuses the light before it strikes the condensing lenses.

The middle part of the enlarger is essentially a camera fastened to the light house, with a slide arrangement to hold the negative, and made light-tight so that it will not expose the paper.

Lenses for enlargers are usually made differently than a regular camera lens. They are especially corrected for the distances generally used in enlarging. Any well-corrected lens of the proper focal length is satisfactory. Remember the rule — *The focal length of the lens must be at least equal to the diagonal of the negative.*

A means of focusing is attached to the lens mount so the distance from the lens to the negative may be adjusted. The negative is flat and the sensitive paper is flat, so there need be little concern about depth of field.

There is usually no shutter in the lens mount. Timing is accomplished by turning the light on and off. A foot control on the floor is very handy. This leaves the hands free to do other things.

Most enlargers have a filter holder which swings in place between the lens and the sensitive paper. This is usually red, unless color separation work is being done. The image can be seen on the sensitive paper, thus making it possible to make final adjustments with the paper in place before the exposure is made.

The last item of the enlarger is a stand for adjusting the distance from the enlarger to the paper. This controls the size of the image.

The diffusion enlarger gives slightly less contrast in the prints than the condenser enlarger. The condenser enlarger gives more contrast, but it also has the fault of enlarging too sharply. Every defect gets its share of attention. Grain is more prominent and every scratch or blemish is shown. Another objection to the condenser enlarger is the need for different condensing lenses. If the condenser enlarger or the diffuse-condenser enlarger is used, better results can be obtained by using paper which is one grade softer than normal.

**Enlarging Papers**

About the only difference between contact papers and enlarging papers is the emulsion. Bromide and chloro-bromide

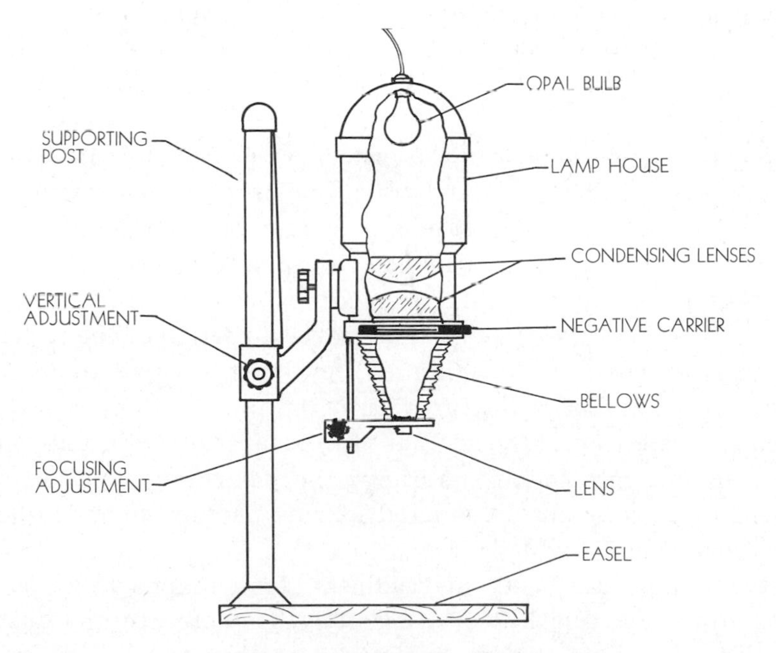


Fig. 11-1. Diagram of an Enlarger

papers are used for enlarging. The bromide paper is more sensitive. Enlarging papers are sold in the same grades, surfaces and weights as contact papers. Enlarging papers cost more than contact papers. In a way this is a good thing as it encourages greater care in making the prints. Making a good enlargement is an art that offers a real challenge. The selection of paper for an enlargement is determined by the kind of an enlargement desired. Samples of different papers can be examined at a photo supply store.

### Preparations for Enlarging

The arrangement of trays, Fig. 10-6, the solutions, and procedure for developing the enlarged print are the same as for contact printing. It is suggested that the sections on "the Darkroom", "Chemicals", and "Photographic papers" in the chapter on Contact Printing be reviewed before beginning enlarging. The only variation of arrangement from contact printing is possibly a tray of clean water between the developer and the stop bath. Some photographers prefer to nearly stop development by washing off surplus developer. They may then apply developer locally to bring out areas that are responding slowly. This pre-rinse also saves stop bath.

The enlarger should first be tested to see that it is in operating condition. Chemicals and trays are prepared the same as for contact printing. The safelight should be an OA (yellow green) or an S-55-X. It is a good idea to run a test to see whether the safelight is really safe. Lay a piece of bromide paper in the working area. Turn on the safelight. Cover a portion of the paper every 15 seconds for two minutes. Develop the paper and see whether you can detect any grey on it. If not, the light is safe. If you can detect grey, the amount of exposure time will tell you how long the light is safe. Arrange the enlarging paper in a convenient place so that it is handy. Some photographers make themselves a light-tight drawer.

Everything else being in readiness, take the negative out of its envelope and look it over carefully. If there are any dust particles on it, they should be removed as they too will be enlarged. Now take a look at the negative holder to make sure it is clean. If the glass is dirty or has finger marks on it, it can be cleaned with rubber cement. Drop a little cement on the glass, spread it around with the finger and after it has dried a minute rub it off with a clean finger. It cleans grease and dust without scratching the glass. The best way to clean the negative is to blow gently across it or use a soft brush. If it is very dirty, a reliable film cleaner should be used. Cleaning should be done rather quickly. *Put the negative in the slide with the emulsion side toward the lens.* It is usually advisable to insert it upside down so that the image will be upright as it is viewed on the easel. Check for cleanliness each time the negative is changed. With everything in readiness put on an apron, get a clean towel, and proceed to make the enlargement.

### Procedure for Making an Enlargement

1. Clean the negative carrier. Some enlargers use glassless negative carriers.
2. Clean the negative.
3. Place the negative in the negative carrier and insert immediately in the enlarger.
4. Place a white piece of paper in the enlarging easel and set the masking guides for the proper size print. Some easels are made for specific sizes of prints and have no masking guides.
5. Turn on safelights and turn off white light.
6. Turn on enlarger light.
7. Adjust the focus with lens wide open until the image is sharp.
8. If the image on the easel is too small, raise the enlarger head and refocus. If too large, lower the head and refocus.
9. When the image size is correct, select a fine line near the center of the picture and adjust the focus so that it is the sharpest possible.
10. Swing the red filter in front of the lens. Close the lens diaphragm until fine detail of the image begins to dis-

appear but the image remains visible. This should be about f/8 or f/11.

11. Place a strip of photographic paper of your choice on the easel so that it will get a good sample of the image.
12. Expose the test strip as follows:
    a. Expose entire strip for 5 seconds.
    b. Cover one-fourth of the strip with cardboard and expose 5 more seconds.
    c. Cover one-half of the strip and expose 10 seconds more.
    d. Move the cardboard to cover three-fourths of the strip and expose an additional 20 seconds.

    This gives exposures of 5 - 10 - 20 - 40 seconds on the one strip of paper. Note that each doubles the previous exposure.
13. Develop the test strip in the same manner as contact prints. Be sure to develop for the time stated on the developer container.
14. After the test strip has been in the fixing solution for a minute or two, examine it carefully. Select the exposure time that gives the best print. If none of the tests are satisfactory, try another test strip with different contrast grades of paper. A good print should have texture in the highlights and detail in the shadows.
15. *Wash your hands thoroughly and dry them.*
16. Take a full sheet of paper of the kind giving the best test and place it in the easel.
17. Expose the print for the time that gave the best print on the test strip.

Fig. 11-2. Determining Proper Exposure Time

Test Strip

5 10 20 40

Photo by Charles Raleigh

Completed Picture Using Twenty Seconds Exposure

18. Develop for the same time that was used on the test strip and fix as indicated for contact prints. Don't forget to agitate by rocking the tray. This is very important.
19. Wash one full hour. This means one full hour from the time the last print was put in the washer.
20. Dry the prints as described for contact prints.

If the prints tend to curl badly they may be soaked in a commercial print flattener before drying (follow directions on the label) or you may prepare your own by preparing a solution of 1 ounce of glycerine in 16 ounces of water. Soak the print in this solution for 3 to 5 minutes before drying. When dry the print should remain reasonably flat.

## PROJECTION CONTROL

The techniques of enlarging present opportunities to manipulate the light to obtain effects not common to contact printing. It offers opportunities to improve one's prints, to make certain desirable changes, and perhaps most of all it is a fascinating challenge to the photographer's skill. The techniques of projection control are not difficult but do require some practice.

### Spot Printing or Burning In

It may happen that a small area of an otherwise good negative needs additional exposure to bring out the detail. Sometimes cloud areas of the sky need additional exposure to show the texture to best advantage. You may deliberately add exposure to the corners to darken them for pictorial reasons. This adding of exposure in selected areas is called *spot printing.* Some photographers call it "burning in".

This type of control is accomplished by cutting a hole in a

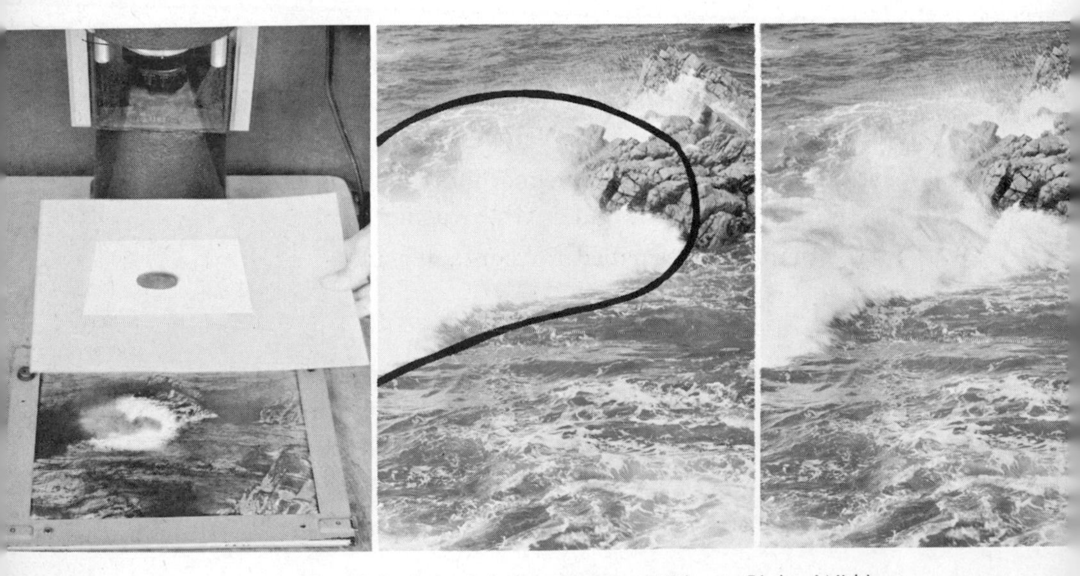

Fig. 11-3. Spot Printing (Center, Without; Right, With)

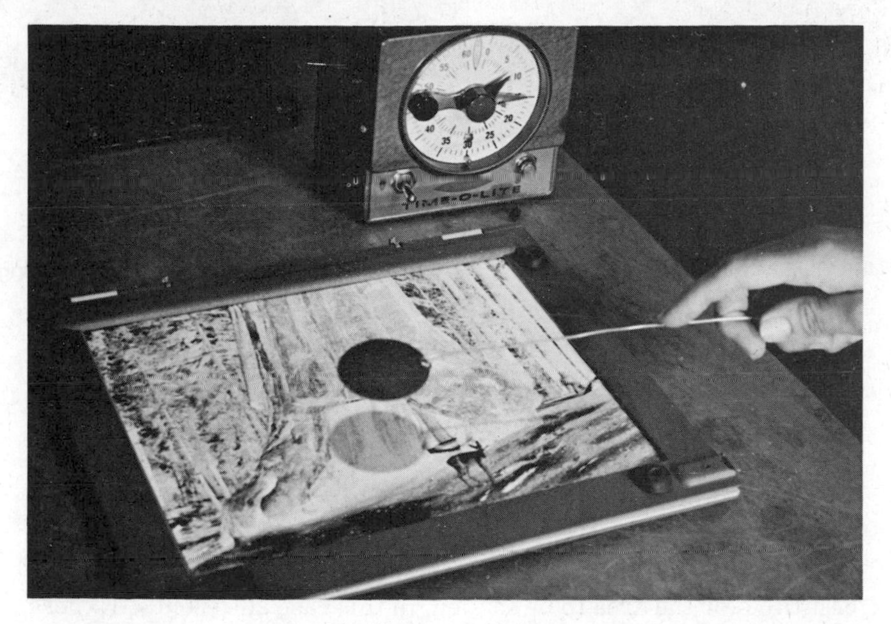


Fig. 11-4a. Dodging

large piece of cardboard or heavy black paper. The card is held between the lens and the paper. This allows additional light to hit the desired area through the hole while the large cardboard prevents the remainder of the picture from being further exposed. Keep the cardboard in gentle motion so that the edges of the area being printed in will blend with the remainder of the picture.

### Dodging

Dodging is just the opposite of spot printing. It occasionally happens that a straight print would make an area too dark. Shading this particular area during part of the exposure reduces the exposure in that area and consequently makes the area lighter when it is developed. The tool for this manipulation is a piece of cardboard to use near the edges (this may be cut to any desired shape), and a small disc of black paper held on a thin stiff wire.

Make a test strip of the area to be dodged to determine the correct length of exposure. It is helpful to regulate the lens opening so that the exposure time is 30 seconds or more. This gives time to do a better job of dodging.

Fig. 11-4b. Print Made Without Dodging or Spot Printing

Fig. 11-4c. Better Print When Dodging and Spot Printing Employed

Hold the dodging tool between the lens and the paper and keep it in constant motion to blend the edges with the remainder of the picture.

*Example:*

Close the lens so that the proper time for the most of the print is 40 seconds. When the test strip is made be sure that it includes the area to be dodged. Determine from the test strip the best time for the area to be shaded, in this case 20 seconds. Expose the entire print for 20 seconds then slip the dodging tool in place, keeping it in constant motion, for the remaining 20 seconds. Some operators use a rotary motion for the dodging tool, others use a vertical motion. It is important to move the wire over different areas of the print so that it will not leave a light line on the print.

### Correcting Distortion

Distortion results when it is necessary to tilt the camera up, or down, to include the desired area. This happens most when photographing tall buildings or tall trees. The base of a building, being closer to the lens than the top, registers wider on the film than the top. This gives a feeling of falling back or of converging at the top. This is a natural law of perspective. We see it every day, but our eyes automatically compensate for it. When we see it in a print, this compensation does not occur and we find it objectional.

We know that when a camera is pointed up, or down, this distortion results. When possible, this should be corrected in taking the picture. We can, however, correct some distortion while making the enlargement.

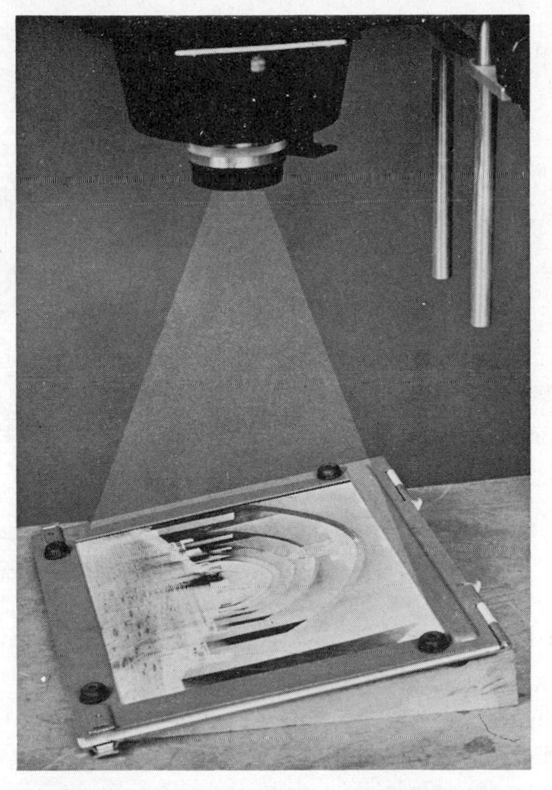

Fig. 11-5. Position of Easel for Distortion Control

The procedure for correcting distortion is as follows:

1. With the negative in the enlarger and a focusing paper in the easel, open the lens to its maximum aperture and turn on the light.
2. Adjust the focus until it is approximately correct.
3. Tilt the easel so that the image of the bottom of the building is closer to the lens than the top of the building. The easel is tilted until the lines of the side of the building are parallel to the side of the easel. There is a practical limit. This slant must not be greater than the depth of field.
4. Prop the easel securely in this position.
5. If the enlarger lens can be tilted, tilt the lens so that it is parallel with the easel. If the lens can not be tilted, select

Fig. 11-6. (a) Photo Before Correction (b) Photo After Correction

an object a little above the center and focus critically with the lens wide open.

6. Close the lens to its smallest aperture. This gives maximum depth of field.
7. Make a test strip to determine the correct exposure. This is necessary because, if the easel is tilted an appreciable amount, the part farthest away requires more exposure than the part closest to the lens.
8. When exposing the finished print, give the entire print the proper exposure for the part nearest the lens. With a piece of cardboard start at the part nearest the lens and gradually shade to the part furthest from the lens. Keep the cardboard in motion at all times. It is well to practice this a few times before exposing the paper so that the rate of moving the cardboard will be correct to give correct exposure to all parts of the print.

### Cropping

One of the biggest problems for the amateur is to know where to stop. The picture should portray just what you want and no more. It often happens that more is included than makes for a good photograph. This may be controlled to a large extent when the final enlargement is made.

A study print of the entire negative is made first. Make two L-shaped pieces of cardboard, similar to Fig. 11-7. Use these pieces of cardboard as masks to move back and forth over the

Fig. 11-7. L-Shaped Cardboards Used to Judge Composition

test print to determine just what part of the picture makes the best composition. Mark this area with a heavy pencil so that it can be used as a reference when composing the picture when the enlargement is made.

Finding the best part of a picture to use is called *cropping*. Frequently, by using only a part of the negative, an interesting photograph can be made out of one that would ordinarily be relegated to the waste basket.

### Vignetting

It occasionally happens that only a small portion of a picture is desired. This is often the case when a group of persons are taken together. Sometimes one person may move as the picture is taken and spoil the picture, but another in the group has an especially good picture. An enlargement can be made of this one person of the group by a little trick known as vignetting.

To accomplish this, take a cardboard or black paper and cut a hole in it to approximate the shape of the image desired, but somewhat smaller. Cut notches all around the hole, Fig. 11-8. Determine the exposure time as previously described, and place the sensitive paper in place as for a regular enlargement. Swing

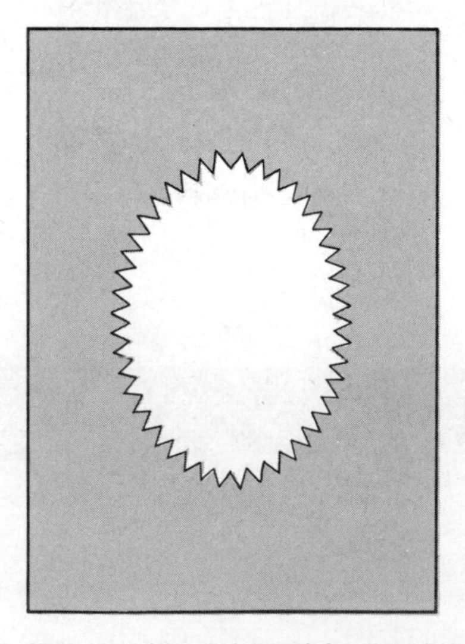

Fig. 11-8. Cardboard Used for Vignetting

Group of Girl Scouts — One Person Removed from Group by Vignetting

the red filter in front of the enlarger lens. Turn on the enlarger so that the image appears on the sensitive paper. Now place the prepared cardboard so that only the image wanted in the finished photograph can be seen. Swing the red filter out of the way and begin the exposure. Rotate the cardboard gently so that the edges fade gradually. Finish the print in the usual manner.

### Diffusing

Certain photographs may look better if not as sharp and with a softer atmosphere. This can be accomplished by placing a *diffusion disc* next to the enlarging lens during the exposure. The disc is a flat piece of glass with concentric rings pressed into it. It scatters the light just enough to break up the sharp edges made by the anastigmat lens.

One thickness of silk hose stretched over a frame is an acceptable substitute for the diffusion disc.

Keep the diffusion disc moving up and down and around in circles during the exposure. The degree of diffusion is controlled by the amount of time the diffusion disc is in operation. Try about half of the normal exposure time for your first print. The exposure with the diffuser requires some additional exposure time — up to 25 per cent more for full diffusion.

### Retouching

No matter how careful one may be, occasional defects such as pin holes or scratches will appear in the negative. This may be corrected by retouching. Skillful retouching can overcome many defects. This requires almost as much skill and artistic ability as that of an artist who spreads his paint on the canvas to get a desired result.

The tools for retouching are four in number; a pencil, a small high-quality brush, retouching fluid, and a special knife. India ink may be used for retouching. There are several commercial retouching preparations available. Small parts can be retouched by a pencil. Very carefully make fine narrow lines over the part which is to appear lighter until the density is correct. Sharpen the pencil so that the lead protrudes at least a half inch. This will give some spring to the lead and prevent marking too heavily. Go over the area several times to obtain the correct density rather than try to do the job the first time over. With care, spots, deep shadows, pimples and wrinkles in portraits can be removed. Do not try to remove freckles in this manner unless there are only a few. If freckles are characteristic of the person they really help to make up the personality that the photographer is trying to capture. If the subject insists that there should be no freckles, just slip the correct filter over the lens and the freckles will automatically disappear.

If the negative has pin holes in it due to dust on the film or poorly mixed chemicals this can be corrected. With a brush carefully apply some India ink to the spot. This will leave a white spot on the print which is corrected by spotting.

To reduce the density of a small part of the negative, very carefully scrape off the emulsion to the desired density. This is a delicate operation and extreme care must be taken or the negative may be irreparably damaged.

Retouching is an art that requires great skill and patience. Much of it can be learned only by watching someone who is skilled. If there is an opportunity to observe a skilled retoucher, by all means do so. Learn to do retouching well, because a poor retouching job is worse than none at all. There will be little need for retouching if proper care is taken in the preceding photographic operations.

### Spotting

Occasionally a particle of dust gets on the negative unnoticed. This results in a small white spot on the print. This can be corrected by touching the spot with a small pointed spotting brush that has been dampened with a spotting fluid. Several companies make spotting fluid under a variety of trade names. The brush should be nearly dry. The spotting colors are diluted with water until they are the same value (darkness) as the area to be spotted. Do not try to eliminate a larger area with a single application. Go over it several times with a weaker color until it is built up to the same value as the surrounding area.

The technique of handling the brush varies with the person using it and the area to be filled in. In general a series of small dots is used for a small area and a cross hatching motion for a larger area.

If there are small holes in the negative, the spot on the print will be black. This can be removed by the application of a reducer, sometimes called spot remover. It is applied in the same manner as described above. To stop the action, use methyl alcohol, or just plain water, on a cotton swab. The cotton swab is a small tuft of cotton twisted on the end of a toothpick or match.

Several commercial preparations are on the market. You can easily make your own from the following formulas:

Solution A

15 grains of Theocarbamide
1 oz. of distilled water

Solution B

15 grains iodine crystals
1 oz. methyl alcohol

To use, mix one drop of each solution on a glass or dish and add 1 or 2 drops of aerosol or other wetting agent. Keep solution A and solution B stored in separate bottles. Mix only enough each time for one spotting job. Once the two solutions are mixed they spoil rapidly.

## PRACTICAL EXPERIMENT

### Making Prints by Projection.

*Materials Required* —

1. Darkroom with suitable safelight.
2. Necessary chemicals.
3. Enlarging paper, grades #1, 2, and 3.
4. A normal negative, a negative slightly less dense than normal, and a negative slightly more dense than normal.

*Procedure* —

1. Place the negative in a properly masked carrier and insert in the enlarger, emulsion side toward the lens.
2. Adjust the height of the enlarger to produce the desired size image.
3. Focus on a piece of white paper.
4. Cut a strip from each of the three grades of paper and place under the enlarger so that, when the enlarger light is turned on, the image will fall on the strips of paper.
5. Place a piece of cardboard or black paper over the strips of paper so that only a small portion of each can be exposed. Turn on the enlarger light and expose this small portion. At the end of five seconds, move the cardboard to expose an additional portion of the paper strips. At the end of ten seconds move the cardboard again. Continue this procedure until you have at least four exposure times on each strip, doubling the exposure each time.
6. Develop the strips for a normal period (about 1 minute for D-72), place in stop bath, wash and transfer to the fixing bath. Note — you will want to keep these strips to mount in your notebook. Examine the test strips and determine which section of the three strips makes the best print.

7. After the grade of paper and exposure time have been selected, take a whole sheet of paper of the grade selected and expose for the full length of time determined from the test strips.
8. Process the print in the same manner as you did your contact prints.

CHAPTER XII

# treatment of imperfect negatives

Preceding chapters told how to develop films by the tray and tank method. How to develop contact prints and enlargements. Information has also been included as to how to compensate for some faulty negatives and balance them by careful printing. Some photographers prefer to watch the development of the negative and, if necessary, to give it some special treatment. If it lacks contrast, it can be increased. If the contrast is too great, it can be reduced. All of the things that have been said about developing still hold, but with a little more information poor negatives can be made into reasonably good ones.

It should be remembered that blue sensitive film and the orthochromatic film can be developed in red light, but that panchromatic film is sensitive to all light and, therefore, must be developed in total darkness. To make it possible to watch negative development, the film can be desensitized.

### Desensitizers

No attempt will be made to tell about the composition of desensitizers. They are very complex compounds with complicated formulas. It is enough to know their names and that they will desensitize the film to such a degree that it may be developed in bright green or orange light. There are two desensitizers which are in common use; pinakryptol green, and pinakryptol yellow.

Pinakryptol green may be placed in the developer. It is a rather expensive chemical, but so little is used that the unit cost is not great. To prepare the solution, add fifteen grains of pinakryptol green powder to a mixture of one pint of water and one pint of methyl alcohol. This is the stock solution. Take 0.7 ounces of stock solution and add to 14 ounces of developer for the proper concentration. This solution must act on the film for two minutes before the light may be turned on. Because it is necessary to develop two minutes in darkness, this desensitizer is not recommended for rapid developers. It is recommended for slow and medium developers. Pinakryptol green may be used as a pre-bath when fast working developers are used.

Pinakryptol yellow is more efficient than pinakryptol green, but it does not agree with developers. The solution is prepared in hot water (follow directions on the label) and is used as a bath before development begins. To use this solution the film is placed in the bath for about two minutes (some additional time does no harm) and then transferred to the developer without rinsing. The green or orange light may be turned on and development watched from the beginning.

For the sensitive panchromatic films a combination of both methods is recommended. Place the film in a bath of pinakryptol yellow for two or three minutes then transfer to a developer which contains pinakryptol green.

Desensitizers make it possible to watch the development of each film and thus get the best possible results.

### Special Development

In regular development it is better to use the time and temperature method. After efficiency in regular development has been acquired you may wish to try the following method to bring out the best possible refinements of your negatives.

Many scenes, such as a beach scene, have extreme contrasts because of the natural lighting. Many are extremely flat, such as those taken on a rainy day. These unusual negatives can be greatly improved by special development. The method of development about to be described is not recommended for some of the extremely fast films. They are quite likely to fog.

Arrange three trays for the developer. Arrange one tray for a slow developer which produces low contrast, such as DK-20 or D-23. Place this tray on the left. Pour a fast working, high-contrast developer such as Eastman D-11 with a desensitizer added, in the tray on the right. The center tray is for the normal developer. Prepare also a stop bath and the usual hypo fixing bath.

Load the tank in the usual way and fill with a soft, slow working developer. For purposes of illustration suppose D-76 is used. For normal development, the time is 17 minutes at 68° F. (20° C.). Instead of developing for the full time, develop it for about half time (8 minutes). Pour the developer from the tank into the middle tray. Immediately fill the tank with a solution of pinakryptol and water and place the films in this tank. (About one ounce of stock solution of pinakryptol to 14 ounces of water.) This will premit the film to remain in the tank for a considerable time without much additional development.

If a roll is to be developed it can be cut apart so that one exposure at a time can be developed. Remove one and examine it. Do not prolong this examination. If the film seems to be developing properly, place it again in the normal developer and watch its development until the regular period of time has elapsed. Dip the film in water to retard development and examine it again. If the brightest highlights need a little more density, place the film for a *few seconds* in the fast working developer, and this will accomplish the desired contrast. At the correct instant, transfer the film to the stop bath. The correct instant is based on one's ability to judge a good negative — an ability which comes with experience. The beginner should make several identical exposures, develop each differently and make a print from each. This may help to acquire the ability to judge the degree of development in each solution. The remainder of the operation is the same as described in Chapter IX.

Take another film from the tank. Suppose that this one was taken in the rain and is very thin and flat. Place it in the fast working, high-contrast developer and carefully watch the development. When the picture "comes through" (begins to show on the back) transfer the film immediately to the stop bath.

With some practice and a lot of attention negatives can be improved. Unless one is a skilled technician, it is better to use the time-temperature method.

No film has ever been made that can register the same as the eye. The best that can be done is to use the average of the total range. Sometimes calculations are inaccurate and overexposure and under-development result in poor negatives. These mistakes sometimes can be corrected by intensifying or reducing the negative.

### Intensification

There is little hope for a negative that has been extremely underexposed. Intensification may help some. It may "save" an otherwise impossible negative. A negative which has been properly exposed, or nearly so, but has been underdeveloped can be made into a fairly good negative by intensification.

There are several kinds of intensifiers on the market. *All of them are poisonous* and some of them are extremely so. Be very careful with this material. It should be kept out of reach of children. Always wash your hands thoroughly after using it.

There are three intensifiers in general use; the mercury intensifier, chromium intensifier, and the silver intensifier.

*Because of the deadly poison in mercury intensifier, and the extreme care with which this material must be used, it is not recommended for general use.*

The *mercury intensifier* is in two parts: the bleach, which is composed of mercuric chloride (poison) and potassium bromide, and the intensifier. The intensifier may be any one of several chemicals. The solution producing the greatest contrast contains *sodium cyanide.* Sodium cyanide is a *deadly poison.* Always use rubber gloves when handling this chemical. *Under no circumstances should one breathe the fumes.* When it is poured down the sink be sure to wash it down with a generous quantity of water. *Never use it in a room that is not well ventilated.*

The *chromium intensifier* bleaches the negatives after which the negative is again developed in a suitable developer. Be sure to follow the instructions carefully, as not all developers are suitable to use after bleaching in this solution. Development can be done in any artificial or natural light except direct sunlight. The process can be two or three times for more intensification. Negatives intensified with chromium intensifier are more permanent than those intensified with the mercury solution.

*Silver intensifier* has an advantage when preparing slides for projection, in that it does not change the color of the image. All others change the image color. This solution intensifies the image proportionately and its action can be easily controlled by the length of time the negative is left in the intensifier. This intensifier is unstable and will spoil in about thirty minutes after it is mixed.

No specific directions will be given for using intensifiers as each is used differently. Full directions will be found on the package. There are two general characteristics of intensifiers: They increase the *contrast* as well as the density, and they usually increase the grain.

Before experimenting with intensifiers use your knowledge of printing to try to make a good print. Intensify only if the results are not satisfactory.

### Reducers

Reducers are used when a negative is too dense to make a good print, or when the whole negative is covered with fog.

There are two general classes of reducers: those which reduce *contrast* as well as density, and those that work by reducing the whole area evenly.

The reducer which greatly reduces contrast, sometimes known as a *flattening reducer,* is composed of ammonium persulfate and sulfuric acid. Remember the caution about mixing acids. *Always pour acid into water — never pour water into acid.*

This reducer takes more silver from the areas which contain the most silver, with a result that the reduced negative is thinner and has much less contrast. Be sure that the negative is fixed and washed *thoroughly* before reducing it in this solution. Judge the density by watching the degree of reduction. Hold it up to the light and look through it. When it is to your liking, put it in running water and wash for an hour.

The other type reducer cuts evenly over the entire surface. It is sometimes called a *cutting reducer*. If the negative is fogged and dense, this will usually clear away the fog and leave a bright negative. One of the best known of this type is *Farmer's reducer*. Its ingredients are potassium ferricyanide and hypo (sodium thiosulfate). This solution decomposes rapidly after mixing; hence it must be used immediately. It is necessary that the process be watched carefully as the tray is rocked lightly. Use a white tray, if available, as it makes it easier to watch the process. When the density is satisfactory remove the negative quickly and wash for about an hour. If there is only one small area that needs reducing, apply the reducer to the area with a cotton swab or pad.

This concludes the description of the mechanical processes involved in exposing, developing and making prints. The remaining chapters are written to give help in making photographs more appealing, more interesting and more beautiful. Some mechanical processes will be described, but the remaining chapters deal more with art, good taste, balance, lighting, general composition, color and the many other things that make photography a pleasure.

CHAPTER XIII

# special treatment of prints

Many photographs are finished in shining black and white. From the artistic point of view, many of these photographs could be improved by changing the color of the image, the paper surface, or the mounting. The portrait of an elderly gentleman is more artistic in a softer warmer tone. *Tone refers to the color of the image.* It can be controlled to a considerable extent by choosing the correct paper and developer. Some papers produce a blue-black image which is cold and of high contrast. Some produce a warm tone. With the materials available, there is great latitude for individual artistic ability.

## Toning

Toning is not a difficult task. There are three principal methods which will be described briefly. Since each solution and method has a different technique, the toning processes will not be described in detail. A general description of each method will be given, together with some suggestions and cautions.

The first method is by direct development. This is accomplished, as has been previously stated, by the proper selection of paper and developer. It is used when only a slight change of color is desired.

The second and most popular method is to replace the silver image with an organic salt. This may sound complicated. The chemical reactions probably would cause trouble, if they had to be derived, but fortunately they have all been tried, and the chemicals are accompanied with definite directions for proper use.

The third method of toning is to place the print in a solution of potassium ferricyanide. This changes the silver image to silver ferricyanide which will absorb many dies. The silver image cannot be satisfactorily dyed.

### Toning by Replacement of Silver Image with Inorganic Salts

There are four general formulas for producing the sepia (rich brown) tone: hypo alum sepia toner, sulfide sepia toner, polysulfide toner, and the gold toner.

In general all prints which are to be toned should be thoroughly fixed and washed. The print need not be dry before toning, but if it is dry, it should be soaked in clean water several minutes before toning.

The *hypo alum sepia toner* is recommended for warm tone papers. It is a single solution which is poured into a tray and heated to 120° F. (49°C.). The print should tone in from ten to fifteen minutes. Prints to be toned in this solution should be slightly darker than normal before toning. After toning is completed, gently wipe the surface to remove any sediment which might have collected and wash for one hour in running water.

The *sulfide sepia toner* is probably most common. It is recommended for all papers except the warm tone papers. The process has two phases: the bleaching, and the toning. The print must be washed thoroughly before placing in the bleach. After washing immerse the print quickly in the bleaching solution. Be sure the print is immersed quickly and evenly. In about one minute the image will nearly disappear. When only a yellowish hint of the picture remains, remove it from the bleach and wash it in cold clear water for at least five minutes. Place the bleached print in the toner solution until the print is restored in its new color. This operation will probably not last much longer than 30 seconds. The print is then immersed in a hardening bath for about five minutes and washed in clear water for about 30 minutes.

The *polysulfide toner* is much simpler to manipulate. It is a single solution and requires no heating. It can be used on most papers. (See note on label for papers for which it is not suitable.) It produces darker sepia tones than some other toners. The time required is about 15 minutes at 69° F. or 3 minutes at 100° F. (38° C.). Just immerse the print in the solution for the required amount of time, remove and wash for thirty minutes. If sediment has collected on the print, remove it with a soft sponge prior to washing.

*Gold toner* has the advantage of producing a variety of brown tones. The print can be removed at any stage of toning when the desired color is obtained. Gold chloride is a rather expensive chemical which makes this solution somewhat more expensive. The toning is done with the bath between 100°F. and 110°F. After toning is complete, the print should be returned to the fixing bath for about five minutes, then washed for an hour in running water.

In all toning operations the tray should be rocked gently. It is better to use a glass tray. A tray with any metal exposed gives unsatisfactory results. The toning solution reacts with the exposed metal causing a mixture of colors.

Other toners are available such as *uranium toner* which produces colors from chocolate to brick red and *iron toners* which produce blue tones. They are all simple to use. Just follow the directions on the label carefully and excellent results are assured. If some other color such as yellow, green, violet, etc., is desired a different process must be used.

### Dye Toning

A silver image will not take dye. It is necessary to change the image so that it will dye. To do this the print is immersed in a bath called a mordant bath. If the print is left in the ferricyanide solution too long the image will be destroyed. To know when to remove the print, another chemical, uranium nitrate, is added to the bath. When the print has remained for a sufficient time in the mordant bath, it will begin to turn brown. This is the cue to remove it. Wash for a half minute to remove the yellow stain from the highlights and transfer to the dye bath. Leave it in this bath until the desired color is obtained, then remove and wash until the extra dye is washed from the highlights. Do not wash too long or the result will be spoiled.

## Hand Coloring

Hand coloring requires considerable skill. It is very closely related to the work of the artist, who with his brush and colors, reproduces his thoughts and emotions on canvas. The difference is that the artist begins with a plain white canvas, while the photographer has the images present and needs only to supply the proper color to each. In general the colors should follow those found in nature. After acquiring a thorough understanding of color harmony and some skill in toning, deviation from nature's colors can be tried.

To describe in detail all of the things one should know to become expert at hand coloring would require a volume in itself. Only a general description will be given here. If prints are to be made for someone else to color it is necessary to know something of the requirements.

Prints to be hand-colored should be less dense than normal and should be on matte or semi-matte paper. Make a normal exposure but stop development before it is completed; about three-fourths of normal time is usually about right. The print must be free from finger prints. The color will not distribute properly if a finger print is present. There are two general methods of coloring prints; with oil colors, and with water colors.

The beginner will probably be more successful with oil colors than with water colors. Transparent oil colors come in tubes. The surface of the print is treated with photo-medium, applied with a cotton tuft or clean cloth. After a few seconds the print is wiped dry and is ready to receive the colors.

The colors are applied with tufts of cotton wrapped around a toothpick or sharpened match stick, or by a larger tuft held in the hand. The colors are usually squeezed onto a small plate of glass. Each time a different color is applied a clean tuft of cotton should be used. If the colors are not satisfactory they may be removed with a tuft of cotton saturated with photo-medium. Oil colors in pencil form are now available. They are true oil colors and may be used with the moist colors from the tubes. They are very good for fine lines. Oil colors dry rather slowly so it will be necessary to lay the print away for two or three days before it can be mounted.

Transparent water colors are very inexpensive and somewhat more difficult to use. To prepare the print either dampen it or coat it with a sizing solution. The colors are applied with a brush. Water colors once applied cannot be successfully removed. The color should be built up by applying a weak color several times instead of trying to get the correct color with the first application. If the print becomes too dry, a moist blotter underneath will keep the print the proper dampness to color well.

Before attempting to do tinting with water colors one should read a good book on color and color harmony. Careful observation of nature will provide many interesting things that may have been overlooked. Notice that the sky is not as blue near the horizon as it is overhead, that distant objects do not appear in their natural color but usually look hazy and blue or blue-purple. Notice the color of leaves in the shade, and where the sun hits them, the color of reflections in water, etc. Nature will supply unlimited lessons in color.

### Mounting Finished Prints

A good enlargement deserves to be seen. There are many ways that they may be used. One very good use is to decorate the walls of your home. This offers a real opportunity to demonstrate good taste and artistic sense. It is well to change the photographs on the wall occasionally. This will keep the walls interesting, and will also help remove earlier photographs that no longer represent your best efforts in photography. The seasons of the year, special holidays such as Christmas, will give ample opportunity to display suitable photographs. Superior photographs should be entered in exhibits.

Whatever the occasion the best prints should be mounted. Salon exhibits almost always require 16 x 20 inch mounts. Prints should be so placed that the mounts can be hung vertically. If the print is made on white paper, the mount should also be white. Warm tone prints usually look better on a cream or ivory mount. A sub-mount which extends about one-eighth of an inch all around the print is in good taste. Black or sepia sub-mounts are good for warm tone prints. You may wish to title your print and sign your name to the work. This should be small, neat and not too conspicuous. Keep it simple, in good proportion, and above all, avoid complicated border designs and drawings.

The remarks about exhibition prints apply equally well for other mountings except for the size of the print and the mounting. See Chapter XIV for ideas of proportion of print size to mounting size. The general rule is: *Allow a generous margin all around the print keeping the margin of the two sides and top equal and the lower margin somewhat larger than the edge.* Pictures to be framed, and those made for salon exhibit may cover the entire 16 x 20 inch mounting board. Mounting paper and board can be purchased in varying surfaces and grades at artist supply stores.

Various methods are used in mounting. In any case, whether mounting with cement, paste, mounting tissue, rubber cement, or other numerous products, follow the directions carefully. When selecting a rubber base mounting material be sure that it is a quality suitable for photographic work. Some rubber contains a sulfide which may damage the print.

As a final refinement on exhibition prints or gifts, fasten a piece of tissue paper, either plain or figured, over the mounted print. The psychological effect of lifting a delicate piece of tissue paper to look at the work gives it a certain sense of value, of expensiveness which it otherwise does not have. The paper will also act as a protection for the print.

## PRACTICAL EXPERIMENT

### Toning

*Materials Required —*

1. Three trays.
2. Necessary chemicals. These may be packaged chemicals ready to mix or a formula may be mixed from appendix.
3. Several good prints.

*Procedure —*

1. Select prints of good contrast and a little darker than normal. Be sure that they have been well fixed and washed. Some toners require the prints to be fixed without hardener. Be sure to determine whether the paper is suitable for the toner to be used.
2. Prepare solutions.
3. A. Sepia toner by bleach and redevelopment.
   a. Place the print in bleaching bath until the image fades to a pale yellow. This will take from 1 to 3 minutes.
   b. Wash the print in running water for about a minute.
   c. Place print in redevelopment solution (sulfide — has a strong odor) until development is complete, or about 1 minute.
   d. Wash for 30 minutes and dry.

   B. Red tones

   There are a number of formulas that will give red tones. Try the following formula. It has been found quite satisfactory.

   Solution A

   Solution A

   Water .................................................. 5 oz.
   (cupric) Copper sulphate ........ 15 grains
   Potassium citrate ........................ 60 grains

Solution B

Water .................................................. 5 oz.
Potassium ferricyanide ........... 12 grains
Potassium citrate ....................... 60 grains

a. Take equal parts of solutions A and B.
b. Place print in this mixture until the desired color is obtained. The color changes from a warm black to a chalky red. You may remove the print at any point.
c. Wash a few minutes and dry.

C. Blue tones.

Prints for the following solution should be considerably darker than normal as this formula produces some bleaching. Try this formula on a snow or water scene.

Solution A

Water .................................................. 8 oz.
Potassium ferricyanide ........... 8 grains

Solution B

Water .................................................. 8 oz.
Ferric chloride .................................. 8 oz.

After dissolved, add formula B to formula A then add $5/8$ oz. of nitric acid. This formula must be used immediately. It loses its action in a short time.

a. Immerse print in above solution until desired tone is obtained.
b. Wash thoroughly.
c. Remove all drops of water. If drops of water are left on the print while drying, they may cause color spots. Dry the prints.

Note: If blue stains are left in the tray or on the hands, a weak solution of sodium carbonate will remove the stain.

## Mounting Prints With Dry Mounting Tissue

*Materials Required* —

1. Print to be mounted.
2. Dry mounting tissue.
3. Dry mounting press or electric iron.
4. A suitable size mounting board. (An 8 x 10 print should have a 12 x 15 or 16 x 20 inch board. An 11 x 14 print should be mounted on a 16 x 20 board.)

*Procedure* —

1. Trim print.
2. Lay off size of print on the mounting board. The sides and top (vertical print) should be equal with a wider space at the bottom.
3. Place dry mounting tissue on back of print and attach it by touching the tip of the iron to the corners. The heat of the iron should be set for "artificial silk" or lowest heat.
4. Trim the mounting tissue, if necessary, and place in position on the mounting board.
5. Place a clean sheet of white paper over the print and apply the iron to one corner. Do not "iron" the print as you would clothing. Press the iron firmly for a few seconds, then move it forward about half its length and press again. Continue this until you have crossed one edge of the print. Repeat this procedure, each time overlapping the area previously put down.

   If a dry mounting press is available, follow the directions given by the manufacturer.
6. You may wish to draw a neat line around the print.
7. Supply a title and sign your name. This is usually done in pencil and should be inconspicuous. Your name should be placed in the lower right hand corner.

CHAPTER XIV

# some principles of art

*"It is sometimes argued that fashion controls taste, but good taste never finds any obstacle in the most arbitrary dictates of fashion, because it is superior to them."*

*Wilson's Quarter Century in Photography,*
*Edward S. Wilson, 1887*

When art is mentioned probably most people think of a famous painting, or something in the museum. True, those great paintings are works of art, but too often people think *only* of paintings and drawings as works of art. Some think of decoration as art, but art is much broader than decoration or drawing or even great paintings. Art is built on certain principles which can be used every day. Which hat to wear? Which tie to select? Which flowers to cut for table decorations? How should items be arranged? The answers to all of these questions have their answers in some of the principles of art. Art is not a thing to be set aside for occasional enjoyment. It is expressed in everyday dress, surroundings in the home, office, parks, etc. and in personalities. The ornate expensive things are not always the most artistic, the most beautiful. On the contrary, the most beautiful things are likely to be the simplest. *Great emphasis should be placed on simplicity.*

Artistic sense is determined by good taste and good taste can be cultivated by the application of some of the principles of art. There are basic reasons why one object may have pleasing eye-appeal while another may not. Some of the principles which are developed in acquiring good taste in art are (1) harmony, (2) proportion, (3) balance, (4) rhythm, (5) emphasis and (6) perspective. All of these principles can be applied in composing photographs.

## Harmony

Harmony is that principle of art which produces an impression of belonging together, of wholeness, the feeling of something in common.

There are five general aspects of harmony; harmony of line or shape, size, texture, idea, and color.

Lines are important in art and photography. *Lines lead the eye.* They can lead the eye out of a picture or they can lead it to the greatest point of interest. When two lines come together, there is opposition or conflict, Fig. 14 - 1 (a) and (b). The effect of this contradiction can be softened by a line of transition, Fig.

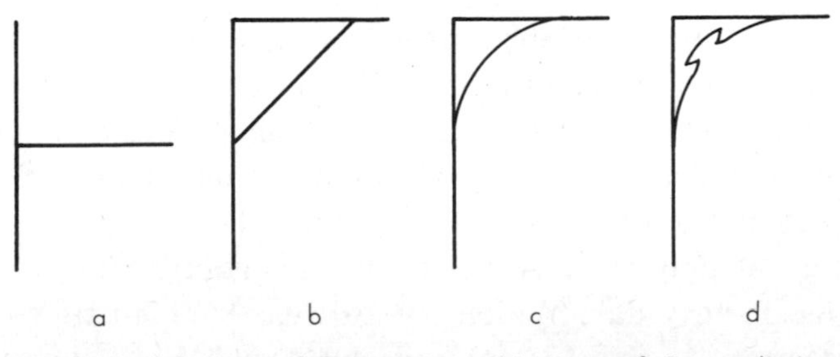


Fig. 14-1. (a) Lines of Opposition (b) Lines of Contradiction (c) Lines of Transition (d) Lines of Transition

14 - 1 (c), and still more by a line of transition as illustrated in Fig. 14 - 1 (d). Curved lines usually make the best lines of transition. A line of transition carries the eye easily from one place to another without the abrupt stop of opposing lines. This is im-

portant to the photographer because it means that he can improve his photographs by the use of these principles in his composition. A tree can be the center of interest with its branches filling the corners and drawing the eye to the tree itself. Before snapping the shutter, walk around looking through the view finder to get the best possible picture. It may be necessary to lie flat on the ground or climb upon a rock or other vantage point to get the desired result.

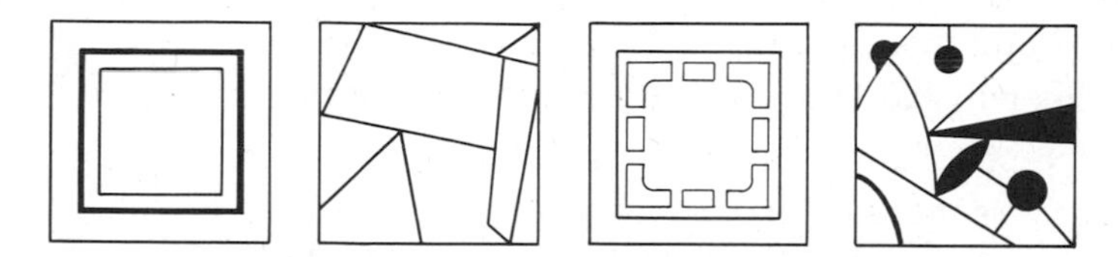

Fig. 14-2. Effect of Lines and Shapes on Harmony

Combinations of lines make shapes, and shapes must also be harmonious. Shapes which are contradictory are usually lacking in harmony. Harmony can often be increased by repetition and good proportion. Proportion will be discussed a little later in this chapter. Look at the squares in Fig. 14-2. Which are most pleasing and which are somewhat annoying? The important thing in composing photographs is to have the objects in the photograph in harmony, things that seem to belong together. A beer bottle would not be appropriate in the same photograph with a sweet little girl. Neither would a vase of beautiful flowers look well in a blacksmith shop. A well composed photograph should have a *single* idea or theme. Improve this single idea by using the correct objects, well placed, of a size and texture which will enhance the single idea. When no further improvement can be made on the single idea, the addition of more objects, lines or ideas will detract rather than contribute to the beauty. Color harmony will be discussed in Chapter XX.

**Proportion**

When two or more things are shown together, there is always a question of relationship or proportion. The Greeks worked out a series of relationships which they considered the most interesting. They considered the "golden rectangle" as one of the most satisfying. It has the proportion of two to a little more than three, 2:3¼ is more exact. Some of the most beautiful buildings of the old world are constructed on this proportion, the Parthenon being an excellent example. Another proportion found pleasing is the proportion of 3: 5. There is a rule of proportion which goes something like this: *when dividing a space into pleasing proportions, divide the space so that the division is more than one half and less than two thirds the distance.* Two of our most popular film sizes (2¼ x 3¼ and 3¼ x 4¼) follow this rule. This proportion should prove pleasing.

The problem of dividing space into two or more parts probably occurs more often than any other single item of composition. Examine Fig. 14 - 3 and determine which division is the most interesting.

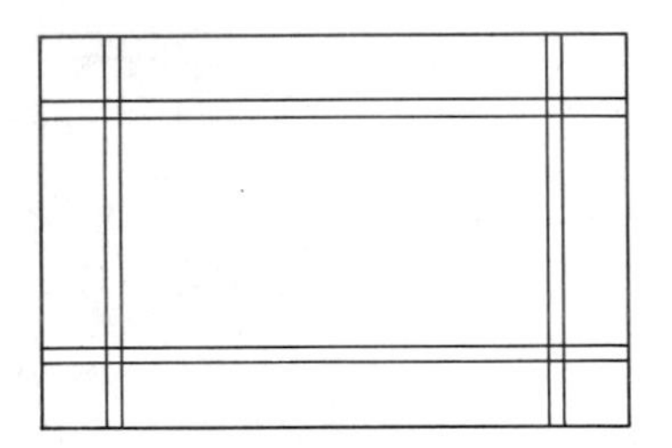

Fig. 14-3. Rectangles Divided into a Number of Parts

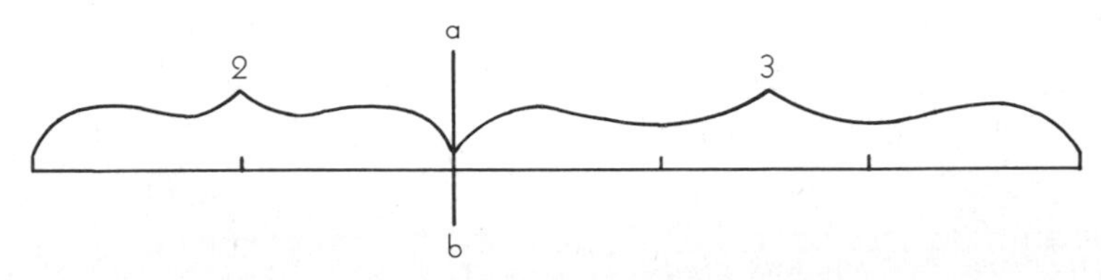


Fig. 14-4. Line Divided in Proportion of 2 : 3

Where should the principal objects in the picture be placed to make them most interesting? How wide a border should be on a mounted print? These are practical problems of proportion. All of the proportions which have been mentioned are pleasing when used in the right way. For purposes of illustration use the proportion of two parts to three parts. If a line is divided into two and three parts respectively, Fig. 14-4, the division line *ab* is the most interesting point to place the principal object. Applying this to photography (Fig. 14 - 5) notice that the horizontal line can be either two spaces up from the bottom or two spaces down from the top. Two spaces up from the bottom and two spaces from the right or left seem to be the most logical

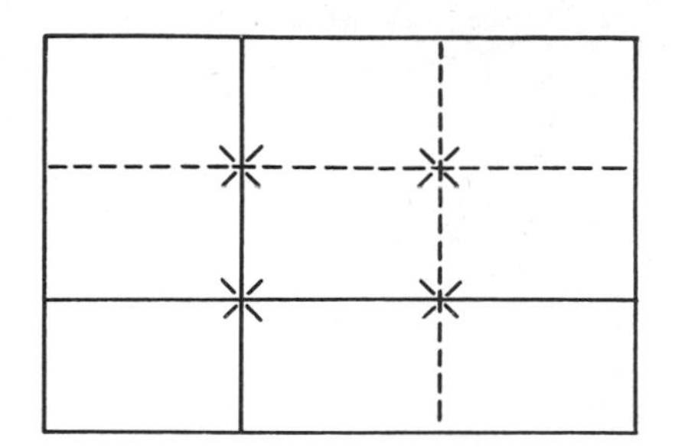

Fig. 14-5. Place Principal Objects Where Proportion Lines Cross

locations for principal objects. An object exactly in the center is in the most uninteresting place of the composition. One does not have to be a mathematician and carry a ruler to get correct positions for pictures. When looking through the view finder or glass, give quick attention to the composition to get the most pleasing arrangement.

Sometimes there is not time for composing. A deer or other wild animal may appear suddenly, so the "shot" must be made quickly without thinking of composition. The composition may be improved when the print is made by using the interesting part of the negative and arranging it in a pleasing manner.

When arranging more than one object in the composition, it is necessary to place the objects where they will be in best proportion. Sometimes it will be the problem of borders for mounting the print. This is the problem of dividing a given space into several interesting parts. Strangely enough, three objects are generally more pleasing than two. Odd numbers of objects or spaces are more interesting than even numbers. Several objects may be grouped together and used as a single unit.

To figure an interesting border for a 5 x 7 enlargement divide the five into three equal parts, which gives 1.6 inches.

ROCKY MOUNTAIN NATIONAL PARK
Snow, Trees, Mountains, Clouds and Sky
Blend Harmoniously to Make a Delightful Scene

(See Fig. 14 - 7.) Consider the width of the print in relation to the total width of the mount. In this case, the side margins would each be $1\frac{1}{2}$ inches, the top margin $1\frac{1}{2}$ inches and the bottom margin about $2\frac{1}{2}$ inches. This will produce a pleasing proportion.

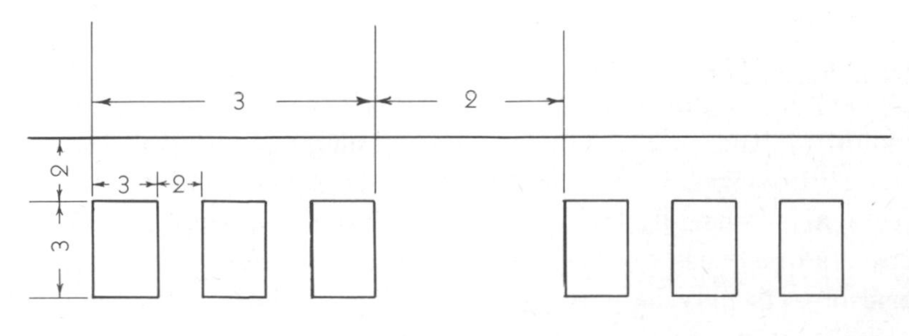


Fig. 14-6. Design Based on the Proportion of 2 : 3

Fig. 14-7. Pleasing Proportion for Mounting Print

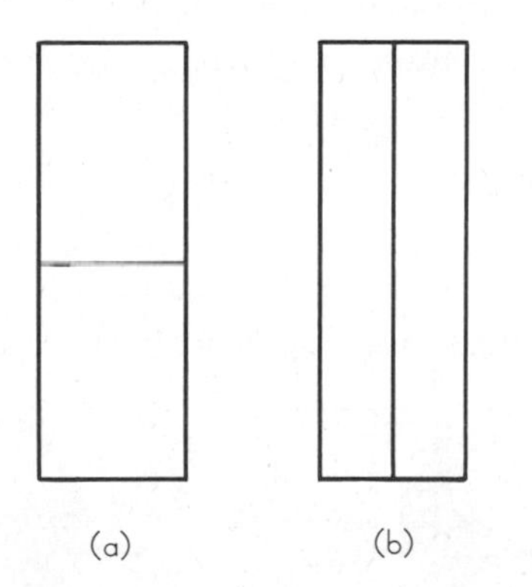


Fig. 14-8. Rectangles Divided Horizontally and Vertically

Before leaving the subject of proportion, there are some other characteristics of lines which affect proportion. Vertical lines tend to make objects look taller, and horizontal lines tend to make objects look shorter and wider. Examine Fig. 14 - 8. The rectangles are exactly the same size, yet (b) seems taller and narrower than (a).

Other interesting and useful characteristics of lines are that horizontal lines give the sensation of quiet, rest, and peacefulness. Vertical lines give the sensation of strength, stalwartness, majesty. Straight lines are usually considered cold and hard while curved lines are softer and more graceful. Contrasting and opposing lines portray strife and struggle.

All of these ideas can be used in composing a photograph. All of them may be found in one composition, but one theme, either horizontal or vertical, should be dominant and the others should lend variety and support to the dominant theme.

### Balance

Working closely with proportion is the principle of balance. A photograph must be balanced or it is not pleasing. Balance is the feeling of rest or repose, steadiness, equilibrium. Consider two boys on a teeter-totter. If both boys are the same weight, they will be an equal distance from the center or point of balance. See Fig. 14 - 9 (a). If one boy moves either closer to or farther from the center, the balance is disturbed, and the teeter-totter no longer operates properly. This type of balance is known as *formal balance or bisymmetrical balance.* This type of balance is, as its name implies, somewhat stiff and formal. Any two objects of equal weight or value must be equally balanced.

If the two boys on the teeter-totter are not of equal weight, the boy that weighs the most must sit closer to the center than the boy that weighs less. See Fig. 15-9 (b), Similarly, a heavy boy

Fig. 14-9. Formal and Informal Balance

Above: Formal Balance
Below: Informal Balance

on one end might balance two or more smaller boys on the other end. This type of balance is known as *informal* or *occult* balance. Informal balance offers more opportunity for interesting arrangements. It is less stiff and usually more pleasing.

Another way to show balance is to have one object closer to the eye than the other. This gives a perspective effect and is useful when it is desired to give the feeling of distance. To have mathematical balance the weight of one object times the distance from the point of balance must equal the weight of the other object times its distance from the point of balance. If more than one object is present on one or both sides, the sum of the weights times the distances on one side must equal the sum of the weights times the distances on the other side. Since this is a course of photography rather than mathematics, it is necessary to reduce it to a more practical application.

Instead of weight the photographer will use areas of lights and darks. The mathematical formula still holds good. A light area in one part of the composition must balance with one or more light areas in another part. Likewise, a dark area in one part needs one or more dark areas in another part for proper balance.

Balance must be applied to value and also to color. Value is the relative lightness or darkness of an object. It takes twice the area of middle gray to balance an area of black, Fig. 14 - 10. Color balance will be discussed in Chapter XX.

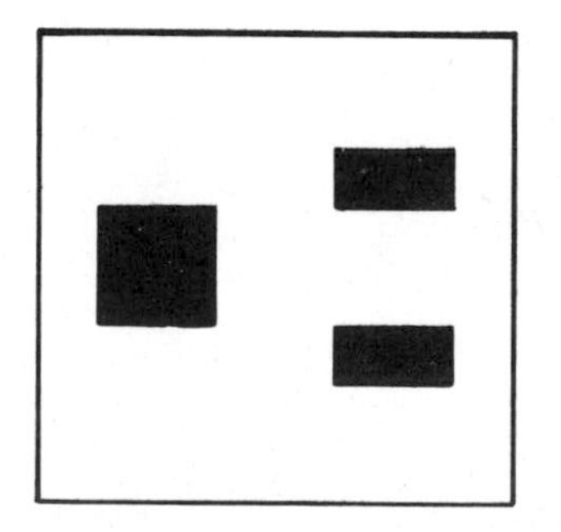
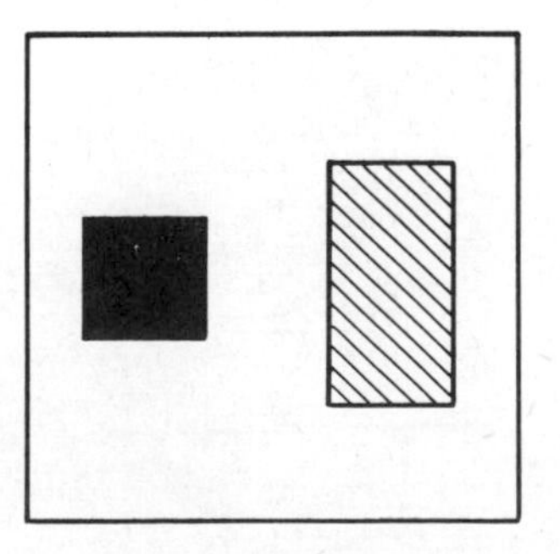

Fig. 14-10. Areas Arranged in Balance

The whole subject of balance is that of spacing. Balance of interest is something which cannot be figured mathematically. A small object of unusual shape or color might have more power to attract attention than a somewhat larger object of simpler, quieter design. A small object which is surrounded by a large empty space has greater attraction for the eye.

The task of a photographer is to balance photographs so that they are attractive, and so that everything seems to belong in the position in which it has been placed.

### Rhythm

Rhythm means an orderly related movement. A line of transition about a corner will carry the eye around the corner rather than let it stop at lines of contradiction and wonder what is going to happen there. Where two lines oppose each other, the eye will stop. By careful composition the eye of the observer can be brought to focus on the object to which his attention is desired.

Artists gain rhythm through repetition of shapes, progression of sizes, and by having the lines of their work in an easily connected line movement.

An illustration of repetition of shapes is the repeated columns of many famous buildings. Probably the best example is the Greek Parthenon with its repetition of beautiful well-proportioned columns. When objects are repeated at regular intervals with good proportion and balance, there is no consciousness of individual items. The eye travels progressively, and space is seen as a unit. Objects wrongly spaced and in bad proportion lead to confusion.

The second way to obtain rhythm is by progression of size. This is closely related to proportion. Progression of size causes rapid movement of the eye. Frequent use is made of this principle in composing photographs. An old fence row, a hedge, a group of trees all catch the eye and cause it to travel along the general lines of composition. Such a theme can add much interest to the photograph, but it can also lead the eye out of the picture. When the effect of great distance or depth is desired it can be accomplished by the use of progression of sizes, the larger objects being closer. If there are no near objects, an individual can be placed in the foreground. This person should be looking in the direction of the principal interest. People are inclined to look where someone else is looking.

The third method of obtaining rhythm is by lines which permit a continuous easy movement of the eye from one part of the photograph to the other. This is closely related to music. It is the pleasant easy movement that makes a waltz attractive. A photograph with good rhythm can be viewed beginning at any point and continuing through the composition without interruption. This type of rhythm calls for the use of graceful curved lines, lines of transition, and enough variety to hold the interest. An object placed where it interrupts the regular lines of composition will disrupt the whole composition.

### Emphasis

It has been said before that there should be *one* main, central idea in each photograph. That one central idea must stand out from all others. The art principle of emphasis is simply that this main idea or central figure should stand out among all the minor ideas or figures. Unless an object or idea adds to the main idea or setting, *it should not be included. Simplicity* is the keynote of emphasis.

Whether it is a delicate flower or a majestic mountain to be emphasized there are some general principles to be followed.

One of the first things to remember is that objects that are close together are seen as a unit. Therefore, if a flower is to be emphasized it should be separated from the group. If it is a beautiful flower, the flower is the center of interest. It is important that the center of interest have the proper *background.* Many of the most famous paintings have left almost all detail out of the background. The detail that is found in the background is only suggested.

One of the principles of emphasis is that a *plain space* around an object gives it emphasis. The background, then, should

MAGNOLIA BLOSSOM

Emphasis Gained by Plain Dark Space as Background

be in harmony with the principal subject, but be subordinate to it, and usually be *plain* and *simple.*

Another way of obtaining emphasis is by the grouping of objects. Objects should be grouped so that the lines of the composition lead to the principal object.

A good position to place important objects is wherever the two-to-three proportion lines cross. To prevent monotony, objects should not appear on a straight line. Vary the spacing to keep a good proportion and balance. Fig. 14 - 11 shows one of many possibilities.

Nature does not always place things in position for the most pleasing pictures. But by moving around the resourceful pho-

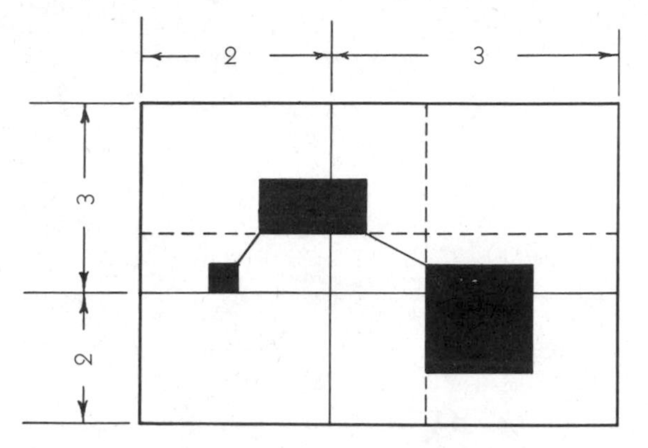


Fig. 14-11. Spacing Varied for Good Proportion and Balance

tographer can usually get a tree or rock or other object in approximately the right place for proper emphasis.

Emphasis may be created by contrast of dark and light or by contrasts of colors. The eye is quick to distinguish between lights and darks. If a very dark object is placed in a light background, it will at once stand out, even without good composition lines. Here is where harmony comes back into the picture. If an object of considerable contrast is placed in a subordinate part of a well-composed photograph there is at once a fight between the principal object and the subordinate object. Conflict of this kind is uninteresting and undesirable. In color photography strong colors attract attention. The improper use of color will disturb the balance and interest in a color photograph.

Emphasis may be gained through *radiation.* Radiation means that all lines have a central axis from which they spread in all directions. An example of this is the spokes of a wheel radiating from the center. This principle is not used as often as some others but it gives strong emphasis.

Remember that the camera lens does not see as the eye. The camera lens records everything, the eye is selective. The photograph should be composed so that the eye naturally selects the important object.

### Perspective

Looking down a long straight stretch of railroad track, the rails appear to come together in the distance. This principle of perspective is important in photography. The principle is quite simple: all parallel lines appear to converge (come together) at a distant point on the horizon. The point at which these lines converge is called the vanishing point. Objects which are the same size appear smaller as they get further away. If depth or a feeling of distance is desired in photographs, they should be composed so that the principle of perspective operates.

Fig. 14-12. Perspective

It is not possible to get "third dimension" on a flat piece of paper. Depth can be suggested by arranging the objects so that some objects are in the immediate foreground and will appear larger than the distance objects. Light objects tend to stand out while darker objects recede. If the nose and cheeks have highlights on them, and the hair and ears are in the shadows, it tends to give a roundness to the face. Perspective is that illusion of third dimension which all photographers attempt to portray. Success at portraying the illusion of depth will depend upon skill in arranging the elements of the scene.

### Applying Art Principles to Composition

All through the discussion of art principles, suggestions have been made for applying them to photography. A perfectly composed picture employs practically all of the principles at the same time. It might be asked how can one think of all of those things at one time? No one will be able to think of all of them but with practice they are subconsciously employed. Look at pictures in newspaper and magazine advertising and try to analyze them. Did they just happen, or did the photographer plan them that way?

"A STREET IN SPAIN"
El Paseo Court, Santa Barbara, California
An Excellent Illustration of Perspective

Practically all still life pictures, advertising illustrations, portraits and the like are planned. Try some deliberate, planned compositions occasionally. Try to practice art principles that will give you better photographs. This will help to insure better pictures that may need to be snapped quickly and without warning. Two or three exposures from different angles should be taken for pictures about which there is uncertainty. Then when the negative is finished, it is possible to select the one with the best composition.

WATER SPOUT IN THE CARIBBEAN
An Example of a Spontaneous Photograph

By Charles F. Snow

LANDSCAPE
Fall River, Rocky Mountain National Park

CHAPTER XV

# landscape photography

Every photographer at some time or other has made a photograph of a landscape. Something prompted him to take the picture. What was that something? From the beginning of time man has worshipped the great out-of-doors, the trees, the sea, the mountains and the plains. Landscapes (including the sea) give a certain feeling, an emotion. It is a landscape photographer's job to try to capture that emotion. If the photograph conveys the feelings and emotions experienced by the photographer when he was inspired to take it, real talent is reflected. The purpose of this chapter is to suggest ways in which the technique and skill may be developed to get maximum emotional appeal in a picture.

The composition of the photograph has a considerable effect upon the observer. The photograph should be well balanced, harmonious and in good proportion. Many schemes of composition have been proposed such as the triangle, the S-shaped curve, the C-shaped curve, Z-shape, the circle, vertical line, curved line, etc. Many good photographs have been analyzed and found to have these principal shapes. If principles of art are followed, it does not matter whether it is N-shaped, Z-shaped or some other form, the composition will be pleasing.

By Charles F. Snow

DREAM LAKE, ROCKY MOUNTAIN NATIONAL PARK
Vertical Lines Suggest Stalwartness, Majesty and Strength
Fog Adds Mystery and Distance

Remember that vertical lines suggest strength, vigor, majesty, and usually give the emotion of grandeur. The majority of forest and mountain scenes come in this classification. To successfully capture this emotion the photograph should have depth.

Horizontal lines suggest calm, rest and quiet. Practically all of these scenes should give the emotion of joy, happiness and satisfaction. Long shadows and warm afternoon light help to portray the feeling of quiet and satisfaction. Evening scenes and sunsets never fail to bring forth pleasant memories and day dreams. A soft focus lens will aid in giving a soft restful effect. Afternoon and evening scenes are usually best portrayed on a soft warm-tone paper.

Ocean and beach scenes are usually a little more difficult than land scenes because the wide expanse of ocean and sky does not provide the variety of interesting objects that are present in land scenes. Birds, boats, and clouds help with the composition. Another way to hold interest is to use some breaking waves. Most people can sit and watch the breaking waves for hours at a time. The sea usually presents a feeling of restfulness and mystery. It stimulates the imagination and sometimes can excite the feeling of adventure. Most land views will have the light back of the camera or cross light, but marine views are often most effective when lighted by strong cross light coming toward the camera from over the water. Special care should be taken to shade the lens or the negative may be full of circles caused by lens flare. The hand or hat should be held to make a shadow on the lens. A shade attached to the lens is always helpful.

Moonlight pictures are usually tricks. To give the effect of moonlight, either on land or over the water, wait until the sun is low enough that it does not hurt the eye to look directly at it. Stop the camera down and shoot directly at the sun. Make the print dark. A filter, and some clouds in the sky will improve the effect greatly. Choose a time when the sun is partly or wholly behind a cloud. If the sun is too bright solarization will take place and spoil the effect. Slightly underexpose and develop for considerable contrast.

A good photograph can be made by the light of the moon by an exposure of ten to thirty minutes at f/8. If a photograph of the moon itself is desired, first make the exposure without the moon and then re-expose with the moon in the proper place. The exposure of the moon itself takes from ten to thirty seconds. Another way is to photograph the moon separately with only the sky, and superimpose this negative with the first in printing.

Morning scenes should give the feeling of awakening. They are usually finished in a cooler tone on a blue-black paper. A little more shadow detail than in midday scenes is usually helpful. Here again cross light will be found more suitable than back light. Sometimes early morning mist will give a very pleasing effect.

Noonday light is not usually as satisfactory for landscape work as morning and evening light. Most landscape photog-

LAKE LOUISE, BANF
ALBERTA, CANADA

Diagonal Lines Suggest M

BAY AT MONTEREY

Horizontal Lines Suggest Calm, Rest and Quiet

raphers prefer not to use the time from ten o'clock in the morning to two in the afternoon for landscape photography.

The illusion of motion is probably the hardest to capture. In general, diagonal lines tend to suggest motion. Suppose a picture is desired of a canoe in a lake or stream. Have the canoe traveling diagonally to the camera. Be sure to include the V-shaped ripples as they tend to project the eye forward. If skillfully done, the canoe will seem to be moving in the picture.

Filters are highly important in good landscape photography. Clouds add greatly to a composition. It may be desirable to cut out distant haze, although a certain amount gives the feeling of distance. See page 200. Such changes in natural views can sometimes be justified to achieve a pictorial result.

A red filter together with infrared film will sometimes achieve the result desired. This combination will produce a black sky with snow white clouds. Green trees and green grass will show a snowy white against the black sky. This can give some striking effects. Remember not to use the red filter with ortho film or the final result will be zero. A green filter will give better definition of trees and grass when using a "pan" film. The standard for landscape photography is a medium yellow or medium green filter with possibly an orange to cut haze and darken skies.

In this high-speed age it is well to take time to observe some of the natural beauty which is so abundant. Take time to *wait* for correct light or clouds. A tramp through the woods might prove most valuable in finding a unique forest scene for a good photograph.

Snow scenes are the most difficult of all landscapes. The snow being white must show detail or the whole scene appears chalky. The darks must also show some detail. A filter is ab-

Snow at Its Best by Strong Side Lighting

solutely necessary for snow scenes. Snow reflects much light which makes it very important to carefully calculate the exposure time. Snow is displayed at its best by strong side light or light coming toward the camera. Long shadows help the effect. The choice of arrangements is unlimited. Winding streams, snowy branches of trees against the sky, weeds, ski tracks, and an infinite number of other effects are possible. One can deviate from true values in snow pictures to obtain pictorial results. A good snow storm offers endless possibilities. Concentrate attention on the foreground. Get some figure bucking the storm with head down and coat tails blowing, or a fishing boat all covered with ice returning to port. The possibilities are limited only by one's imagination and skill.

## PRACTICAL EXPERIMENT

### Studying Landscape Photography

*Materials Required* —

1. Camera (preferably a view camera).
2. Film.
3. One or more filters.

*Procedure* —

1. Study the illustrations in Chapter XV of this book together with the remarks. Collect some additional landscapes and analyze them for composition and artistic value.
2. Make a pencil sketch of the landscape you propose to take.
3. Determine the best time of day to make the photograph.
4. Go on location and make your set up. *Do not hurry.* Select a time when you can leisurely wander around with your camera. Try several angles.
5. Process film and make a print of each negative.
6. If you have a print of sufficient merit, make a 11 x 14 enlargement for mounting and exhibition.

CHAPTER XVI

# still life photography

Still life photography usually brings to mind such old pictures as the dead ducks hanging by their necks, or a big slice of watermelon. This is not the still life that this book is designed to stimulate. Still life is sometimes referred to as table-top photography. It may require the use of the table top, or make necessary lying on the floor, or a trip to the woods. Still life includes such things as flowers, vases, statuettes, interesting arrangements of silver, books and many other subjects. It is planned, deliberate photography. Many interesting arrangements can be created. The only limitation on the photographer is his own imagination, ability and skill. Unusual lighting effects often give the photograph more interest if done in good taste.

Still life gives plenty of time. There is no need to hurry. Lighting can be either natural or artificial. Most photographers prefer artificial light because they can control it. So far we have been accepting light as it happened, planning our shots accordingly. To be most successful as a photographer, it is necessary to fully understand the use of artificial light and to know how to produce the desired tones, shadows, and highlights. This provides further opportunity to employ the principles of art, i. e., balance, spacing, rhythm, emphasis, and harmony.

The first and most important rule is *simplicity*. Do not clutter the composition with too many details. Plain backgrounds add emphasis. Contrast lighting adds interest and depth.

Take plenty of time to plan the scene. It will prove advantageous to set up the composition and just study it. A camera

Ted T. Trainor, Brooks Institute of Photography

STILL LIFE STUDY

Simplicity and Plain Background Add Emphasis and Beauty

with a ground glass to focus upon is preferred. An arrangement for a picture may appear entirely satisfactory, but to really see how it will look in the finished picture, it is necessary to see it through the eye of the camera. Take plenty of time to change the arrangement and adjust the camera. Experiment with the lighting until the view is absolutely satisfactory. Do not be hurried because the extra time and patience will be worth the effort. This is further opportunity to study and put into practice the principles of art which have been previously discussed. Some photographers purposely throw the camera out of focus for the purpose of studying space relationships and balance. In this way detail will not influence them in arranging the composition.

For a subject use anything that presents an idea, a decorative design or an interpretation of some mood or emotion. The motion picture industry has created whole cities in miniature. Some of the great sea scenes have taken place in relatively small tanks. Mountains crumble, trains wreck, houses are smashed by prehistoric animals all in a few square feet or square yards. Miniature soldiers, dolls, ships, etc., are used. Many photographers have used toothpicks, shavings from a carpenter's plane, and sometimes a section from just a plain egg crate. Flowers offer a challenging subject since they have beauty in themselves, and can be arranged to make beautiful photographs.

An interesting addition to still life photography is photographing cold blooded animals. Strictly speaking it is not still life because the animals are alive and they will move. They can be made to stay "still" by refrigerating them. Put them on ice for an hour or two, then place them in their proper setting for photographing. The warm light is pleasant to them, and they will perform beautifully in slow motion. Frogs, toads, lizards, and harmless snakes are the best subjects. They are not harmed by the refrigeration experience.

Since the arrangement is usually the center of interest, backgrounds are usually plain. If Christmas cards are being made, a photograph may be used as a background.

Lighting is usually soft with soft contrasts. Expensive lighting equipment is not necessary. Beautiful still life photography

DELICATE FLOWERS
Soft Lighting is Best
One Piece of White Cardboard and a 25-Watt Table Lamp Were Used

has been done with a single light plus one or two reflectors. The reflectors are usually white cardboard. An ordinary table lamp is sufficient. If a spot light is needed, take a cardboard and cut a small round hole in it. The camera should be on a support, a tripod is best, but a stack of books will do. Exposures are usually rather long. Time exposures are most common.

## PRACTICAL EXPERIMENT

### Photographing a Still Life Subject

*Materials Required* —

1. Camera with a ground glass back.
2. Necessary film.
3. Subject to be photographed.

*Procedure* —

1. Select a subject to photograph. A flower, some pottery or old silver pieces are suggested.
2. Make an artistic arrangement.
3. Move your camera around to discover the best camera angle.
4. Arrange the lights to get the most out of the composition. Lights should be soft and of low wattage for flowers. Do not worry if the exposure time is several seconds. A cross light of about 45° is a good average. Arrange the light so that it skims the surface of a flower. A tent may be required for silver. A white cardboard will be needed for a reflector. The background should be plain and in contrast to the subject.
5. Process negatives and prints. If you have a good print, make an enlargement for exhibit.

CHAPTER XVII

# portraiture

Every reproduction of the human face is a portrait. It matters not whether it be a snapshot taken on a picnic, or a serious attempt in the studio. The task of the photographer is to capture the personality of the person whose portrait is taken. There is no phase of photography that comes closer to true art than portraiture. No definite rules can be given. Each subject is different and will require a different treatment. Some suggestions, however, can be made which should be helpful in making better portraits. Study some good portraits. Go to the library or the museum of art and look at some of the old masterpieces. Study some paintings of Rembrandt, Frans Hal, Velasquez, Titian, and as many other famous painters as possible. While studying the work of the old masters try to decide what makes them good.

### Equipment

The equipment for taking outdoor portraits is a camera and perhaps a reflector. The reflector can be a white luncheon cloth or white cardboard.

The equipment for indoor work is the same as for outdoor with the addition of a source of light. The camera can be any

By Charles F. Snow

An Example of Excellent Composition in Portraiture

size or make, but a camera with a full-size ground glass for focusing is far superior. If possible, the lens should be of long focal length, and for many types of portraits, a soft focus lens

Simplicity Is the Keynote to this Madonna Study

is desirable. The price is not the basis for judging the lens. Many prize winning portraits have been made with an inexpensive, simple meniscus lens.

For indoor work a background is necessary. Backgrounds for portraits should be very simple in design or entirely plain. One should never be conscious of the background. A dark, a medium, and a light background will be sufficient. Sometimes drapes can be used to good advantage. Sometimes an unobtrusive object in the background will lend atmosphere.

Backgrounds for outdoor portraits should be simple and in keeping with the idea to be presented. The clear sky is excellent. When using the sky as a background, use also a yellow or green filter. Such things as the siding of a house, bricks, shrubs, and the like do not usually make good backgrounds.

Film for portraits should have one special quality. This quality is softness. Most panchromatic films of moderate speed are suitable. Most companies make a special portrait film. An "ortho" film can sometimes be used to good advantage for portraits of men. A soft-working developer is recommended.

### Outdoor Portraits

The first suggestion for outdoor portraits is to keep them simple and true to life. Keep the background simple and unobtrusive. Some of the miniature cameras have great depth of field and will produce sharp background details.

The second suggestion is to use close ups. This does not mean that the camera should be in the subject's face. Use an auxiliary lens, if necessary. Be careful that the angle of the shot does not offend. If the subject is sitting, be sure that his feet and hands are not extended toward the lens. This gives a very bad perspective and results in distortion.

The next item, and probably the most important, is to *put the subject at ease*. Most people try to pose when they are having a picture taken. This results in an unnatural and stiff expression. Probably the best solution is to give them something to do. Try to think of some way to get their mind off the camera. This may take some tact and knowledge of human nature. The attempt to make people at ease should never be obvious. Keep the subject happy and in a jovial mood.

The source of practically all outdoor light is the sun. Sunlight, when used directly, produces harsh shadows which are usually undesirable for portraits. The noonday sun is especially

Norcross Studio

Outdoor Portrait — Light Reflected into Shaded Side of Face

offensive in this way, producing very dark shadows under the eyebrows, nose and mouth. The slanting rays of the morning or evening sun are best. Lighting can help portray the character of your subject. Use soft delicate lighting for feminine subjects with a stronger cross light for men.

PORTRAIT OF A YOUNG LADY

Natural North Light from a Large Window

The shade, with open sky as a source of light, produces a soft light suitable for portraits. A reflector or two should be used to help distribute the light where it is needed.

As a general rule, light should strike one side of the face giving it full illumination and cross to illuminate small areas on the other cheek. The remainder of the face would then be in deep shadow. Use a reflector to lighten the dark side of the face. One caution is appropriate for taking portraits in the shade. If the shade is cast by a tree, be careful that scattered light does not produce spots on the subject. Those spots are very annoying.

Another method is to use a small flash bulb along with the natural light. (See Chapter V for instruction for flash.) The flash bulb will illuminate the harsh shadows made by natural lighting.

Portraits in color should have a flat lighting. The ratio of the bright side of the face to the shaded side should be about 2:1. Let the color furnish the contrasts. Hazy days usually give best results. Be careful of deep shadows, which contain a large amount of blue and may give an unnatural and unpleasant result. Early morning and late afternoon sun contains an over abundance of red, which is usually objectionable. In general, color photographs are not taken until the sun has been up two hours, nor during the two hours preceding sunset.

### Indoor Portraits

The main difference between an outdoor portrait and an indoor portrait is the source of light and the consequent control of it. Indoor portraits usually fall in two classes: the informal portrait in the study or living room, and the studio portrait. Expensive lighting equipment does not insure pleasing results. A studio may be so cluttered up with wires and stands and lights that the subject has difficulty getting to the chair without tripping over something. The real job for the photographer is to portray a person, his likeness and personality, not to impress him with equipment and conversation.

By Charles F. Snow

A Portrait of Excellent Quality
The Subject is at Ease and Off Guard
Fluorescent Lighting

The light should be soft and cast no harsh shadows. A fluorescent light source is excellent. Use a reflector or an additional light to lighten the other side of the face and perhaps a spot to add highlights to the hair. Photo-flood lights may be used, but they cast deep shadows. This can be corrected by using a thin white spun glass screen between the light and the subject.

Probably the most accepted lighting for portraits is a principal light source placed on one side to strike the face at an angle of about 45° and illuminate one side of the face. The light should be so placed that the shadow of the nose falls between the cheek and the mouth, and illuminates a small triangle on the opposite cheek. On the other side place a reflector so that it will illuminate the dark side of the face, but so that it will be darker than the principal illumination. Another light of less intensity or one of the same intensity at a greater distance may be substituted for the reflector. There should be some detail in the deepest shadows and in the lightest highlights. No spot should be perfectly black or perfectly white. Arrange the spot light in any way that will add life to the hair. Additional lights will seldom be needed. Be careful of reflections in the eyes and from glasses. Only one bright reflection should show in each eye. Many studios are changing their lighting to electronic flash.

When the lighting is satisfactory, no further change is necessary to make a back lighted shot. Simply move the camera to the appropriate place and leave the lighting as it is. There may be need for a shade or hood over the lens.

When doing color work in the studio, be sure to get the proper type of film for the lighting.

Unless the subject is a professional model, he will be a little uneasy and perhaps a little nervous. Expect people to come to the studio in this uneasy state. If they are rushed into the studio and promptly "baked" with a battery of lights, it makes matters worse. This is a real test for a photographer. The success of the portrait will depend upon the photographer's knowledge of human nature and skill in making the subject feel at ease. Make them forget the purpose for which they came. Each person is different. It is a good idea to talk with them before

Joseph W. Sprung —
Brooks Institute of Photography

A Fine Example of Back Lighting

entering the studio. Find out their interests; sometimes a conversation eases the nervous tension and helps the individual be natural. Soft music is usually soothing. Give them time and a place to freshen up a bit. While they are freshening up, get everything ready.

To simplify the manipulation the operations should be well standardized. Use the same film, the same exposure time (1/25 second is recommended for portraits) and the same developer. In the studio the f-opening can be fairly well standardized also. Of course, *the posing is never standardized.* Have the main light on, the films near the camera in their holders, camera in approximate position; have as little manipulating as possible to do after the subject enters the studio. When everything is ready invite him to come in.

Do not be in a hurry. Let the subject ask questions or get him interested in something. A magic trick or two, a well chosen joke, or a friendly argument will sometimes help. Be sure that he is comfortable and happy. Rapidly, but without any appearance of excitement or confusion, set the camera, adjust the lights, and then wait for the exact expression wanted. The subject should never know the exact instant that you are going to snap the shutter. A long release which permits walking around is a big help. The longer the better. Smiles should be spontaneous and natural, never forced. When the print is finished, cover up the nose and mouth with the hand, and look at the eyes. If the eyes sparkle and are full of life it reflects personality.

Make up for portraits should be natural. Too much rouge and lipstick is not good. Occasionally a little face powder on a shiny spot is necessary so that it will not show flat in the print. If a little highlight on the lips is desired have the subject moisten the lips just before releasing the shutter. Vaseline may be used for this same purpose.

The things which have been said about studio portraits hold equally well for those informal shots in the home. The matter of putting the subject at ease is probably simpler. Excellent home portraits can be taken with natural light and a reflector.

### Portraits of Children

Children are usually easy subjects, because they forget to be artificial. They are usually natural and nearly always active. The danger is that they may be afraid of the equipment. Give them something to do, play with them and make them happy, and little difficulty will be experienced. If they must be "posed" they still must have something to do. Expect to spoil some films by their movements. Usually they will be reasonably quiet for a few seconds if entertained. Children like to kick so some difficulty may be experienced in keeping their feet still. One good method with children who are more than a year old, is to fold one leg under and let them more or less sit on it while the other hangs free. Smaller babies are best photographed by playing peek-a-boo over the basket or crib.

Strong light should be avoided. Sometimes a back light works well with reflectors to lighten the face. A somewhat flatter light is recommended for small children.

By Charles F. Snow

CHARACTER STUDY
Use a Well Chosen Joke or a Friendly Argument

KATHLEEN — PORTRAIT OF A CHILD
Taken on Plain White Background
Pattern Background Worked Onto an 8 x 10 Print
Printed Through a Texture Screen From a Paper Negative

BATH TIME
An Excellent Time
To Capture Baby's Moods

Electronic flash is ideal for children. There are no glaring lights, and the flash is fast enough to stop any of their motions.

### Animal Portraits

Animal portraits (heads of dogs, horses, etc.) are made much like portraits of people. Most of them are made out of doors. Small animals, such as pets, are often well trained and well behaved and can be posed in much the same manner as a human. Food seems to be their main interest. A few bites of the proper food will do wonders with animals. Tame animals respond to stroking the head or a gentle pat.

Wild animals are difficult to photograph. A thorough knowl-

By Jay M. Clark

AN ANIMAL PORTRAIT

edge of their habits is essential. One will need a long focus or a telephoto lens. There are some tricks in making wild animal pictures and portraits. For example a deer will always look in the direction of a slight sound just before running away. Compose the picture, set the camera with a finger on the trigger ready to shoot, then with the foot break a twig. This will cause the deer to look in the direction of the camera for a perfect picture. Many other tricks of feeding, making blinds, etc. are used, but that is beyond the scope of this book. There is one precaution in taking animal pictures, and that is one of perspective. If the full body is photographed be sure to get a pleasing angle. An angle nearly perpendicular to the direction of the camera is usually most satisfactory. Animal portraiture is a specialization in itself. Those who love and understand animals usually can take good portraits of them.

Carefully study the portraits illustrated in this chapter. They have been selected with great care. Several have won many prizes. Study their composition and lighting.

A portrait photographer is limited only by his own imagination and ability. No phase of photography will give more pleasure than a portrait well done. If artistically inclined, you may wish to try some art work in connection with your portraits. A paper negative or a texture screen or both may add interest to some portraits. Attempt a serious portrait occasionally. Analyze the results, study people, and try again until you get the thrill of a portrait well done.

## PRACTICAL EXPERIMENT

### Studying the Effect of Lighting on a Portrait

*Materials Required* —

1. Model (one of your classmates or family).
2. Camera with a ground glass for focusing.
3. Two lights of equal intensity and a spot light.
   Note — For the purpose of this experiment two G-E Reflector Photoflood No. RFL-2 and one G-E Reflector Photospot No. RSP-2 will be found satisfactory.

*Procedure* —

1. Set up camera and place one light close to the camera on one side about the same height as the camera or very slightly above. This is the basic light and the one for which the exposure is calculated.
2. Place model near a simple non-distracting background about six feet from light and camera. Expose one film at this setting.
3. With camera, model and main light in same position place a second light in the following manner:

   Draw a line from model to main light. Set this distance at six feet. From the main light draw another line at 45° to the first line. This line will pass in front of the camera. Measure 4 feet and 3 inches along this line and place the second light. This light should be placed higher than the first light so that the shadow of the nose falls between the cheek and lips. (The lights must be on opposite sides of the camera.) Using the same exposure as before, expose one film with lights in this position.
4. Leave the lights as you have them and add a third light in the following manner:

   Draw a line from your second light to the model and extend the line behind the model. Place the third light on this line the same distance behind the model as your number two light is in front. Place the light high. This is the place for the spot. It may be necessary to protect the lens from the direct rays of this light before making the exposure.
5. Expose the third film using this arrangement. No increase in exposure time is necessary.
6. Develop the negatives and make a print from each. Note carefully what each light does for the portrait. This is a basic lighting arrangement used by several well known photographers for taking portraits in color. It works equally well for black and white.

7. Make a study of several lighting situations and record them in your notebook. Experiment by changing the lights to create any effect you wish.

   (The author suggests that the student examine a good book on portrait lighting. Try several of these situations with some of your friends.)

CHAPTER XVIII

# silhouettes

A silhouette is a photograph of a person or object made against a very light background and showing no gradation in value. It is usually a profile view which resembles a shadow. All objects are black against a light background. There are two general classes of silhouettes; those in which all objects are black against a plain light background, and those in which one or more objects are black against a photographic background.

Silhouettes in which all objects are black are made in the following manner. Place a screen, such as a sheet or curtain, across a frame or open doorway and stretch it fairly tight. Behind the screen place the light source. It can be bright daylight or an artificial light. Place the subject near the screen and the camera facing the light source See Fig. 18 - 1 for diagram.

The composition may be improved by pinning objects on the screen. For example, fasten branches from a tree, placing them to present the best balance and design. Objects can be cut of dark paper such as the old covered well, or a windmill, or an infinite number of things. The many tricks possible are a constant challenge to individual initiative and imagination. As an

By Charles F. Snow

BRIDE AND GROOM
A Studio Silhouette

Silhouette With a Natural Background

experiment make up a screen to indicate a circus and have a friend juggling a half dozen balls. The person in the picture might not be able to juggle two balls, but round pieces of paper can be pinned on the screen in the proper place thus giving the appearance of balls in the air. Such stunts are a source of much entertainment and fun at parties. Making silhouettes is not limited to tricks and fun. Many beautiful serious silhouettes have been created by people with a little skill and imagination.

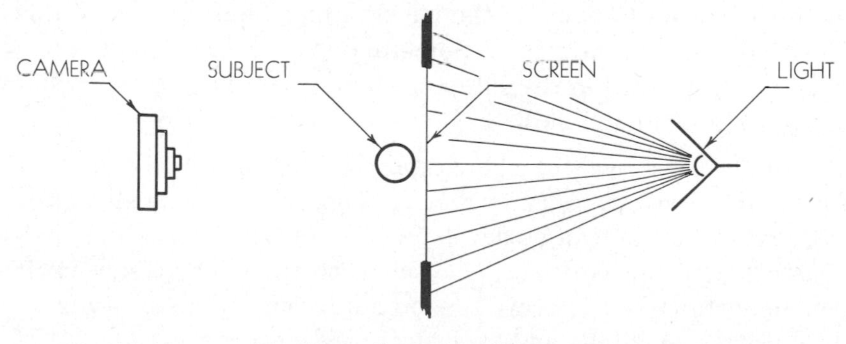


Fig. 18-1. Setting for Silhouettes

By Charles F. Snow

A SILHOUETTE IN NATURE
Taken at Rocky Mountain National Park

The other type of silhouette is accomplished by placing the subject between the camera and the principal scene so that the light is not sufficient for any detail. See illustration of silhouette with the Grand Canyon as the background. Photographs of this kind can be very beautiful. Sometimes you may wish to show a very slight detail in the subject. This too can be charming, but it requires taste and skill.

In the first type of silhouette, color blind (blue sensitive) film can be used since a contrast of black and white is all that is required. The film can be developed for contrast and a high contrasty paper can be used. The exposure time for this work is not important, but it is well to be guided by previous study on this matter. A slight overexposure does no harm.

In the second type of silhouette calculate the exposure for the scene which is to make up the background. Choose the film for the scene rather than for the silhouette. Develop and print in the usual manner.

Try silhouettes occasionally. They are interesting and lend variety to photographic work.

## PRACTICAL EXPERIMENTS

### Photographing a Silhouette.

*Materials Required*—

1. Camera with ground glass focusing.
2. Film.
3. Screen (A bed sheet will do very well).

*Procedure*—

1. Stretch the screen so that there are no wrinkles.
2. Place a light behind the screen.
3. Place camera on opposite side of screen facing the light.
4. Place the subject on the camera side of the screen about two feet from the screen.
5. Attach any decoration to screen.
6. Make exposure. In this case it is better to overexpose slightly.
7. Process the film for good contrast.

CHAPTER XIX

# motion picture photography

The term "motion picture" is somewhat misleading. The pictures on the screen at the movie theater do not move at all. A fortunate physical characteristic of the eye gives the sensation of movement. The eye retains the impression of a picture for a fraction of a second after the picture is gone. Projecting another picture on the screen while the eye still retains the previous one, produces the sensation of a continuous motion. It has been found that sixteen pictures per second will give the illusion of continuous motion. Most silent films are taken and projected at sixteen pictures (frames) per second.

With the development of sound recording on the film, the speed was increased to twenty-four pictures per second. The reason for the increase in speed is that the sound recording works much better at this speed. As long as the pictures are taken and projected at the same speed, the apparent motion will be the same as that of the original objects.

Increasing the speed of the camera to 128 or 64 pictures per second and then projecting them at normal speed produces the illusion of slow motion. Athletic coaches find this very useful for analyzing plays and showing each player just what happened. By reducing the speed of the camera to eight frames per second and projecting at standard speed, the apparent motion is speeded up.

### Motion Picture Film

There have been many sizes of motion picture film in the past. At the present time it is standardized in three sizes: 35 mm for professional work, 16 mm for educational films and amateurs, and 8 mm for the home movie. The 35 mm film is usually on a cellulose nitrate base. This is flammable and must be handled with caution. The 16 and 8 mm films are made on a cellulose acetate base and will not burn readily.

Motion picture films are usually purchased in rolls. Some companies pack film already threaded in a magazine, and all that is necessary is to push the magazine into its chamber. Roll films must be loaded into the camera by the photographer. This should not be done in bright sunlight, but in the shade of a tree or one's own body. Some of the 8 mm films come 16 mm wide. When the roll has been exposed (through the camera once) it is necessary to remove the film from the camera, turn it around and reload it. An exposure is made on both edges of the film. When this film is processed, it is cut the full length of the film. The two pieces are then spliced together.

The emulsions of the various films are the same as for still cameras. Exposure is calculated in the same manner as for still pictures. The shutter speed varies according to the make of camera. Be sure to look in the book of instructions that comes with the camera and find out the exact speed of the shutter. Some shutters have a speed of 1/25 of a second at 16 frames per second, some have 1/30 of a second, and some have 1/43 of a second. Some cameras have a release which makes it possible to take single frames. The shutter speed is different for these single exposures. Consult the instruction book for the exact amount. Motion picture films are seldom processed by the amateur photographer. They are usually returned to the company which made the film.

### Lenses

Various focal length lenses can be purchased for movie cameras. Two general classes of lenses are the fixed focus lenses and the focusing mount. Wide angle and telephoto lenses are available for those who want them. Most amateurs get better results with the fixed focus lens. The depth of field of these lenses is very great. For example, "an f/2.7 lens at full diaphragm opening will produce sharp images from 15½ feet to infinity."* If this same lens is stopped down to f/16, objects as close as 3 feet will be reasonably sharp. Practically all lenses for modern motion picture cameras have an iris diaphragm which is marked in the f-system. Filters may be used with motion picture cameras in the same way that they are used on still cameras.

Lenses mounted in a focusing mount must be focused for the proper distance. Most amateur motion picture cameras do not have a coupled range finder. It is necessary to estimate or measure the distance and set the lens by turning a focusing ring. An individual range finder is desirable for accurately determining the distance. Some instruction books recommend keeping the lens set at 25 feet and using it as a fixed focus lens. Other instructions suggest setting the lens at infinity and using it as a fixed focus lens for objects at a distance greater than 25 feet, focusing only for close objects. The best advice is to follow the directions of the company which makes the lens or the directions which come with the camera.

### Holding the Camera

By far the best pictures can be made with the camera mounted on a tripod. A tilting head on the tripod is very convenient. Excellent results may be obtained by holding the camera in the hand *if it can be held steady.* Take the camera and practice with it to determine the most satisfactory method. It can usually be held steadier by keeping the elbows as close to the body as possible and the camera steadied against the cheek or forehead. If a strong breeze is blowing, probably it will be necessary to lean against a tree or some other steady object. Practically all 35 mm cameras are supported by a tripod.

* *How to Make Movies with the Bell and Howell Filmo.* — An instruction book which accompanies Bell & Howell cameras.

**What to "Shoot"**

Remember that the movie camera is made to show motion. If there is no motion in a scene, take it with the still camera and save the movie film. Movies are most interesting when they tell a story.

Everyone likes a good story. Most good stories are planned. Planning a picture story is not difficult. Some stories (such as a fishing trip) almost unfold by themselves. The vacation trip is another natural. Just think through the natural order of sequence. A fishing trip might be started with dad looking over or repairing the fishing equipment. This might be followed by loading the car or boat, launching the boat, etc. Almost every fishing trip has something of a humerous nature. Don't miss it. The conclusion of the sequence might be dad with a six-inch fish indicating the size of the one that got away.

In general, long distance shots give a setting to the story. They are used sparingly. Middle distance sequence take up a fairly large percent of the film footage. Then move in for close-ups. It has been said that variety is the spice of life. It is also the spice of any movie. Every scene should have a purpose. Be sure that the scene tells the full story. Every story has a climax. This should be true of the movie story. Mix the scenes but have them connected.

The best scenes will be those in which the actors are not conscious of the camera. Be sure to get real action in the pictures. Try to avoid posed pictures but get several close-ups. They add variety, interest and emphasis. Many interesting and beautiful close-ups of flowers, portraits (moving), etc., can be arranged. Lighting for these scenes should follow the same principles as for still pictures. Be sure to make the scene long enough. Beginners are inclined to make scenes too short and regret it later. The average scene should be not less than three feet of film for 16mm cameras or about seven or eight seconds of time.

Linking the scenes together may be done in several ways. First you may use titles. These may be lettered by hand, perhaps on a postcard. They may be typed, or perhaps best of all, they may be produced on location, *e.g.*, written in the sand at the beach, or in the snow in the mountains. Some of the best titles are natural ones — road signs, signs at interesting places.

The second way to link scenes together is to use a scene as a connection between past action and that which is to come. The car speedometer for the passing of miles, the hands of a clock for the passing of time. Packing the picnic basket gives the audience a clue as to what is to follow. The case of the missing cookies is an example of how mother may go to the cookie jar to obtain cookies for her party only to find the jar nearly empty. Where did they go? The next scene could logically be little mister mischief with bulging pockets passing out cookies to his many little friends.

Another way to keep sequence is to cut the film and splice it together to tell the story. Missing views and titles can be taken and placed in the proper place.

Panoramic (pan) pictures, unless carefully done, are not recommended. The eye is selective and does not see everything on the horizon in one look. The eye stops to examine small areas. Likewise, when taking scenes with a movie camera, time should be taken for individual scenes. If it is necessary to "pan," do it slowly. Pivot the whole body slowly. Move the camera slowly and, when an interesting scene comes into view, pause for a few seconds to let the eye absorb the full meaning, then continue moving the camera slowly on to the next interesting scene. In order to prevent a jerky motion when taking a panoramic view, it is advisable to use 24 frames per second instead of 16. In this case, it is necessary to open the lens diaphragm one half stop more than for the 16 frame per second speed.

Swiftly moving objects, such as races of various kinds, speed boats, ball games, etc., are filmed by pivoting the camera to keep the moving object in the view finder. The moving object should be near the center or a little behind the center. Always have moving objects move into the picture rather than out of it. It is usually best to avoid rapid action which takes place at right angles to the camera. If it is necessary to take a cross action picture, the camera should be at least 30 feet away from the action, and further if possible. The background will be blurred when photographing swiftly moving objects, but this is not a serious objection because the eye is on the moving object, which is the center of interest. Shortening the length of the scenes of fast action and showing them in rapid sequence adds to the feeling of excitement.

By all means include a sunset in your motion picture work. Sunsets are best when the sun is partly or wholly behind a cloud. To photograph the full sun is to invite lens flare. The sun can usually be photographed without difficulty when you can look at it without hurting your eyes. A very impressive trick is to use the single frame shutter release and take individual frames at intervals. There are 40 frames per foot on 16 mm film which would be 120 frames for a normal scene. This would be ten frames per minute for twelve minutes. When projected, the full sunset will be shown in all of its colors. The sun will be seen to set in only one scene, going down very rapidly with all of the color changes which took place in the actual sunset.

### Presenting the Show

A movie to be appreciated must be presented properly. In order to insure that the show will be a success, you must practice. Try it once. Be sure that people are seated where they can see well. Have everything ready. Fooling with photographic equipment while your audience waits is a show killer. Be sure that the projector to screen distance is correct. Have electrical connections tested and ready. Have a spare bulb. After a reel has been projected do not rewind it until your guests have gone. A very important factor is to be sure that the show is not too long. Leave your guests wanting more and they will be anxious to return for another show. If they are tired and bored, they will not want to return.

The above statements are just some of the more important points of good showmanship which have been learned "the hard way" by people in show business. Remember — an average film well presented will be enjoyed more by your friends than an excellent film poorly presented.

### Prints From Motion Picture Film

Occasionally you may want a black and white print of a scene taken with the motion picture camera. Prints can be made from motion picture film in several ways. If the film being used is a negative film, it can be placed in the enlarger in the usual way. Most films are reversed (positive). For positive film a negative can be made by contact printing, or by projection, or a print can be made directly on direct positive paper.

### Defects — Their Cause and Remedy

The best of photographers will get poor results occasionally. Most defective pictures are a result of carelessness or neglect. This section is devoted to some defective motion pictures and the reason for the defect.

Pictures that are too dark have been under-exposed. The remedy is to set the lens to a larger opening or increase the light source.

Pictures too light with no color are over-exposed. The cause is too large a lens opening.

Pictures with fuzzy edges usually indicate dirt around the camera aperture. The aperture plate should be thoroughly cleaned after each roll or magazine of film is removed. Follow the directions which come with the camera.

Fine lines or streaks the full length of the film are usually caused by sand or grit on the aperture plate. Sand is the number one enemy of good pictures and equipment. Frequent cleaning is necessary.

Pictures not sharp are usually the result of an improperly focused lens. If the lens is a fixed focus lens, it is probably dirty or has moisture on it. Severe temperature changes sometimes produce condensation on the lens. Another cause is improper assembly of the lens. To overcome these problems consult an expert at a camera store.

Jerky panoramic pictures are caused by moving the camera too rapidly. A slower movement should overcome this problem.

Prints From
Kodachrome
Motion Picture Film

Blurred pictures are caused by a movement of the camera. If it cannot be held steady, it will be necessary to use a tripod.

No pictures at all are usually caused by failure to remove the lens cap or by under-exposure.

Close ups that are off center or with part of the subject cut off are caused by the view finder being at one side and above the lens. Most view finders have lines or notches to indicate the part of the view finder to use for close-ups.

An occasional blank frame is caused by allowing the spring motor to run down. When this happens the shutter may stop with the open section over the lens. This results in extreme over-exposure on that particular frame, which causes it to process clear. There is nothing wrong with the camera. Winding the camera after each scene insures against running down in the middle of an interesting scene.

Scenes that are too short are very disappointing. All scenes should be at least seven or eight seconds long. Longer scenes are desirable when especially interesting. When photographing titles, read the title twice while the camera is in operation.

CHAPTER XX

# color photography

The subject of color is so extensive that a single chapter cannot begin to do it justice. Everyone is sufficiently aware of color to know that some color combinations are pleasing and some are not. Most of us have spent far too little time studying color to know why certain combinations are pleasing and why others are not. Those who are seriously interested in color photography should study at least one good book on the subject. A brief summary of some of the principles of color will be given in this chapter, but the principles presented here are only a fundamental beginning.

This discussion of color will be limited to the color in light. *Do not confuse this with the mixing of pigments. Mixing colored light and mixing paint are quite different.*

## THE THEORY OF COLOR PHOTOGRAPHY

Colors that we "see" are sensations caused by certain wave-lengths of radiation falling on the retina of the eye. Sunlight contains all of the wave lengths that the eye can detect. We call sunlight *white light*. If a glass prism is placed in a beam of white light, certain of these wave lengths are refracted (bent) more than others and we see several individual wave lengths. Our eyes record these as different colors. These are the colors of the spectrum, the main ones being blue, blue green, green, yellow, orange, and red.

The scientist distinguishes colors by the length of their waves. Starting with the blue end of the spectrum, blue light has wavelengths which vary from 400 to 470 millimicrons. (A millimicron is a millionth of a milimeter, usually abbreviated m). Green has wavelengths of between 500 and 570 m and red 600 to 700 m. It is important to note that blue, green, and red each occupy nearly one third of the spectrum.

The color of objects around us is a result of absorption and reflection of various wavelengths of light. If an object reflects all of the wavelengths, we get the sensation of white. If an object absorbs all of the wavelengths, the result is no reflection. No wavelengths strike the retina of the eye, hence no color and we say that the object is black. An object which we see as red absorbs blue and green wavelengths and reflects the red. Green objects absorb red and blue and reflect green. It is the property of objects to absorb or reflect certain wavelengths of radiation that gives the object the color. Some people have difficulty with the receiver of certain light waves (the retina of the eye). If the eye does not react to a certain wavelength, the person cannot see that color and is said to be colorblind.

The problem of color photography is to reproduce the wavelengths that appear in nature. Scientists as early as 1855 showed that all of the colors of nature could be imitated by mixing together the proper amounts of three colored lights — red, green, and blue. This suggests the probability that all of the colors that we see consists of mixtures of these three colors. These colors, then might be called the primary colors. Now if a record of each color could be registered on photographic film showing the proportion of that color that appears in the original object, it should be possible to put them back together again on a suitable surface to reproduce the original colors in their true proportion.

In 1862 *Ducos du Hauron* wrote a paper called "Solution physique du probleme de la re'production des couleurs pour la

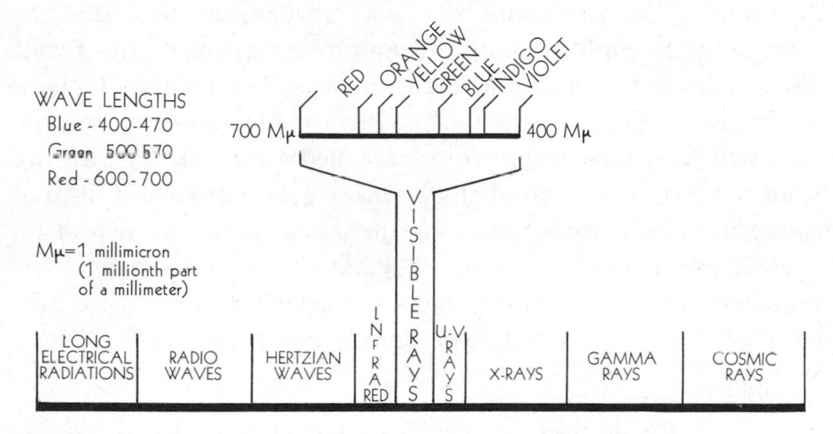


Fig. 20-1. Chart of Radiation Wavelengths

photographie". The paper was published in 1897. It describes a process of making three photographs each through a different filter — red, green, and blue. These record the proportionate amount of each color reflected by the subject. The negatives separate the colors and are called *separation negatives*. Transparent positives were then made. Each positive was put in a separate projector and arranged so that the three projected images coincided on a screen. The blue filter was placed on the projector with the positive from the blue filter negative. This is the same filter that was used to make the negative. The original green and red filters were placed on the projectors with the positives from the green and red-filter negatives respectively. When the lights of the three projectors were turned on, a picture in its original colors resulted. Where all of the positives were black, no light hit the screen and the result was black. Where all three positives were clear, thus allowing the light from the three filters to hit the screen on the same spot, the result was white.

Use a flashlight or projector in a dark room. If the light is projected through the red filter, the screen will appear red; projected through a green filter the screen appears green; projected through a blue filter the screen appears blue. With three flashlights or projectors, project all three colors on the screen at the same time. It no doubt will be a big surprise to see that the screen appears white. If only red and green are used the result will be *yellow*. If green and blue are used the result will be a blueish green which is called *cyan*. Project blue and red and the result will be a pink color which is called *magenta*. By varying the amounts of any or all of the primary colors any color desired may be produced. *Notice that one primary color was placed on the other and viewed together*. They have been blended together. This is a fundamental principal of some color film processes, such as Dufaycolor, which are known as *additive processes*.

### The Additive Process

This principle can be easily demonstrated by a simple experiment.

Suppose a colored object is photographed using a red filter. The red filter passes all red reflected by the object. Without changing either the object or the camera, expose another film using a green filter, and still another using a blue filter. A separate image is formed by each of the primary colors. These negatives are called *separation negatives*. This is the first step of a color printing process known as the *dye transfer process*. Now take each of these negatives and make a print on another piece of film. The result is a positive print of each primary color.

Take each positive film and place it in a projector together with the same filter of the proper color, *i.e.*, a red filter with the film in which the clear area represents red, green for the film which represents blue. Turn on the projector with the red filter and a red image is on the screen, This red image represents all red light which was reflected by the original object. Remember that yellow is made up of red and green so that a part of the yellow will be represented by the red image. Now turn on the projector with the green filter and superimpose it on the red image. A yellow object in the original scene will now appear yellow but a magenta colored object still appears red and a cyan colored object still appears green. Now turn on the third projector and superimpose the image on the other two. This produces a picture of the original subject in all of its true color.

By adding the primary colors in varying proportion all colors have been reproduced. You may wish to try the experiment described above.

If all this process could in some way be incorporated onto a single piece of film, and viewed or projected, an image of the original object in all of its true colors would be revealed. Through years of study and experiment a process has been developed which does give all colors from one piece of film. This is known as the screen plate process.

Instead of using a single filter on each of three negatives, a pattern of exceedingly small red, blue, and green spots covers the entire film area. Each spot of color acts as a filter for the small area of film under it. When exposed and developed the spots of color remain. By a special process the film is reversed (made a positive image instead of a negative) and when white light comes through these thousands of tiny filters, each transmits its proportionate amount of color. They are so close together that the human eye does not see each individual filter but sees a picture of the original scene in its full color.

There are some quite serious objections to this process, one being that when the color transparency is enlarged to a considerable degree, the tiny color spots (screen) can be seen individually. Another objection is that these tiny filters absorb so much light that the projector must have a much more intense light to project them properly.

### The Subtractive Process

A filter, as we learned in chapter VII, absorbs certain wavelengths of light. Instead of starting with primary colors and adding them together, assume that we start with white light. If no filter is present we see white. If a cyan (blue-green) filter is placed between the eye and the light, it will remove (subtract) red. A magenta filter will subtract green, and a yellow filter will subtract blue. If cyan and magenta filters are superimposed between the white light and the eye, the cyan subtracts red and the magenta subtracts green, leaving only blue to come through. Likewise, if magenta and yellow filters are used, the magenta subtracts green and the yellow subtracts blue, leaving only red to come through. If all three filters (cyan, magenta, and yellow) are superimposed and placed between the eye and white light, all light is absorbed and the result is black. Try it and be convinced. These three colors — cyan, magenta, and yellow — are called subtractive primaries and films using this method of obtaining colored images are said to be *subtractive process films.*

Films made by the subtractive process contain three sensitive layers instead of one as in black and white. Each layer is sensitive to a single primary color which results in three separation negatives on one film.

The three separate images are developed as a negative. The negative is then exposed to light and again developd. During the second development a dye image is formed along with the positive silver image. The dye formed in each case is the complement. The dye which is formed in the red-sensitive layer is cyan (blue-green). Magenta is formed in the green-sensitive layer and yellow is formed in the blue-sensitive layer.

Fig. 20-2. Principle of Subtractive Color

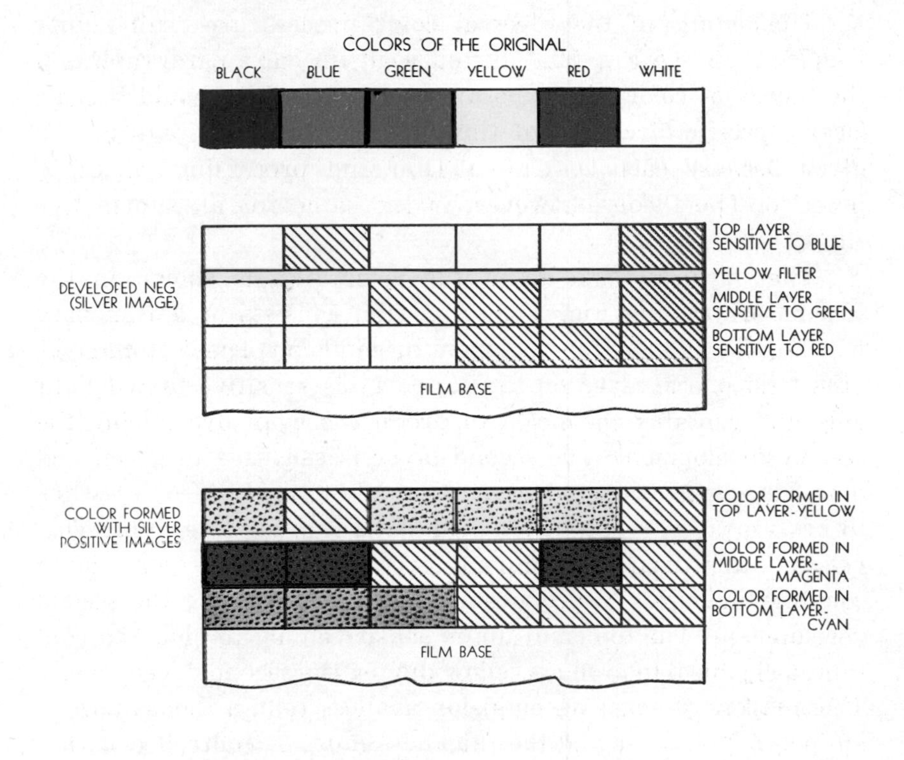


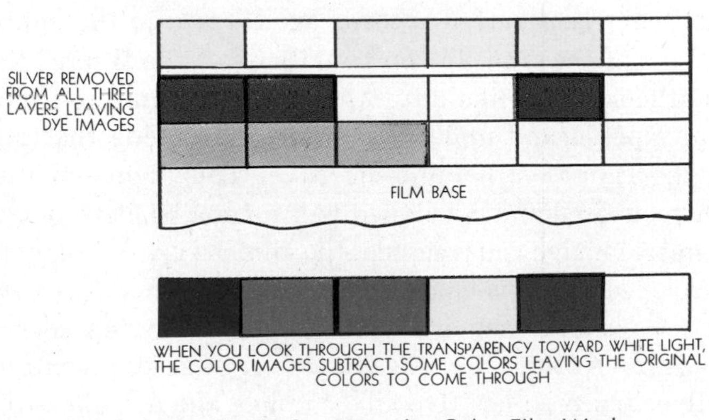


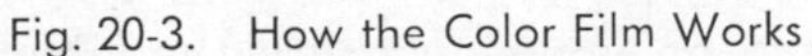


Fig. 20-3. How the Color Film Works

The details of the reversal color process are really quite simple. Examine Fig. 20-3 as you read the next paragraph and the theory of color film exposure and processing should become clear. Specific directions of time, temperature, etc., will not be given because each company's film and processing varies in practice. The theory, however, is the same for all subtractive films.

The physical make-up of the color film is shown in the schematic drawing Fig. 20-3. The film consists of a film base which is the support for the layers of emulsion. The bottom layer (the first one sprayed on the support) is sensitive to red light only and contains chemicals to produce a cyan dye during the second development. The second layer is sensitive to green and blue. Since we wish it to be sensitive only to green it is necessary to next spray a yellow filter over it to stop all blue light. This yellow filter disappears during processing. This second layer contains chemicals to produce a magenta dye during the second development. The top emulsion is sensitive only to blue and contains a chemical to produce yellow during the second development. These layers of sensitive emulsion are less than a thousandth of an inch in thickness and the thickness must be controlled within very accurate limits or variations of color will result.

After the film is exposed and developed as a negative (first development), color separation records are formed in the appropriate emulsions of the film. If you could look at the film at this point it would look much like any other negative that you have made. The unexposed and undeveloped silver bromide that still remains on the film is still light-sensitive. This light-sensitive emulsion when exposed and developed will form a positive image. After the negative image is developed, the film is exposed to white light and developed in a developer that produces both a silver and a dye image — yellow, magenta and cyan dyes in the correct layers of emulsion. At this point the film is very dense. It contains a negative silver image, a positive silver image and a positive dye image in each layer of emulsion. Both the silver negative image and the silver positive image are bleached out in one simple operation which leaves only the positive dye images in their respective layers, yellow in the outside layer, magenta in the middle layer, and cyan in the bottom layer.

There is no red dye in a film made by this process. How then does it appear red? It works in this manner: the red in the original object has exposed two layers of color, yellow and magenta. The yellow filters out the blue and the magenta filters out the green which leaves only red to pass through. A green object in the original scene also will have two layers of color, yellow and and cyan. The yellow filters out the blue and the cyan filters out the red, leaving only green to come through. Certain colors are filtered from white light which leaves the color desired to pass through. If all three colors, yellow, magenta, and cyan are present, they filter out all of the colors leaving black.

Most of the color films made in the world today are made on the subtractive principle. Dufaycolor is the only successful color film on the market that uses the additive process. All of the others have been designed for or have changed to the subtractive process.

The most popular color films using the subtractive reversal process for the amateur are Kodachrome and Ektachrome made by Eastman Kodak Company, Anscochrome and Super Anscochrome made by Ansco. Several foreign color films are becoming available. Probably the most successful to date is Agfacolor which is manufactured in Germany. All of the above films, when exposed and processed according to the directions, are capable of producing excellent results.

### Negative Color Films

Reversal color films do have some limitations. It is difficult to make a satisfactory color print on paper directly from a positive transparency. A much more satisfactory method is to use negative-positive materials. This process is similar to the process just described for reversal color films by the subtractive process. Instead of developing a negative, re-exposing and developing a positive color image, the color developer is used in the first development. This produces a color image opposite to the original color of the subject (negative). If this color negative is then printed or enlarged on a multi-layer positive paper or film and processed in a manner similar to the negative, a positive color print in the original colors of the subject is produced. If the positive material is transparent, a transparency suitable for projection is the result. Paper base positive material results in a color print on paper. The color negative may be used in the contact printer or enlarger in the usual way to produce regular monochrome (black and white) prints.

Negative color film has much more latitude than the reversal film. It also permits the photographer to make corrections in

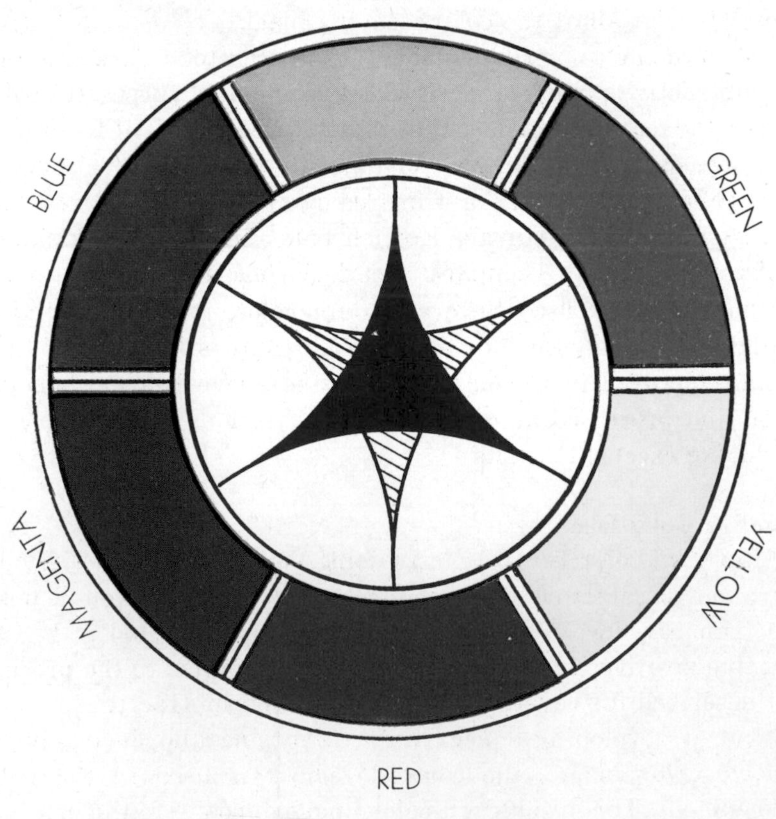


Fig. 20-4. Color Wheel

printing. It has much to commend it but it is not yet the perfect answer. There are many technical difficulties in manufacture to overcome. Remember too, that transparencies are shown in a darkened room where there is no opportunity to compare the colors with the surroundings or the original. Color prints may be viewed in natural sunlight or by tungsten light. There is opportunity to compare it with surroundings or the original. People are very much more critical of color prints than they are transparencies. Paper cannot reproduce as great a tone range as a transparency, so the transparency seems to be more brilliant than the print. This, at present, is the best that can be done. A transparency can give as high a tone range as 1 to 1000 while a print cannot do much better than 1 to 50. Much progress has been made in recent years to make better color prints. Much more progress is to be expected in the years immediately ahead.

Eastman Kodacolor is the favorite of American-made negative color films for amateurs. In Europe, Agfa negative color film seems to be most popular. Both of these films are capable of producing excellent color prints on paper.

### Principles of Color

Most people know red when they see it, or green, or blue. A person knows when a color is pleasing or irritating, whether he likes or dislikes certain combinations, but that is about the extent of an untrained individual's knowledge of color. To talk intelligently about color one should understand some of the terms used and understand some of the principles which determine whether a color is pleasing.

Color has three qualities; hue, value and chroma. Hue is almost the same word as color. It is used to designate a particular color such as blue, red, green, yellow, purple and all other variations which are given a name.

Value represents the lightness or darkness of a color. Think of a scale graduated from white to black; now transpose this to any given color. This lightness or darkness of a given hue is what is meant by value.

By chroma is meant the purity of a color; the extent to which it is free of gray. Another word which might be used instead of chroma is purity.

There are several systems in use for classifying color accurately, probably the most common of which is the Munsell system.

### Color Harmony

Almost all of the principles of art can be applied directly to color. By far the most important is harmony. Harmony in color is produced by applying many of the other principles of art. The following expression is often heard, "Those two colors just do not go together." Perhaps it is correct in one sense but wrong in another. The artist can take these same colors and by a special treatment make them pleasing. Too many writers have left *color fitness* out of their discussions and have considered only color combinations. It is true that certain color combinations are more pleasing than others.

There is proportion, rhythm, radiation, and balance in color as in black and white composition. The question then becomes, "which color will balance another color?" Construct a color wheel similar to Fig. 20-4. Some color schemes have been worked out which tend to be harmonious. The first is the complementary color scheme. Consult a color wheel and notice any colors which are directly opposite. Any combinations of opposite colors are said to be *complementary*. These colors form a contrast, and one will balance the other. Colors may be divided in several other ways. They have been classified as warm and cool colors, advancing and receding colors. Blue-green, blue, violet and blue-violet are the cool colors while red, orange, yellow, and yellow-green are the warm colors. The warm colors have a tendency to stand out and advance while the cool colors seem to remain in the background. Complementary colors balance each other and form the highest contrast.

Again consult the color wheel and note the colors touched by the triangle. These colors usually tend to be harmonious. Rotate the triangle to obtain other combinations.

A group of colors close together on the color wheel is sometimes known as an *analogous color scheme* which produces harmonious results. Any group of analogous colors (closely related on the color wheel) produces a quiet appeal. The high contrasts are lacking. Such a color scheme can produce definite moods. An autumn scene with its reds, yellows and orange gives a quiet feeling of warmth. The bluish shadows of evening and night give a feeling of coolness and quiet. Perhaps these schemes have been derived from nature. Observe nature and she will give some wonderful lessons in color.

The story about waving a red flag in front of a bull is an old one and quite commonly believed to be true. The bull does get angry, but not because of the red. This story is partly the reason for the belief that red has the emotional effect of disturbance thus producing anger. The truth of the story is that the red is easily and quickly seen, thus attracting the attention of the bull. The waving motion is what disturbs him. A white flag will do the same thing once he sees it. Red is used to wrap Christmas gifts, and there it gives the feeling of cheerfulness. The point of this discussion is that some colors are appropriate for some occasions and not for others.

A few of the principles of color and their appropriateness will aid you greatly in making good color photographs. As an example, suppose a young lady with fair complexion and golden hair is to be photographed.

A little thoughtful planning and application of principles already discussed will enable one to see that the background should be in contrast to the face and hair. Further reflection will reveal that the face is the item of importance in the photograph, and that the clothing should add to rather than detract from the attention to the face. After all, the real object is a portrait of the young lady with all her charm and personality. *Keep the composition simple.* Ask the young lady to dress in a light, soft color. Since her hair is golden, a soft blue dress would be appropriate. The make-up should be quiet and in keeping with her personality. The background should show some contrast and harmonize with her dress and hair. Perhaps a darker shade of blue or gray might be appropriate. Arrange her to give the best composition and balance, then make the exposure. The result should be a portrait with quality and beauty.

### Film

Color film is made by several companies. It is made for daylight and for artificial light. Be sure to get the correct film for the lighting to be used. Artificial light contains much more red than sunlight. Photographs taken in daylight with film compensated for artificial light will not give a true color.

Most films may be sent to the company that made them for processing, although some color films are now made that can be processed in your own darkroom.

### Filters

No filters are needed for most color films although a scene of distant mountains which has a blue haze sometimes may be improved by a haze filter. This is a colorless filter which absorbs most of the ultraviolet rays thus giving a more natural color. It can be used also in marine scenes, on cloudy days, and for some snow scenes.

A filter known as a skylight filter which is nearly clear, but has a detectable trace of color, may sometimes be used to advantage in high altitudes, near the sea, and in the shade. It absorbs ultra violet, and a little blue. This gives a slight warming effect to the transparency.

The polarizing filter may be used with color films. It has two purposes. First it may be used to reduce or eliminate reflections. The second use is to make the blue sky very much darker than normal thus producing a dramatic effect. It does not change the other colors. This filter has a filter factor which must be calculated when making an exposure.

If a prize transparency has a color-cast (an overall tendency toward one of the colors), a color compensating filter may be bound with the transparency and projected together to correct the off color. Color compensating filters are available at most photo stores. They will advise you of the proper filter to correct a particular transparency.

A film intended for artificial light may be used in daylight, if a compensating filter is used. Similarly, a film made for daylight may be used in artificial light, if the proper compensating filter is used. Consult your photo dealer to obtain the proper filter.

### Lighting for Color Photographs

Lighting for color photographs is somewhat different from lighting for black-and-white. The composition must be properly balanced in color as well as otherwise. Unless each color gets its share of light, its value and chroma will change. Therefore lighting should be flat. Let the colors furnish the contrast. A slight variation may improve the photograph, such as having the light come slightly from one side, but to violate this rule to any great degree is inviting disaster. Use a reflector, if necessary, to lighten deep shadows.

Remember that sunlight has an orange color in early morning and just before sunset. This can be used to good advantage for making sunrise or sunset pictures but should be avoided for portraits.

Lighting for portraits is similar to that for black-and-white except that more light is needed on the dark side of the face. Outdoor portraits are most pleasing when taken on a hazy day or in open shade. Consider the color of nearby objects. A red brick wall reflects red light and will give the subject a reddish cast. Likewise green leaves will reflect green and give the subject a greenish cast.

Correct exposure is necessary, therefore care must be exercised in calculating the exposure for color film. The exposure should be correct to within half a stop, or the result will not be satisfactory. Under-exposed color films appear too dark while over-exposed films appear too light and the colors appear washed out.

### Mistakes and Their Causes

Anyone may make mistakes. Even professional photographers sometimes make mistakes. So don't be discouraged if some of the color transparencies turn out poorly. The important question is to find out what caused the mistake. Following is a list of thc more common mistakes and their causes.

*Dense transparencies* with heavy dark shadows and no brilliant highlights, colors not true — underexposure.

*Thin transparencies* with colors washed out— overexposure.

*Transparency blue over entire area* — probably used a film made for artificial light for an outdoor picture.

*Transparency red over entire area* — daylight film used indoors with artificial light without using a color balancing filter.

*Yellow transparencies* — probably left a yellow filter on the lens. A red filter will make the transparency red. A green filter will make the transparency green, etc.

*Red or green fog* — Sheet color film loaded in a darkroom with a red or green light.

*Two pictures on one film* — failure to turn the winding key after one exposure.

*A part of the picture has no detail* — your thumb or finger probably extended over part of the lens.

### Black-and-White Prints from Color Transparencies

Black-and-white prints can be made from color transparencies in two ways. The first is on direct positive paper, and the second is by making a negative.

Black-and-white prints from color transparencies are relatively simple provided the transparencies are normal. Place the transparency in the enlarger and focus on a piece of white paper. Next take a test strip of direct positive paper and make several exposures. Follow the directions for development carefully. Direct positive paper requires different development from regular enlarging paper. Full directions accompany each package.

The other method is to use a convenient size film instead of paper. Expose it then develop it in the regular way. Color transparencies tend to have very high contrast so do not prolong development. A short development may be helpful. With a negative properly exposed and developed, contact prints or enlargements can be made.

WASHINGTON MONUMENT AND CHERRY BLOSSOMS
Print Made From a Kodachrome Transparency on Direct Positive Paper

**Color Prints**

There are several ways to make color prints. Full directions will not be given in this book. Some of the processes are rather long and complicated. Some are rather short. In all of the methods absolute accuracy is necessary. Temperature, exposure, and development time must be very accurate. Prints in various sizes may be obtained by sending transparencies to the company that made the film.

Processes will be mentioned which are suitable for the amateur, provided he is a careful, accurate worker. No doubt other simplified methods will be released from time to time.

The first method which promises to be suitable for the amateur is called *printon.* It was developed by the Ansco Company. This material (printon) is used like an enlarging paper. The exposure is made directly on the printon and developed according to the formula supplied by the company. Several filters are needed. By using the correct filter, considerable control may be exercised in correcting faulty color in the original. Success will depend upon accuracy.

Another method which will produce excellent color prints is the *dye transfer process.* In this process it is necessary to make three color separation negatives from which three positive matts are made. Separation negatives can be made from color transparencies or directly in the camera by using the proper filters. The matts are placed in their proper dye and transferred to a treated paper. It is necessary to transfer them in register, i. e., so that one is directly on top of the other. The Eastman Kodak Company has a small booklet of complete directions for making prints by this process.

The Eastman Kodak Company produces a color print material to be used with their negative color films which is within the ability of the advanced amateur. This material, when properly processed, produces excellent color prints on paper.

There is something fascinating about color photography. There is a decided thrill with each beautiful transparency or print produced.

CHAPTER XXI

# professional photography

It is beyond the scope of this book to develop a professional photographer. Some of the basic processes have been explained in considerable detail and, if the instructions are carefully followed one should be able to make good photographs. This book is only a humble beginning. Much lies beyond for any who might wish to pursue the subject further. Many people make their living by photography. These people are called professional photographers. There are many branches of professional photography. A few will be described briefly to provide a glimpse of the field.

### Press Photography

The camera plays an important place in newspapers and magazines. Practically every newspaper or magazine has one or more photographers. Their job is to get the story in pictures. Most of the work is assignment work although many times the photographer brings in material of his own. The press photographer must be an expert in the fundamentals of photography. His work is varied, ranging from pictures of grasshoppers to portraits and social events. He works under any and all conditions, and is expected to bring back a good picture suitable for reproduction.

By R. C. Jacobson

SOUTH SEA SUNSET
Steamship Lines Use Photos of This Type for Advertising

The press photographer should know people, and things which interest people, as well as how to take pictures. Human interest stories accompanied by a suitable photograph attract many readers. The newsman's photograph should tell a story which will interest other people. He should be able to write the accompanying article.

Large companies such as railroads, airlines, steamship lines, and many others employ photographers to take pictures for advertising. This may be color work, black-and-white, still, or movie. This work of the photographer in news and advertising is almost unlimited.

### Photostats

There are many opportunities for photographers in the special field of reproducing documents or printed matter. The work is not difficult and requires no camera. Merely place the document to be duplicated on the bench or table face up. Place a hard bromide paper (photostat paper) over this with the emulsion side against the document. Place a glass on top to press them together and expose to a strong light such as a photoflood.

The light penetrates the paper, the emulsion, and is reflected back to the emulsion except where it is absorbed by the black ink of the document. When this is developed, the document will be recorded as white on a black background. It is also in inverse order. Repeat this process placing fresh paper over the first photostat and a correct reproduction of the original document will be produced.

This may prove useful since photostats when notarized are accepted as originals. The method is not expensive.

### X-Ray

X-ray photography makes use of an invisible ray. No camera is used to make x-ray pictures. X-ray photography is a special science of its own. It is used extensively in medical work. The pictures are really shadows of objects in the path of the x-ray. The intensity of the shadow depends upon the density of the object. Objects which are more dense cast heavier shadows. Bones cast heavier shadows than flesh so appear whiter in the negative. Since some detail is lost in making positives, they are seldom made. Negatives are used almost exclusively for diagnosis. If the lung or some other part of the body is infected, the parts will be filled with liquid which is more dense than air or normal muscle. This liquid will cast a shadow and can be detected. It is a wonderful discovery which makes it possible

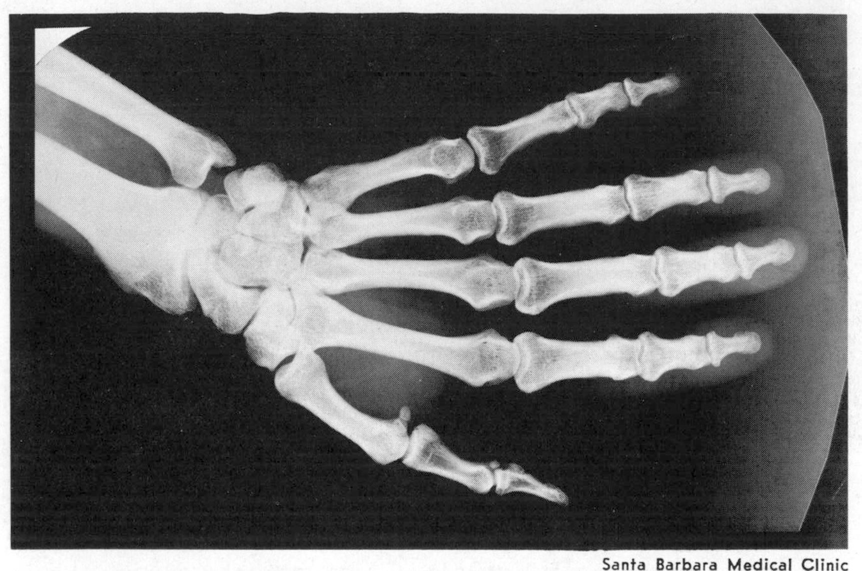

Santa Barbara Medical Clinic

Fig. 21-1. X-Ray Photograph

to save many lives every year. X-ray photography is interesting work.

### Infrared Photography

Just below the red color (longer wave length) is a wave which cannot be seen. It has been named infrared. The camera lens can see this wave and film has been made which is sensitive to it. Pictures can be taken in a room which appears to be pitch dark. This ray is being used more and more in the treatment of human ailments. It can be used with spectacular results in landscape work. Infrared photography has many possibilities.

### Stereo-Photography

Photographs taken with the ordinary camera are in two dimensions. The illusion of depth can be given by proper perspective. In viewing a scene a person obtains third dimension by seeing a different picture with each eye. The pictures seen with each eye register the perception of depth or distance. Look at some nearby object with one eye. Notice the relative position of objects. Now close this eye and look at the same scene with the

Above: Infrared Film, Leaves Photograph White, Sky Black
Below: Same Scene With Normal Panchromatic Film

other eye. The relation is not quite the same. Pictures can be made to show the illusion of the third dimension.

The eyes are approximately 2½ inches apart. A camera with two lenses spaced about 2½ inches apart and arranged so that they both take a picture at the same time functions similarly to the eyes. The lenses are arranged so that when one is set the other is automatically set. Such a camera is called a stereoscopic camera.

Negatives are developed in the same way as other black-and-white negatives. Enlargements can be made from either negative. When the prints are finished and ready for mounting there is one important thing to remember. The optic nerves cross each other before registering an impression on the brain. This means that *the print to be seen by the right eye must be made from the left negative.* When the prints are mounted and viewed through a stereoscope they will look real and natural. Transparencies are more natural than prints. Color transparencies give a full impression of naturalness. It is surprising that this type of photography has not been more popular.

Composition for stereo-photography differs only slightly from ordinary photography. There is one principle which must be remembered. Distant objects do not appear in third dimension to any great extent even when seen with both eyes. Near objects give the greatest third dimensional effect. It is *necessary* to have nearby objects to obtain the best effect. This means, in addition, that the lens be stopped down to get a good depth of field.

It is not absolutely necessary to purchase a stereoscopic camera. Two other methods are possible by use of attachments. The first is done by the use of an attachment, called a stereotach, to fit over the lens. This device has two windows about 2½ inches apart and, by a system of prisms or mirrors, two stereoscopic pictures are taken on the one film. Each window uses one half of the lens.

The other method uses a homemade device. It works very well for scenes which have no moving objects. Make a box or frame for the camera so that it is 2½ inches wider than the camera. Fasten this to the tripod. If one picture is taken with the camera to the extreme left of the box, then another with the camera to the extreme right of the box, it is possible to get a good stereoscopic effect from the two negatives. Make a practice of taking these scenes in the same order so that it will be easy to know which is the right and which is the left negative. This simple device can be made in a short time and costs only a few cents.

### Photography in Science and Industry

Much pleasure is to be experienced from photography as a hobby but amateur photography does not scratch the surface in comparison with the importance of photography in science, industry, commerce, and research. Photography has made the progress of civilization much more rapid. Doctors and dentists make frequent use of photography. The struggle of a tiny plant for life can be observed by the use of delayed photography. The man in the laboratory of a steel plant makes use of photography to detect flaws that cannot be seen with the eye. The aviator can map an area for many purposes. The police can photograph printed matter after it has been burned to ashes, reproducing it so that it can be read again. Pictures through the microscope and the telescope have revealed untold discoveries. The advertising man uses attractive pictures to sell his products. An event which happens in Asia, Africa, or Europe can be seen in newspapers in cities thousands of miles away on the same day of the incident. The possibilities of photography seem almost limitless.

### Pictures Through the Microscope

The science student and teacher often find it necessary to take pictures through the microscope. Both slides for projection and prints on paper may be made, either in monochrome or color. A microscope camera is a rather expensive piece of equipment and not always available. Any ordinary camera may be used and no extra equipment is necessary.

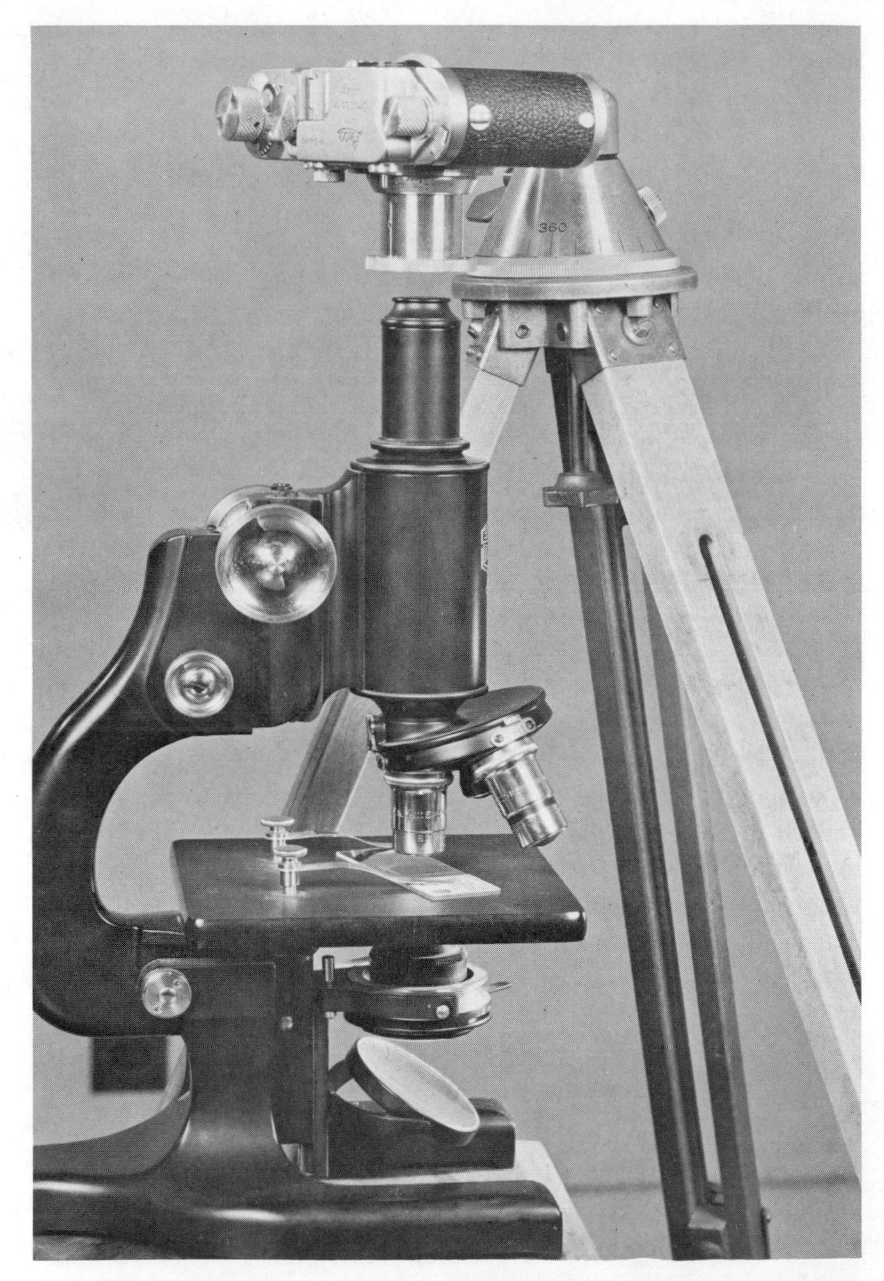


Fig. 21-2. Camera (35 mm) in Position for Photographing Through Microscope

The procedure for making pictures through the microscope is as follows:

1. Focus the microscope in the usual manner. It is assumed that the photographer who takes microphotographs can manipulate the microscope. If he has had no experience with the microscope, he should seek aid from someone who is proficient with it.
2. Adjust the camera with the lens over the microscope which has been visually focused. The lens of the camera should be set at infinity and at its maximum aperture. Good photographs result if proper adjustment is made. There are two precautions:
    1. The eye should be relaxed as it looks into the microscope much the same as looking at distant objects. If there is any tendency to strain the eye in focusing, the distance scale may have to be set at 50 feet, or in extreme cases, to 25 feet to make the picture sharp.
    2. The position of the camera lens should be such that the eyepoint of the microscope falls in the center of the camera lens. The eye point can be found by placing a thin piece of paper above the eyepiece of the microscope and moving it up and down until the circle of light is the smallest. When ready to make the exposure, wrap a cloth around the lens so that stray light will not enter.
3. If a camera with a ground glass is used, the image is focused on the ground glass and the exposure made.

Exposure time will depend upon the film used, intensity of the light source, the filter factor, if a filter is used, and the density of the material under the microscope. It is best to make trial exposures. If 50 watt spot light is shining on the microscope mirror or specimen at a distance of two feet, the microscope lens combination magnifies sixty diameters, the specimen has a medium density, and film with an A.S.A. rating of 50 is being used, an exposure time of $\frac{1}{2}$ second should prove a good starting point.

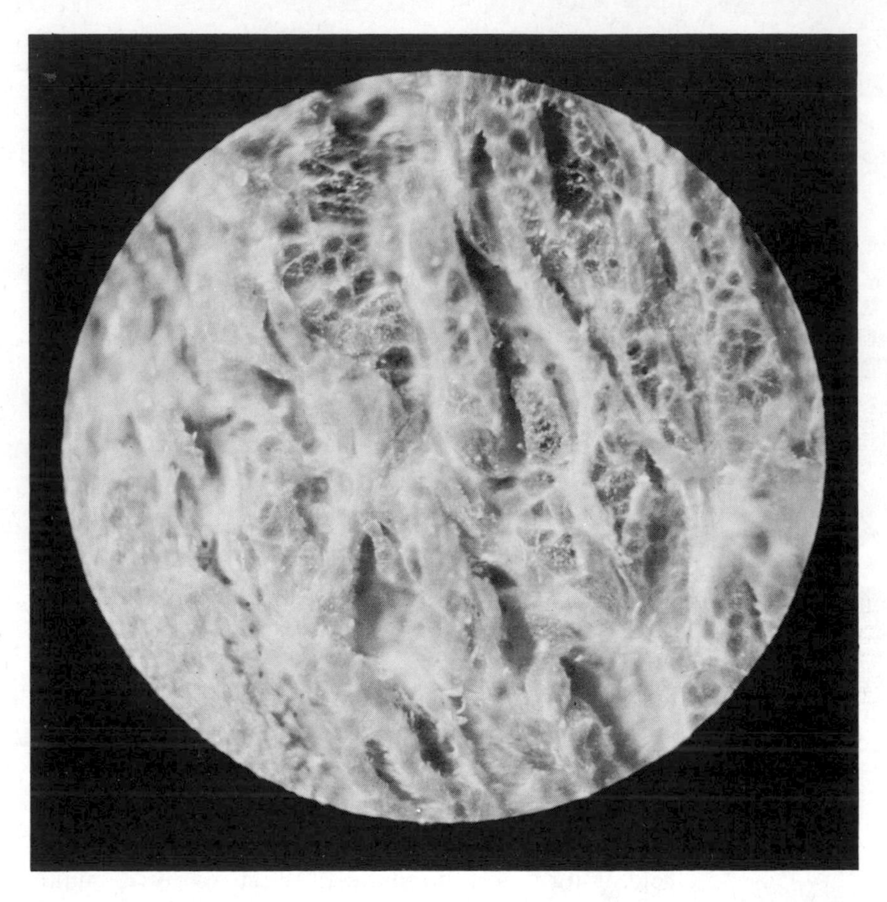

Fig. 21-3. Microphotograph

Fig. 21-3. Microphotograph of a Piece of Leather. Microscope Lens Set to Magnify 40X, Elmar 3.5 at Full Aperture, 1/4 Second Exposure on Adox 14 Film. Specimen Illuminated from Top and Side with a 50 Watt Spot. Field of View about 3MM.

## PRACTICAL EXPERIMENT

### Reproducing a Page of Printed Copy

*Materials Required* —

1. Camera with double or triple extension bellows and a ground glass back.
2. Commercial film.
3. Printed matter to copy.

*Procedure* —

1. Attach copy to support.
2. Arrange a light on each side at an angle of 45°.
3. Place camera between the lights and focus on ground glass. Center the camera on the copy. The camera back must be parallel with the copy.
4. Check the image to see that it is square (not distorted). Be sure to calculate the correct exposure. Take into account the extension of the bellows.
5. Process film for maximum contrast.
6. Print on contrast paper.

APPENDIX A

# selected bibliography

ABEL, CHARLES AND FALK, S. *Practical Portrait Photography, for Home and Studio*. New York: Am Photo, 1958.
A new book on portrait lighting.

*Basic Photography, Technical Manual TM 1-219*. Washington, D.C.: U.S. Government Printing Office, 335 pages.
This book is edited by the War Department and contains almost everything necessary for the practical photographer. The information is somewhat technical but is not difficult to understand. It sells for less than one dollar.

CHAMBERLAIN, KATHERINE. *An Introduction to the Science of Photography*. New York: The Macmillan Company, 1951.
A beginning book with special emphasis on the physics necessary to understand the scientific why's of photography. This book requires some knowledge of the physical sciences and of mathematics.

*Defender Formula Book*. Wilmington, Delaware: Photo Products Department, E. I. du Pont de Nemours & Co. Inc.

DESCHIN, JACOB. *Say It With Your Camera.* New York: McGraw-Hill Book Company, 1950.

This an approach to creative photography. It is an inspirational treatise by the author to help the amateur be creative with his camera, express himself through the medium of photography.

FLYNN, JACK O. AND OTHERS. *Develop, Print and Enlarge your own Pictures.* New York: McGraw-Hill Book Company, Inc. 1952.

A how to do it book made up largely of pictures. Much like a film strip on paper.

GREENLEAF, ALLEN R. *Photographic Optics.* New York: The Macmillan Company, 1950.

This book gives a clear comprehensive appraisal of the merits of lenses of different types. Mathematical computation is kept at a minimum. A good book for those who are curious to know more details of the function and operation of photographic lenses.

KELLSEY, LEWIS L. *Corrective Photography.* Chicago: L. F. Deardorff & Sons, Publishers, 1947.

An excellent book on the subject of camera swings and their use in corrective photography. The book is well illustrated with good photographs and working diagrams.

*Kodak Reference Handbook.* Rochester, New York: Eastman Kodak Company.

This handbook is a complete reference for all photographic materials manufactured by the Eastman Kodak Company. It contains technical data pertaining to their products together with suggestions for improving results. The binder opens to remove obsolete material and insert new.

LARMORE, LEWIS. *Introduction to Photographic Principles.* Englewood Cliffs, N. J.: Prentice-Hall, Inc., 1958.

This book deals with the scientific principles of photography.

McCombs, Kenneth M. *Commercial Photography.* Chicago: American Technical Society, 1951.
This book is primarily instruction in advertising, news, illustrative, pictorial and magazine cover photography. It is easily understood by the amateur.

Miller, Thomas H., and Brummitt, Wyatt. *This is Photography.* Garden City, New York: Garden City Publishing Company, Inc., 1952.
The authers assume some knowledge of photography but it is not a technical encyclopedia. It is written in a simple understandable manner. Recommended for the amateur as well as the advanced worker.

Neblette, Carroll Bernard. *Photography, Its Materials & Processes.* New York: D. Van Nostrand Company, Inc., 1953.
The latest revised edition is a storehouse of photographic information. The book contains most of the everyday facts of photography together with up-to-date advanced scientific information. It is written as a textbook at the college level.

Sussman, Aaron. *The Amateur Photographer's Handbook,* 4th Edition. New York: Thomas Y. Crowell Company, 1952.
An excellent book for the beginner. It is written in an easy-to-understand language.

APPENDIX B

# formulas

These formulas are for the convenience of those who prefer to prepare their own solutions. Unless otherwise noted, the chemicals should be mixed in the order listed. These are some of the basic formulas which are most used. Many other formulas are available for special purposes. Each company that manufactures photographic supplies publishes their formulas together with directions for preparation and use.

The formulas listed were taken from *Kodak Reference Handbook,* published by the Eastman Kodak Company, and *Defender Formula Book,* published by E. I. du Pont de Nemours & Co. Inc., Photo Products Department, and are reproduced here with their permission.

## Formulas for Processing Films

### Kodak Developer D-11

### For High Contrast on Films and Plates

| Material | Avoirdupois | Metric |
|---|---|---|
| Water, about 125°F. (50°C.) | 16 oz. | 500 cc. |
| Elon | 15 gr. | 1.0 gm. |
| Sodium Sulfite, desiccated | 2½ oz. | 75.0 gm. |
| Hydroquinone | 130 gr. | 9.0 gm. |
| Sodium Carbonate, desiccated | 365 gr. | 25.0 gm. |
| Potassium Bromide | 73 gr. | 5.0 gm. |
| Cold water to make | 32 oz. | 1.0 l. |

Dissolve chemicals in the order given.

For process photography use without dilution. For development of copies of continuous-tone subjects, dilute with an equal volume of water. Develop about 5 minutes in a tank or 4 minutes in a tray at 68°F. (20°C.)

Kodak Fine Grain Developer DK-20

For Films and Plates

| Material | Avoirdupois | | Metric | |
|---|---|---|---|---|
| Water, about 125°F. (50°C.) | 96 | oz. | 750 | cc. |
| Elon | 290 | gr. | 5.0 | gm. |
| Sodium Sulfite, desiccated | 13¼ | oz. | 100.0 | gm. |
| Kodalk | 116 | gr. | 2.0 | gm. |
| Sodium Thiocyanate | 58 | gr. | 1.0 | gm. |
| Potassium Bromide | 29 | gr. | 0.5 | gm. |
| Cold water to make | 1 | gal. | 1.0 | l. |

Dissolve chemicals in the order given.

Average development time about 15 minutes in a tank at 68°F. (20°C.). See individual recommendations listed for each material.

Kodak Developer DK-50

For Professional Films and Plates

| Material | Avoirdupois | | Metric | |
|---|---|---|---|---|
| Water, about 125°F. (50°C.) | 64 | oz. | 500 | cc. |
| Elon | 145 | gr. | 2.5 | gm. |
| Sodium Sulfite, desiccated | 4 | oz. | 30.0 | gm. |
| Hydroquinone | 145 | gr. | 2.5 | gm. |
| Kodalk | 145 | gr. | 10.0 | gm. |
| Potassium Bromide | 29 | gr. | 0.5 | gm. |
| Water to make | 1 | gal. | 1.0 | l. |

Dissolve chemicals in the order given to form the stock solution.

For tank development of portrait negatives, dilute with an equal volume of water; develop about 8 minutes at 68°F. (20°C.). For tray development, use without dilution; develop about 4 minutes at 68°F. (20°C.).

For commercial work, use without dilution. Develop about 8 minutes in a tank or 6 minutes in a tray at 68°F. (20°C.).

### Kodak Developer DK-60a

For Photofinishing and Professional Photography

| Material | Avoirdupois | Metric |
|---|---|---|
| Water, about 125°F. (50°C.) | 96 oz. | 750 cc. |
| Elon | 145 gr. | 2.5 gm. |
| Sodium Sulfite, desiccated | 6 oz. 290 gr. | 50.0 gm. |
| Hydroquinone | 145 gr. | 2.5 gm. |
| Kodalk | 2 oz. 290 gr. | 20.0 gm. |
| Potassium Bromide | 29 gr. | 0.5 gm. |
| Water to make | 1 gal. | 1.0 l. |

Dissolve chemicals in the order given.

Average development time for deep tank about 7 minutes at 68°F. (20°C.). See recommendations listed for each film.

### Kodak Developer D-76

Maximum Speed at Normal Contrast on Films and Plates

| Material | Avoirdupois | Metric |
|---|---|---|
| Water, about 125°F. (50°C.) | 24 oz. | 750 cc. |
| Elon | 29 gr. | 2.0 gm. |
| Kodak Sodium Sulfite, desiccated | 3 oz. 145 gr. | 100.0 gm. |
| Kodak Hydroquinone | 73 gr. | 5.0 gm. |
| Kodak Borax, granular | 29 gr. | 2.0 gm. |
| Water to make | 32 oz. | 1.0 l. |

Dissolve chemicals in the order given.

Average development time about 17 minutes at 68°F. (20°C.). See individual recommendations listed for each material. The useful life of this developer can be increased 5 to 10 times by use of the Kodak replenisher D-76R.

### Defender 3-D Metol-Hydroquinone Developer

A Cold Tone Developer for Films

| Material | Avoirdupois | Metric |
|---|---|---|
| Water (125°F. or 52°C.) | 16 oz. | 500.0 cc. |
| Metol | 45 gr. | 3.1 gm. |
| Sodium Sulfite, desiccated | 3 oz. | 90.0 gm. |
| Sodium Bisulfite | 30 gr. | 2.1 gm. |
| Hydroquinone | 85 gr. | 5.9 gm. |
| Sodium Carbonate, monohydrated* | 193 gr. | 13.5 gm. |
| *If desiccated, use | 165 gr. | 11.5 gm. |
| Potassium Bromide | 24 gr. | 1.7 gm. |
| Add cold water to make | 32 oz. | 1.0 l. |

Dissolve all chemicals in the order given to form the stock solution.

Defender 3-D is a rapid working, all purpose developer that produces brilliant negatives with a cold blue-black tone. 3-D has excellent keeping qualities and is ideal for tank development when used with replenisher 3-DR. 3-D produces negatives of a grain size intermediate between 1-D and 6-D.

For tray use: Take 1 pt. of stock solution to 1 pt. of water.

For tank use: Take 1 pt. of stock solution to 3 pts. of water.

### Defender 4-D Borax Metol-Hydroquinone Developer
### For Semi-Rapid Development of Films

| Material | Avoirdupois | Metric |
|---|---|---|
| Water (125°F. or 52°C.) | 24 oz. | 750.0 cc. |
| Metol | 37 gr. | 2.5 gm. |
| Sodium Sulfite, desiccated | 2½ oz. | 75.0 gm. |
| Hydroquinone | 45 gr. | 3.0 gm. |
| Borax, crystals | 75 gr. | 5.0 gm. |
| Add cold water to make | 32 oz. | 1.0 l. |

Dissolve chemicals in the order given to make stock solution. Use full strength. Develop 6 to 9 minutes at 68°F. (20°C.) with intermittent agitation.

This developer is especially well suited for the processing of "Defender Arrow" pan film since the maximum effective emulsion speed of the film is obtained with this developer. In addition, this developer is very satisfactory for use with all "Defender" films and produces fine grained cold tone negatives very similar to the "Defender" 6-D formula.

Use full strength.

### Defender 6-D Borax M-H Fine Grain Developer
### Basic Developer for All Films

| Material | Avoirdupois | Metric |
|---|---|---|
| Water (125°F. or 52°C.) | 24 oz. | 750.0 cc. |
| Metol | 29 gr. | 2.0 gm. |
| Sodium Sulfite, desiccated | 3¼ oz. | 98.0 gm. |
| Hydroquinone | 75 gr. | 5.0 gm. |
| Borax, crystals | 29 gr. | 2.0 gm. |
| Add cold water to make | 32 oz. | 1.0 l. |

Dissolve all chemicals in the order given.

The 6-D formula is the basic developer for all "Defender" films. It produces cold tone negatives with maximum emulsion speed and moderately fine grain. However, 5-D will produce finer grain than 6-D.

6-D is especially recommended for tank development because of its long working life and excellent keeping qualities.

Negatives for color work are handled to advantage in 6-D because the neutral gray image permits accurate sensitometric control.

Use full strength. Develop 9-13 minutes, 68°F.

## Formulas for Processing Papers

### Kodak Developer D-52
### Defender Developer 51-D
### For Warm Tone Papers

| Material | Avoirdupois | Metric |
|---|---|---|
| Water, about 125°F. (50°C.) | 16 oz. | 500 cc. |
| Elon | 22 gr. | 1.5 gm. |
| Sodium Sulfite, desiccated | ¾ oz. | 22.5 gm. |
| Hydroquinone | 90 gr. | 6.3 gm. |
| Sodium Carbonate, desiccated | ½ oz. | 15.0 gm. |
| Potassium Bromide | 22 gr. | 1.5 gm. |
| Cold water to make | 32 oz. | 1.0 l. |

Dissolve chemicals in the order given.

For use, take 1 part of stock solution to 1 part of water. Develop about 2 minutes at 68°F. (20°C.).

Note: More bromide may be added if warmer tones are desired.

### Kodak Developer D-72
### Defender Developer 53-D
### For Papers, Films, and Plates

| Material | Avoirdupois | Metric |
|---|---|---|
| Water, about 125°F. (50°C.) | 16 oz. | 500 cc. |
| Elon | 45 gr. | 3.1 gm. |
| Sodium Sulfite, desiccated | 1½ oz. | 45.0 gm. |
| Hydroquinone | 175 gr. | 12.0 gm. |
| Sodium Carbonate, desiccated | 2¼ oz. | 67.5 gm. |
| Potassium Bromide | 27 gr. | 1.9 gm. |
| Water to make | 32 oz. | 1.0 l. |

Dissolve chemicals in the order given.

For dilution and development times, see individual recommendations listed for each material.

### Kodak Stop Bath SB-1
### Defender Stop Bath 1-S
### For Papers

| Material | Avoirdupois | Metric |
|---|---|---|
| Water | 32 fl. oz. | 1.0 l. |
| *Kodak Acetic Acid, 28% | 1½ fl. oz. | 48.0 cc. |

Rinse prints for at least 5 seconds. Capacity: about 20 8 x 10 inch prints per quart (liter).

## Formulas for Fixing Baths

### Kodak Fixing Bath F-5
### For Films, Plates, and Papers

The Kodak fixing bath F-5 has the advantage over the older type of fixing baths, which do not contain boric acid, in that it gives much better hardening and has less tendency to precipitate a sludge of aluminum sulphite.

In warm weather and in inadequately ventilated darkrooms the odor of sulfur dioxide given off may be objectionable. This can be eliminated almost entirely by omiting the boric acid and substituting twice its weight in Kodalk. This modification is known as Kodak fixing bath F-6.

| Material | Avoirdupois | Metric |
|---|---|---|
| Water, about 125°F. (50°C.) | 20 oz. | 600 cc. |
| Kodak Sodium Thiosulfate (Hypo) | 8 oz. | 240.0 gm. |
| Kodak Sodium Sulfite, desiccated | ½ oz. | 15.0 gm. |
| *Kodak Acetic Acid, 28% | 1½ fl. oz. | 48.0 cc. |
| **Kodak Boric Acid, crystals | ¼ oz. | 7.5 gm. |
| Kodak Potassium Alum | ½ oz. | 15.0 gm. |
| Cold water to make | 32 oz. | 1.0 l. |

* To make approximately 28% acetic acid from glacial acetic acid dilute three parts of glacial acid with eight parts of water.

**Crystalline boric acid should be used as specified. Powdered boric acid dissolves only with great difficulty, and its use should be avoided.

Films or plates should be fixed properly in 10 to 20 minutes in a freshly prepared bath. The bath need not be discarded until the fixing time becomes excessive, that is, over 20 minutes. Fix prints 5 to 10 minutes.

The hardener may also be mixed separately as a stock solution.

### Kodak Fixing Bath F-6

Odorless Bath for Films, Plates, and Papers

| Material | Avoirdupois | Metric |
|---|---|---|
| Water, about 125°F. (50°C.) | 20 oz. | 600 cc. |
| Kodak Sodium Thiosulfate (Hypo) | 8 oz. | 240.0 gm. |
| Kodak Sodium Sulfite, desiccated | ½ oz. | 15.0 gm. |
| *Kodak Acetic Acid, 28% | 1½ fl. oz. | 48.0 cc. |
| Kodalk | ½ oz. | 15.0 gm. |
| Kodak Potassium Alum | ½ oz. | 15.0 gm. |
| Cold water to make | 32 oz. | 1.0 l. |

Dissolve chemicals in the order given.

This bath should be used in conjunction with a stop bath such as Kodak SB-1 or SB-1a, or an acid hardening bath such as Kodak SB-3 to obtain the full useful hardening life. The hardening life (capacity) is equal to that of Kodak F-5 provided an acid stop bath is used. With a water rinse the life is about one-half that of Kodak F-5.

### Defender Fixing Bath 2-F

Standard White Alum Fixer

| Material | Avoirdupois | Metric |
|---|---|---|
| Water (120°F. or 48°C.) | 26 oz. | 850.0 cc. |
| Sodium Thiosulfate (Hypo) | 8 oz. | 240.0 gm. |
| After hypo has been dissolved, add the following hardening solution to the cool hypo solution: | | |
| Water (120°F. or 48° C.) | 2½ oz. | 75.0 cc. |
| Sodium Sulfite, desiccated | ½ oz. | 15.0 gm. |
| *Acetic acid, 28% pure | 1½ fl. oz. | 47.0 cc. |
| Potassium Alum | ½ oz. | 15.0 gm. |

* To make 28% acetic acid from glacial acetic acid dilute 3 parts of glacial acetic acid with 8 parts of water.

The 2-F fixing bath will tend to show a white flocculent precipitate as its exhaustion point is near. When this precipitation occurs the hypo should be discarded.

The 2-F fixing bath, prepared as instructed, will fix approximately fifteen 8 x 10 prints per quart (liter) or their equivalent in other sizes if a water rinse is used; or approximately thirty 8 x 10 prints per quart (liter) if the acid rinse bath (formula 1-S) is used between development and fixation. The temperature of the bath should be kept as near 68°F. (20°C.) as possible.

If desirable the hardening solution may be concentrated to four times the strength given in the formula for use as a stock solution.

When it is necessary to mix fresh fixing solution use 1 part hardening solution to four parts plain hypo solution 25% strength. 25% plain hypo solution may be obtained by dissolving 8 oz. (250 grams) of hypo in 1 qt. (1 liter) of water.

### HYPO ELIMINATOR HE-1

Hypo Eliminator HE-1

| | U.S. Liquid | Metric |
|---|---|---|
| Water | 16 ounces | 500 cc |
| Hydrogen Peroxide (3% solution) | 4 ounces | 125.0 cc |
| *Ammonia Solution | 3¼ ounces | 100.0 cc |
| Water to make | 32 ounces | 1.0 liter |

CAUTION: Prepare the solution immediately before use and keep in an open container during use. Do not store the mixed solution in a stoppered bottle, or the gas evolved may break the bottle.

*Directions for Use*: Wash the prints for about 30 minutes at 65° to 70°F (18° to 21°C) in running water which flows rapidly enough to replace the water in the vessel (tray or tank) completely once every 5 minutes. Then immerse each print about 6 minutes at 68°F (20°C) in the Hypo Eliminator HE-1 solution, and finally wash about 10 minutes before drying. At lower temperatures, increase the washing times.

* Prepared by adding 1 part of concentrated ammonia (28%) to 9 parts of water.

*Life of HE-1 Solution*: About fifty 8 x 10-inch prints or their equivalent per gallon (4 liters).

*Occasional Effects When Using the Peroxide-Amonia Treatment ment (HE-1)*

1. Slight tendency for prints to stick to belt on belt dryers. To prevent this effect, bathe the prints about 3 minutes in a 1 percent solution of formaldehyde prior to drying.

2. An almost imperceptible change in the image tone. To prevent this effect, add 15 grains of potassium bromide to each quart (1 gram per liter) of the peroxide-ammonia bath (HE-1).

3. A very faint yellowing of the whites (undetectable on buff papers). To minimize this effect, bathe the prints in a 1 per cent sodium sulfate solution for about 2 minutes immediately after treatment in HE-1 and prior to the final wash.

# index